LEGENDS
of the
JUNGLE

LEGENDS
of the
JUNGLE

Introducing the
Initial Candidatesfor a Possible
Cincinnati Bengals Hall of Fame

MARK POWELL

LEGENDS OF THE JUNGLE
INTRODUCING THE INITIAL CANDIDATES FOR A
POSSIBLE CINCINNATI BENGALS HALL OF FAME

iUniverse books may be ordered through booksellers or by contacting:

iUniverse
1663 Liberty Drive
Bloomington, IN 47403
www.iuniverse.com
1-800-Authors (1-800-288-4677)

Because of the dynamic nature of the Internet, any web addresses or links contained in this book may have changed since publication and may no longer be valid. The views expressed in this work are solely those of the author and do not necessarily reflect the views of the publisher, and the publisher hereby disclaims any responsibility for them.

Any people depicted in stock imagery provided by Thinkstock are models, and such images are being used for illustrative purposes only. Certain stock imagery © Thinkstock.

ISBN: 978-1-5320-1990-6 (sc)
ISBN: 978-1-5320-1991-3 (e)

Library of Congress Control Number: 2017904569

Print information available on the last page.

iUniverse rev. date: 03/25/2017

This book is dedicated to Toni Al, for without her endless support and encouragement, this passion project of mine would never have happened. I love you with all my heart.

"Tell fans to start pushing the Bengals to get a Ring of Honor...If we don't honor our own guys, why should anyone else?

Willie Anderson
Offensive Tackle
Cincinnati Bengals
1996-2007

INTRODUCTION

Lounging in my self-described man cave watching the NFL divisional playoffs on my television has been, unfortunately for a Cincinnati Bengals fan like myself, an annual tradition. For the past 24 years, and in particular the last four, this weekend has been a mixture of watching eight other teams besides the Bengals continue their season interspersed with the voice inside my head asking, "what might have been?" As you can imagine, it is a scene that even Sybil might consider somewhat unbalanced.

So as the 2015 NFL divisional playoffs began, the stage was set for another weekend of loathing and contempt as someone other than the Bengals continued their quest for a Super Bowl championship. That the weekend started with the New England Patriots hosting the Baltimore Ravens made it even more aggravating. Unless you're a Patriots fan, wanting New England and the NFL's version of Darth Vader, Bill Belichick, to win is akin to rooting for Cruella de Vil in 101 Dalmatians. The fact that the Death Star Patriots were facing the Ravens, an AFC North Division rival the Bengals defeated twice in the regular season, made the prospect of watching the playoffs even more galling.

But a funny thing happened on the way to driving myself crazy with hypothetical questions about the Bengals chances of succeeding had they made it this far.

Coming back from a commercial break in the first quarter, the NBC broadcast showed a panorama of what I would later discover to be the Patriots Place Plaza, a tribute to the team's great players of the past. There, pylons recognized each member of the Patriots Hall of Fame, at the time, it seemed like a harmless segue back to the game. Shortly thereafter, however, my focus shifted from asking out loud why the Ravens were still playing and the Bengals were not to asking myself a more important question.

Why don't the Bengals have their own Hall of Fame?

At first, trying to determine why the Bengals had no Hall of Fame didn't distance me from the fact that the Ravens had jumped out to a 14-0 lead over the Patriots. Watching a team the Bengals had beat twice in the regular season completely dominate the favorite to represent the AFC in the Super Bowl temporarily made me forget why Cincinnati had no official place or means to recognize the franchise's best players in team history. Besides, while the game provided the easiest motive for ignoring the absence of a Bengals Hall of Fame, it wasn't very hard to come up with several viable and self-justified reasons for why no such place existed.

First and foremost, it seemed fairly obvious that the main reason why there's no venue to honor the greats of the Bengals' history was the team's owner, Mike Brown. Anyone who follows the NFL is fully aware that when it comes to frugal ownership, Brown not only tops the list but is simply in a class all by himself. At times, it seems that if it were left up to him, the players would pay the organization for the privilege of playing in the NFL. Admittedly, in recent years, Brown has dusted off his checkbook to pay the going rate for better players. But the stigma of being the league's top penny-pincher has never completely gone away, especially in the minds of Cincinnati residents. To prove their animosity and their lingering doubts towards Brown and his self-proclaimed dilemma of not being flushed with cash, like his big market competition, they suggest you look no further than the home of the Bengals, Paul Brown Stadium.

By 1993, Brown was tired of losing money, and his franchise was dying on the vine, the team ranking last in the NFL in gross revenue. He believed that with the league's new and more expensive free agency system allowing veterans to sign to the highest bidder already in place, he couldn't compete with the big market teams and their never-ending stream of money. Brown realized he needed not only to generate a steady and consistent flow of cash, but more of it as well. Desperate to acquire the additional revenue he needed, the son of the legendary Paul Brown decided the key to his team's survival was a new stadium, with its revenue generating private suites and club seats.

At the time, the Bengals' current home, Riverfront Stadium, provided none of those perks. Built in 1970, the Bengals shared Riverfront with the Cincinnati Reds, and any changes to the stadium required the Reds' approval. More importantly to Brown, Riverfront was more of a liability than an asset. In addition to paying $2.5 million in annual rent, the Bengals received no parking revenue and only a portion of the concession sales on game day. In essence, Brown saw Riverfront as a money pit with no future.

"We were in an economic dead end at Riverfront," Brown said in a 2000 interview. "It just could not be made to generate the necessary income to maintain an NFL franchise once free agency came."[1]

Given the economic outlook in 1993, no one, not even Brown's harshest critics, could fault the Bengals' owner for wanting a new home. It's his methods that to this day, anger thousands in and around Cincinnati.

In late 1993, the NFL announced that the cities of Charlotte and Jacksonville would receive an expansion franchise and begin play in 1995. The decision surprised many, especially those in Baltimore and St. Louis, who felt they would receive the offers since they had previously been NFL cities before their respective owners packed up their bags and unceremoniously left town. Knowing there were two cities who desperately wanted back into the NFL, and who were willing to pony up serious cash and serve up a lucrative stadium deal, Brown saw and seized the opportunity to make the Bengals financially solvent. It also provided the ability for the team to compete with the big market franchises like Dallas and Denver.

Brown focused his attention on Baltimore and their promise to the NFL expansion committee to provide a new franchise with a money-making stadium deal. Baltimore, along with the Maryland Stadium Authority, was willing to build a new $200 million football-only stadium next to Camden Yards, the Baltimore Orioles' home. They were prepared to offer guarantees that the new ownership would keep 100 percent of the revenues generated by the 100 luxury boxes inside the stadium, and by advertising, parking and concessions produced on game day. Additionally, the primary tenants of the new stadium would keep 50 percent of all revenues resulting from any concerts, college football games or any other event held at the facility. It was an offer that Brown believed was essential for the well-being of his business and he made every effort to assure the city of Baltimore that he was seriously considering moving his team to their town.

"We were in very heavy discussions with [Brown], to the point where documents were changing hands," said John Moag, then the chairman of the Maryland Stadium Authority.[2]

With negotiations for his potential new home moving at full speed, Brown set his sights on leveraging his relationship with the city of Baltimore with his current home, Cincinnati. Simply put, Brown threatened to pull the Bengals out of town if the city and Hamilton County didn't build him a new, football exclusive stadium. Considering his serious dalliances with Baltimore, the county believed they had no choice but to build Brown his Field of Dreams if they wanted to keep the Bengals in Cincinnati. And make no mistake, the county wanted to keep the NFL in town. More importantly, Mike Brown knew that as well.

To ensure that the NFL and the Bengals stayed in Cincinnati, Hamilton County voters approved a sales tax increase of half of one percent in 1996 to fund the construction of not only a new stadium for Mike Brown, but one for the Reds as well. While on the surface it appeared that two businesses were being served, it soon became apparent that Brown wanted the county to understand that if the stadium deal wasn't to his satisfaction he wouldn't hesitate to leave town, regardless of the stadium they intended on building. After all was said and done, the county apparently took Brown's threats seriously.

By the time Paul Brown Stadium opened in August 2000 with its 114 private suites and 7,600 club seats, Brown had engineered what the Wall Street Journal called in 2011, "the worst professional sports deals ever struck by a local government, soaking up unprecedented tax dollars and county resources while returning little economic benefit."[3]

The Journal reported that the lease signed by Brown and the Bengals with the county included the latter picking up nearly all operating and capital improvement costs as well as paying for all security costs on game day. That's a cost of nearly $8 million a year for the county and doesn't include the $7.5 million they would pay for a new scoreboard and the $3 million in public funding they spent for the $3.5 million cost of installing Wi-Fi at the stadium. Meanwhile, the Bengals would pay a relatively low lease payment and retain the right to keep 100 percent of the annual parking revenue generated by events at the stadium.

The county also agreed in the lease to cover all cost overruns in construction of the stadium, a provision that has cost them nearly $175 million. And the spending doesn't stop there. The lease also requires the county to provide and finance any upgrades to the stadium that other NFL teams have already received or will receive in the future in their homes. It's a lease, according to the Wall Street Journal that is "unusually lopsided in favor of the Bengals."[4]

To be fair, Brown's critics don't begrudge him the deal he made with the county. To many, it was a shrewd business decision, regardless of its lopsidedness, and blame was pointed at the Hamilton County commissioners for agreeing to such a fiscally stupid deal. What grates on his critics and on Bengals fans alike, is what Brown has done with his financial windfall.

When he was angling (or holding the county hostage, depending on your personal point of view) for a new stadium, Brown contended that he needed the extra cash so he could compete with the larger market teams, and teams in pursuit of the free agents he needed to bring a championship to Cincinnati. In theory, it made sense.

In reality, it hasn't happened.

Since the stadium opened for the 2000 season, the Bengals have failed to sign any impactful, unrestricted free agents. In fact, since 2006, the list of unrestricted free agents signed by the team certainly hasn't included any future Pro Football Hall of Famers or even a potential Bengals Hall of Fame. The illustrious list includes:

> QB-Anthony Wright
> DT-Sam Adams
> S-Dexter Jackson
> DT-Kendrick Allen
> DT-Michael Myers[1]
> DE-Antwan Odom

---

[1] Not the Halloween movie killer, although you could make the argument that he would have been a better signing

WR-Laveranues Coles
QB-J.T. Sullivan
DT-Tank Johnson
WR-Antonio Bryant
TE-Bo Scaife
LB-Manny Lawson
G-Max Jean-Gilles
LB-Thomas Howard
QB-Bruce Gradkowski
DE-Jamaal Anderson
RB-BenJarvus Green-Ellis
G-Travelle Wharton
TE-Alex Smith
G-Mike Pollak
S-Taylor Mays
QB-Jason Campbell
OT-Marshall Newhouse
DE-Sam Montgomery

One look at this list and it's no wonder a larger number of Cincinnati fans believed Brown had engineered the biggest bait and switch in sports ownership history. For many, it is an unforgivable sin, and they have attempted to make the Brown family pay for their transgressions by refusing to support the team through the purchase of season tickets, club seats, and luxury suites. Much to the dismay of those who believe Brown fleeced the county, their efforts to shrink the team's bottom line has had no effect. From 2003-2010, the Bengals had 57 consecutive home game sellouts and from 2010-2014, the team averaged 90 percent capacity in their regular season home games.

While his track record of signing free agents is indefensible, it's worth noting that Brown hasn't shied away from paying his current roster of players the going market rate. In 2014, the Bengals' payroll was $73.25 million, including multi-year, multi-million dollar contracts to Andy Dalton, Geno Atkins, Carlos Dunlap, Leon Hall, and Andrew Whitworth. On the surface, it appears Brown is not exactly stashing money in mason jars and burying them at the 50-yard line at Paul Brown Stadium. However, when you find out the Bengals were $26.85 million under the salary cap in 2014, you start to wonder if Brown buried the jars in the end zone instead.[5]

It's this backdrop that would seem to indicate Brown has no interest in building a Cincinnati Bengals Hall of Fame. If the owner isn't willing to pay consistently for the current and future players of the franchise, which in turn directly affects his net profits, what hope is there for him to pay for a tribute to the players of the past that would have little or no effect on the company's bottom line? History would suggest that question is easily answered. And considering what Hamilton County has laid for the construction and upkeep for Paul Brown Stadium, you can't expect them to fund anything they're not obliged to pay for when it comes to the Bengals.

Besides Mike Brown's inclination to err on the side of frugality, another reason why the Bengals Hall of Fame isn't in place is quite frankly because the team's history is far from being rich in tradition or worthy of a home to fete the club's accomplishments. In their forty-eight years of existence entering the 2016 season, the Bengals have a regular season record of 338-399-3, reaching the playoffs in only fourteen of those forty-eight seasons.

On these infrequent occasions when they did qualify for the post-season, the Bengals haven't fared any better, despite reaching two Super Bowls. Cincinnati is a miserable 5-14 in the post-season, a record made even worse if you remove their two Super Bowl seasons. Take those two years out of the mix and the Bengals playoff record is 1-12. True, the team has recently won some divisional championships (2005, 2009, 2013 and 2015) but they haven't won a playoff game since 1990, losing their last eight playoff games. No matter how you try to spin it, the Bengals narrative over the past forty-eight years doesn't immediately command a Hall of Fame.

With a dubious team history like the Bengals possess, it's not a stretch to question whether or not the franchise had enough Hall of Fame-worthy players to make the entire enterprise worthwhile. Granted, there have been a few stalwart players who wore the Bengals uniform, including two who are currently enshrined in the Pro Football Hall of Fame. Nevertheless, when you look back on the forty-eight years of the team's history, it doesn't appear there is enough product to warrant a full-fledged museum dedicated to the team some national pundits refer to as the Bungals. It seemed like it was time to return back to the suffering of watching the Patriots and the Ravens play for a spot in the AFC Championship game.

So, as Darth Belichick employed tactics such as a running back reporting ineligible on the line of scrimmage and calling for his wide receiver to throw downfield on a backwards pass from Jabba the Brady, the idea of establishing a Bengals Hall of Fame initially faded away amidst the multiple reasons why it wouldn't materialize. Besides, the Ravens and Patriots were playing an epic playoff game.

But another funny thing happened on the way to dismissing the thought of a Bengals Hall of Fame. Even though the Patriots/Ravens contest was compelling television, I kept thinking about a way to honor the best of the Bengals past despite the evidence suggesting it was little more than just a pipe dream. In fact, the more I thought about it, the more I was determined to either establish a plan to make it happen or put it to rest once and for all.

If I was truly going to move forward with building a foundation for a Bengals museum of sorts, then, at the very least, I needed to prove whether or not the reasons I believed it couldn't happen were valid, and determine if it was possible to overcome them. It also meant that if I wanted to pursue this venture, I would have to tackle, head-on, the biggest elephant in the room, Mike Brown.

At first, the obstacle that is the stinginess of Mike Brown, seemed insurmountable. Getting Brown to pay for something that provides no tangible effect on this team's profit margin is the equivalent of asking Michael Corleone if he would consider forgiving Carol Rizzi for his involvement in the murder of his brother, Sonny, once he had admitted to his complicity. Sure, he'd think about it, even giving you the impression he might agree to your overtures. But just when you think you convinced the boss to keep you and your ideas alive, he kills you with a wire garrote. While Brown certainly wouldn't conduct his family business the same way Corleone did, there is no question he considers a Hall of Fame for this team an unworthy expenditure.

"We have no statues. We have no Hall of Fame. We have no Ring of Honor," Brown said in a 2015 interview. "We do have large pictures of the players in the foyer of the west side [of the stadium]. But is that enough?

Probably not. I confess it isn't. Maybe someone who comes after me can do better with this."[6]

Given this prospect, it seemed this was a good as place as any to stop these notions of a Bengals Hall of Fame and return to the agony of watching the Ravens give the Patriots more than they bargained for in the early stages of the fourth quarter. In reality, the whole notion should have ended right there and then. Instead, it only gained momentum.

Maybe I was channeling my inner Bluto Blutarsky, defying Dean Wormer's authority and control. Maybe I thought I was Ray Kinsella and somehow subconsciously heard, "If you build it, they will come." Or maybe, just maybe, after many exasperating years, this frustrated Bengals fan was ready to tell Mike Brown, "Keep your money and I'll just do this on my own!" Regardless, I decided I didn't need Brown and his financial support to create and develop the foundation to honor the history of the franchise. Quite frankly, given the infancy of this idea, I'm not looking to build something similar to Patriot Place Plaza.

Realistically, before starting the groundbreaking on an actual building, I needed to assess whether there was any merit to the argument that the team's history deserved a Hall of Fame. The easiest test was to compare the Bengals' past with a team that already has a Hall of Fame, the New England Patriots. As you can imagine, considering the Pats' recent performance, the comparison between the two franchises certainly seemed to confirm why the Bengals had no such gallery, a fact that was underscored as I witnessed New England wrap up their victory over Baltimore, sending them to their fourth consecutive AFC Championship game. The Bengals, on the other hand, haven't played in the AFC Championship game since the 1988 season.

But as Belichick walked across the field to shake the hand of Ravens coach John Harbaugh after the hard earned win, it occurred to me that while the Patriots are arguably the NFL's best franchise now, that wasn't always the case. In fact, it wasn't too long ago that New England was far from being the elite team they are today.

The current New England Patriots began as the Boston Patriots in the AFL in 1960, eight years before Cincinnati entered the AFL. Even though they had an eight year head start on the Bengals, the Patriots did very little to establish themselves as a model franchise.

From 1960-1967, the Patriots were a mediocre 55-48-9, reaching the playoffs only one time, in 1963, going 1-1 and losing in the AFL Championship Game. Once the Bengals joined the AFL in 1968 and participated in the NFL merger three years later, the two teams had similar records prior to Belichick's arrival in New England in 2000. From 1968 to 1999, the Patriots were 220-264 while Cincinnati was 214-269-1 during those same 32 seasons. Both teams made occasional appearances in the post-season during this time span as well. The Patriots qualified for the playoffs nine times, finishing with a 6-9 record, while the Bengals made the playoffs seven times, compiling a 5-7 record in those playoff games. Both franchises appeared in two Super Bowls prior to 2000 as well, with both teams losing each time they played for the Lombardi Trophy.

The big point, however, is what New England has done since the beginning of the 21st Century. During the Belichick era, the Patriots' record is Hall of Fame-worthy: 12 AFC East Divisional titles, including six consecutive from 2009-2014, 6 AFC Conference championships and four Super Bowl victories. You could build a separate Hall of Fame for just this cycle of play.

So while you can't dismiss what the Patriots have done since Belichick's arrival, their history prior to 2000 compares to the Bengals'. When you factor in that the Patriots started their Hall of Fame in 1991, nine years prior to the start of their dominance, and five years before making their second Super Bowl appearance, you begin to believe that the Bengals have enough positive history to merit their place to honor the team's past.

But what about those who wore the Bengals uniform? Are there enough quality players in the team's history to create and sustain a Hall of Fame? Subjectively, of course, there is. Every Bengals fan has their favorite player or players of all-time and I'm no exception. But having a favorite player doesn't necessarily make him an all-time great.

On the other hand, looking objectively at the Bengals of the past and their impact on the team and the NFL is an entirely different proposition. It becomes much tougher to successfully argue if a player is Hall of Fame-worthy once you remove your fan-based biases and make your case solely based on someone's performance on the field. Given the Bengals' forty-eight seasons of mostly below-average results, it makes that task even more difficult.

But as was the case when comparing the two teams' season-by-season records to determine if the Bengals deserved a Hall of Fame like the Patriots have established, it's worth taking a look at who is in the Pats' Hall of Fame and see if a comparable list of former Bengals exist. After reviewing the list of Patriot Hall of Fame enshrines, the answer seems fairly obvious. Since it was created in 1991, 23 players have been elected to the Patriots' Hall of Fame. Those 23 players are:

John Hannah
Nick Buoniconti
Gino Cappelletti
Bob Dee
Jim Lee Hunt
Steve Nelson
Babe Parilli
Mike Haynes
Steve Grogan
Andre Tippett
Bruce Armstrong
Stanley Morgan
Ben Coates
Jim Nance
Sam Cunningham
Jon Morris
Drew Bledsoe
Troy Brown
Tedy Bruschi
Ty Law
Houston Antwine
Willie McGinest
Kevin Faulk

Three of those players, John Hannah, Nick Buoniconti, and Mike Haynes, are also members of the Pro Football Hall of Fame. It's important to note, however, that Buoniconti and Haynes played at least half of their careers with another team. Additionally, only six of the 23 (Drew Bledsoe,

Troy Brown, Tedy Bruschi, Ty Law, Willie McGinest and Kevin Faulk) played for Belichick and earned a Super Bowl title. Finally, the average NFL career for these 23 players was 13.13 years, with an average of 11 years spent in a Patriots uniform.

Looking at the list of players in the Patriots Hall, it's not a stretch to imagine that the Bengals have a similar complement of players to establish their own place to honor the best who have played for the franchise. For starters, the Bengals have their own Pro Football Hall of Famer in Anthony Muñoz, a player who spent his entire career with the team, a more than favorable comparison to the Patriots' Hannah. While the Bengals don't have many players in their history who averaged nearly 13 years in the NFL, they also have played eight fewer seasons than New England. Based upon the Patriots numbers in combination with the number of seasons Cincinnati has played, a solid Bengal Hall of Fame candidate would have played in the NFL for 11.04 years while playing 9.26 years in a Bengals uniform. While numbers aren't etched in stone, they at least provide a solid baseline to determine who deserves enshrinement. Better yet, the numbers appeared to indicate that a Bengals Hall of Fame seemed justifiable.

So, as I prepared for the next game on Saturday's schedule, Carolina at Seattle, what at first seemed an implausible notion, creating and developing a plan for a Cincinnati Bengals Hall of Fame became more than just a dream. In fact, despite knowing that Mike Brown wasn't going to write me a check to start breaking ground, the idea of a Bengals Hall of Fame started to begin taking shape.

As fate would have it, or as if I were destined to make this thought a reality, any lingering doubts I had that the Bengals warranted a Hall of Fame disappeared as the Panthers and Seahawks divisional playoff game at Seattle unfolded.

In a deja-vu moment that seems fitting for what eventually transpired, when the Carolina-Seattle game returned from a commercial break, the camera inside Century Link Field panned to the Seahawks Ring of Honor. The Ring of Honor is a prominent display of those individuals who the franchise has determined to have made an impact and a significant contribution to the team and the National Football League. Despite having only joined the league in 1976, the Seahawks have nine members in their Ring of Honor that includes one head coach and one broadcaster.

At that point, the idea of Bengals Hall of Fame went from, "It will never happen" during the Patriots game to "This has to happen" midway through the Seahawks game. If the Patriots and the Seahawks have a spot to recognize what they believe are their greatest players, then the Bengals deserve a similar point of appreciation. In essence, if Dave Krieg, Jim Zorn, and Sam Cunningham can be venerated by the team they played for, then the Bengals, albeit with a lack of perceived candidates, too many poor seasons, and thrifty ownership, are worthy of their own Hall of Fame or Ring of Honor.

In fact, it's irrelevant what it's called. It's just time, after forty-eight seasons, for the Cincinnati Bengals to pay homage to their past and recognize those players who contributed to the success of the franchise.

By the time the second half of the Seahawks game started, I was no longer interested in its outcome and was instead focused on how to compile the components necessary to bring a Bengals Hall of Fame together. Yes, I knew from the outset that a physical building, having jersey numbers retired, or displaying names on the façade inside Paul Brown Stadium wasn't going to happen. That wasn't the point of what was now, a project.

The real work would start with a full-fledged effort to dissect each year in the team's history, not only looking for those seasons that stood out, but for the players who made their mark while wearing the orange and black stripes.

It's a task requiring an objective review of everyone who played for the Bengals, including the development of a methodology which will serve as the model to determine who qualifies for the initial class as well as future inductions into the team's Hall of Fame.

It's a task so herculean but passionate in nature, that there wasn't time to keep watching NFL playoff games that do not involve the Bengals. It's a task I decided to start on immediately, while the iron and the desire to see this through was white hot.

So now you know how this project was born. Over the next several months, the criteria for consideration was created and the list of nominees was examined. Each individual who qualified was thoroughly vetted statistically. The result is my initial list of candidates and my inaugural class of the Cincinnati Bengals Hall of Fame.

The key phrases here are "my initial list" and "my inaugural class".

The list is by no means sponsored by the team or in any way an official lineup of Hall of Fame inductees. This is simply the opinion of a long-time frenzied Bengals fan who believes it's time for the team to enter the 21st Century like the rest of the NFL by recognizing the great players in the team's forty-eight-year history.

Anytime someone comes up with a list of all-time players in any sport, lively debate is sure to follow. Coming up with what is essentially a short list of the Bengals all-time best players is no exception. And make no mistake, not only do I mind the discussion and criticisms, I welcome and encourage it. It's the only way, moving forward, for me to improve and enhance the qualifications and selections of future Hall of Fame inductees. Consider this, then, your green light to let me know your thoughts and opinions on the initial list of candidates, finalists, and selections for the Cincinnati Bengals Hall of Fame.

Before you can begin to agree or disagree with my processes and selections, you need to know how the candidates for induction were determined and ultimately selected. For that, we need to start with how I determined the list of initial candidates to consider for the inaugural class.

So enough of how I came to the point of writing this book. It's time to see who the initial class of inductees are and how they were selected. Hopefully, you'll receive just as much enjoyment reading this book as I did writing it.

CHAPTER ONE

DETERMINING
WHO QUALIFIES

The first place to start with this immense project was to create a model or formula to determine statistically, analytically, and objectively, which former Cincinnati Bengals were worthy of Hall of Fame consideration. With the advances in technology, the abundance of hard core information available on the internet, and the overall embracing of outside-the-box analysis, obtaining the necessary statistical and analytical data wasn't difficult. The hard part was ensuring the candidates were chosen objectively.

Considering that I have been a fan of the team for more than forty years, it was only natural that I gravitated first toward those players who were and are my favorite Bengals. That's why it was so important to establish an unbiased and objective measuring tool to firstly determine who qualified for induction and to then select the first and potentially future classes of the Bengals Hall of Fame.

Establishing the criteria was the first order of business. I determined that the best way to decide who would initially qualify for the Hall of Fame was to examine the existing NFL teams with their own Hall of Fame or Ring of Honor that have played the equal, fewer, or close to the same number of seasons as have the Bengals. Of the other 31 NFL franchises, 14 began play in either the AFL or NFL since 1960 and each have their own Ring of Honor or Hall of Fame. Those 14 teams have inducted a total of 196 players as of 2016 into their special places of recognition with an average of 10.08 years of service wearing the team's uniform for each player honored (A detailed list of the 14 teams and the players honored by each franchise is located in the Appendix section).

Using these numbers as a baseline, I determined that to qualify for the Cincinnati Bengals Hall of Fame, a player must have played for the franchise a minimum of eight years. The duration of eight years was used instead of nine or ten for three reasons. First, nine of the 14 comparable teams examined were established and playing games prior to the Bengals inaugural 1968 season. In most cases, those nine teams played seven seasons prior to the Bengals' first game. Taking one or two seasons of service from the 14 team average seemed a fair adjustment.

Second, according to a 2011 NFL Management Council Study of players who entered the NFL between 1990 and 2002, the average career length for a player who is on the club's opening day roster as a rookie is 6.0 years with a first-round draft choice averaging a nine year career (As a matter of full disclosure, the NFL Players Association claims the average is 88 percent lower at 3.2 years).[7] Adding two more years to the NFL playing career average in order to qualify for the Bengals Hall of Fame, a 33 percent increase, made logical sense.

Finally, playing for the Bengals a minimum of eight years equates to playing for the franchise for close to 20% (17.02% actual) of the team's existence through 2014. This percentage of service time with a team compares favorably to the other nine teams with the same or greater number of professional football seasons as the Bengals and who have their own form of a Hall of Fame. The players who are members of those nine Halls of Fame, on average, played for less than 20% (19.10 actual) of their team's existence through 2014. The closeness of these two percentages solidified the eight year minimum requirement a player needed to have played in a Bengals uniform in order to qualify for consideration into the team's Hall of Fame.

The next step in the qualification process was to create a statistical platform for all of the positions on a team that not only measured the accomplishments of each player and their position, but to differentiate between those who were good and those who are Hall of Fame-worthy. For the skilled positions such as quarterback, running back, wide receiver, and tight end, this was, initially, a very easy assimilation of statistical information. Access to those type of statistics is easy thanks to such online databases like pro-football-reference.com.

But when it comes to the so-called non-skilled positions like the offensive line, special teams, and the entire defensive unit, traditional stats like touchdowns, points scored or yards gained either don't apply equally or even at all. Fortunately, specific and detailed statistics for these positions are now readily available, dating back to the early 1970s, as well.

While individual statistics are important to measuring the performance of each player, failing to judge the impact each Hall of Fame candidate had on their offensive or defensive unit and the team overall would not yield the true value each individual delivered to the franchise's history and success. That's why the team's regular and post-season records as well as the overall performance of either the offensive, defensive, or special team units during a player's tenure was also factored when considering someone's Hall of Fame candidacy.

Finally, all eligible candidates were sorted by the positions they played during their career with the Bengals. Those positions included:

- Quarterback
- Running Back
- Wide Receiver
- Tight End
- Offensive Line (Center, Guard, and Tackle)
- Defensive Line (Tackle and End)
- Linebacker
- Secondary (Cornerback and Safety)
- Kicker
- Punter[1]

With the statistical framework in place, all those who played a minimum of eight seasons in a Bengals uniform were subjected to a performance review depending on the position they primarily played. Every potential candidate, regardless of their position, were reviewed considering the following criteria:

---

[1] Any special team statistics earned by a player is considered in addition to their performance at one of the primary positions.

- NFL Awards Received
- All-Pro Selections
- Pro Bowl Selections
- Cumulative Regular Season Record
- Cumulative Post-Season Record
- Bengals Regular Season Individual Records
- Bengals Post-Season Individual Records
- Bengals Regular Season Team Records
- Bengals Post-Season Team Records

All of the candidates who played offense were also measured against the team's yearly rank during the time they played in the following categories:

- NFL Total Offense
- NFL Points Scored

Each offensive player was then broken down by the primary position they played. In each category, reviewed, regular and post season statistics were considered. While no category was weighted more than any other, the totality of the player's resume did carry significantly more influence. What follows is the specific statistical platform for each offensive position:

Quarterback

- Season and Career Yards Passing
- Season and Career Touchdown Passes
- Season and Career Interceptions
- Season and Career Completion Percentage
- Season and Career Quarterback Rating
- Yearly NFL Passing Rank

Running Back

- Season and Career Yards Rushing
- Season and Career Touchdowns
- Season and Career Total Yards Gained
- Yearly NFL Rushing Rank

Wide Receiver and Tight End

- Season and Career Receptions
- Season and Career Receiving Yards
- Season and Career Touchdowns
- Yearly NFL Passing Rank

Offensive Line

- Yearly NFL Passing Rank
- Yearly NFL Rushing Rank
- Yearly Yards Rushing Per Carry
- Yearly Sacks Allowed

On the defensive side of the ball, all potential candidates were vetted for the team's yearly rank during the time they played in the following categories:

- NFL Total Defense
- NFL Points Allowed

Like the offensive players who qualified, each defensive player was screened by the primary position they played, and the position categories previously established. As was the case with the positions on offense, both regular and post-season records and statistics were considered for each statistical point. The following is the specific statistical platform for each defensive position:

Defensive Line

- Season and Career Solo Tackles
- Season and Career Total Tackles
- Season and Career Sacks
- Season and Career Passes Deflected
- Season and Career Forced Fumbles
- Season and Career Fumble Returns and Yards[1]

---

[1] Regular season statistics for Solo and Total Tackles, Forced Fumbles, Fumble Returns, Sacks, and Passes Deflected do not exist until 1976. Post-season numbers do exist for these statistics beginning in 1970.

- Yearly NFL Rushing Defense Rank

Linebackers

- Season and Career Solo Tackles
- Season and Career Total Tackles
- Season and Career Sacks
- Season and Career Passes Deflected
- Season and Career Forced Fumbles
- Season and Career Fumble Returns and Yards
- Season and Career Interceptions
- Season and Career Touchdowns
- Yearly NFL Rushing Defense Rank
- Yearly NFL Passing Defense Rank

Defensive Backs

- Season and Career Solo Tackles
- Season and Career Total Tackles
- Season and Career Sacks
- Season and Career Passes Deflected
- Season and Career Forced Fumbles
- Season and Career Fumble Returns and Yards
- Season and Career Interceptions
- Season and Career Touchdowns
- Yearly NFL Passing Defense Rank

As for the special teams unit, the focus was on the placekickers and punters and their regular and post-season statistics. The following is the criteria used to judge both of these positions:

Placekickers

- Season and Career Field Goals Made and Attempted by Distance
- Season and Career Points Scored
- Yearly NFL Field Goal Rank
- Yearly NFL Points Scored Rank

Punters

- Season and Career Yards Per Punt Average
- Season and Career Punts Blocked
- Season and Career Touchbacks
- Yearly NFL Punting Rank

It's worth mentioning at this point, the consideration given to the recent rise in advanced statistics and matrices as fostered by the group at Pro Football Outsiders. While the type of analysis provides invaluable insight and greater detail regarding a player's performance than traditional statistics offer, the problem is that they only date back to 1988. That being said, despite not encompassing the history of the franchise--when applicable--these advanced stats were used in determining the value of many of the qualified candidates (The definitions of the advanced statistics used are located in the Appendix section).

Even with this strongly objective performance review in place for all of the eligible candidates, it's only fair to admit that some of the final evaluations did contain an occasional personal or subjective inspection. Since I am a die-hard Bengals fan, it's only natural that my personal bias towards certain players and moments would seep through on an intermittent basis. Overall, though, the player reviews and final determinations are strongly rooted in the cold, hard facts and performances each eligible individual exhibited during their career with the franchise.

But before the finalists for the Bengals Hall of Fame is revealed, it's necessary to clean up a couple of housekeeping issues regarding who makes the final cut.

CHAPTER TWO

THE FINAL CUT

A fter reviewing *Cincinnati's all-time roster*, spanning from 1968 to the present day, 60 players initially qualified for consideration to the team's Hall of Fame by wearing the Bengals uniform for at least eight seasons. While completing 60 player performance reviews seems in order, it is not practical or effective to do so for a couple of reasons.

First, five of the 60 players are either still active with the Bengals or another NFL team as of the end of the 2014 season. It just doesn't serve the purpose of a Hall of Fame to induct or consider a player for admission while they are still actively playing for either the Bengals or any other NFL team. It is with this thinking in mind that the following players were not considered at this time for the Bengals Hall of Fame:

- Carson Palmer
- Leon Hall
- Andrew Whitworth
- Robert Geathers
- Domata Peko

It should be noted that, barring some unforeseen circumstances, all five of these active players will become eligible for the Bengals Hall of Fame once they retire from the NFL.

Secondly, several of the remaining 55 eligible players, despite being members of the Bengals roster for at least eight seasons, did not play a significant role or were primarily reserve players during their time with the team. Without dismissing their contributions to the history of the franchise, players were not considered who were:

- Not a usual starter at any of the 11 starting positions on offense
- Not a usual starter at any of the 11 starting positions on defense
- Not the usual starting placekicker or punter

In the future, these players may become eligible for induction. In the present, though, these 10 players were eliminated from consideration for the initial class of the Bengals Hall of Fame due to not being a usual starter for at least half of their seasons in Cincinnati:

- Erik Wilhelm
- Turk Schonert
- Essex Johnson
- Robert Jackson
- Brad St. Louis
- Leo Barker
- Gary Burley
- Brian Blados
- Steve Kreider
- Bruce Coslet

After making these operational adjustments, there remained 45 players to consider. The final step in establishing the first list of inductees was to determine how many former Bengals to include. Taking a page from the inaugural Baseball Hall of Fame class, the first class enshrined in the Bengals' Hall will comprise five players.

Now that the eligibility rules, the statistical methodology, the final adjustments, and the number of initial players in the first ever class of the Bengals Hall of Fame have been decided, it's time to reveal the performance reviews conducted on the players who qualified. All told, 45 players wore a Bengals uniform for a minimum of eight seasons and met the final qualifications, while 29 others just missed the cut by playing for seven years in Cincinnati.

So, without further ado, here is the list of candidates, along with their performance reviews, eligible for induction into the initial class of the unofficial Cincinnati Bengals Hall of Fame.

CHAPTER THREE

JIM BREECH

Destiny's Bengal

*L*ife coach and motivational speaker Tony Robbins once said, "It is in your moments of decision that your destiny is shaped." Those words best encapsulate how placekicker Jim Breech became a Cincinnati Bengal for 13 seasons and a candidate for the team's Hall of Fame.

A native of Sacramento and a graduate of the University of California, Breech in two seasons as the Golden Bears placekicker, scored 154 points with a 62.7 field goal made percentage. Those numbers helped him become a member of the University of California's Athletic Hall of Fame in 1999.

Breech was chosen in the eighth round and the 206th overall pick of the 1978 NFL Draft by the Detroit Lions. His career with the Lions, though, was over before it started as Detroit cut him before the start of the 1978 season. To make matters worse, no other NFL team expressed any interest in signing him for the 1978 season.

Breech's fortunes changed the next season when he became the kicker for the Oakland Raiders in 1979. He played the entire season for the Raiders, who finished 9-7 but failed to make the playoffs when they lost to Seattle at home in the final weekend of the season. Breech had a more than respectable season, leading the team with 95 points scored and converting on 18 of his 27 field goal attempts (66.67%).

Unfortunately, in the bizarre mind of Raiders general manager and principal owner Al Davis, Breech's performance wasn't good enough, or else he believed there was someone else who could do a better job. Regardless, Davis triggered the first in a series of events that would, in the end, pave the way for Breech to become an all-time Bengals legend.

Upon learning that the Bengals had released Chris Bahr, their kicker of the last four seasons, Davis didn't hesitate to unceremoniously cut Breech and sign Bahr to replace him. Despite being shown the door by the quirky Oakland owner, Breech didn't have to wait long, unlike in 1978, for another NFL team to want him as their team's kicker. In fact, two teams would become seriously interested in signing Breech, the Bengals and their in-state and divisional rival, the Cleveland Browns. Breech faced a dilemma, and his decision with whom to sign ultimately determined what Tony Robbins called, "that moment of decision that your destiny is shaped."

Breech was first approached by the Browns, specifically assistant personnel director Paul Warfield. The Browns were looking for a replacement to their injured and long-time kicker, Don Cockroft, and Breech was intrigued enough to visit Warfield to discuss the opportunity. That's when the wheels of fate intervened.

Before he made the trip for his scheduled visit with Cleveland, Bengals assistant personnel director, Frank Smouse, called Breech to inquire about whether he would consider replacing Bahr as Cincinnati's kicker for the 1980 season instead.

The recently but soon-to-be shortly unemployed Breech now faced choosing between two franchises that were, on the surface, heading in different directions. The Browns had finished the last four seasons 32-28, and they would finish 11-5 in 1980, winning the AFC Central Division in the process. Meanwhile, the Bengals' record in the previous four seasons was 26-34, including back-to-back 4-12 seasons in 1978 and 1979.

Those last two sub-par seasons cost Bill Johnson and Homer Rice their head coaching jobs respectively, leading general manager and principal owner, Paul Brown, to hire former Green Bay Packer great Forrest Gregg as the Bengals' new head coach for the 1980 season. To the most casual observer, it appeared Breech's decision was simple: sign with the team moving up the competitive ladder, the Cleveland Browns.

Thankfully for Bengals fans, Breech bucked conventional wisdom.

Whether or not Breech would have achieved any success or acclaim with the Browns or the Raiders, we'll never know. For what it's worth, Cockroft recovered from his injuries to lead the Browns in scoring in 1980 with 87 points, only to retire at the end of the year. Meanwhile, Bahr had a successful nine-year stint with the Raiders that included two Super Bowl championships, the first coming in 1980, and the year following Breech's departure from Oakland.

What we do know is that once he arrived in Cincinnati in 1980, Breech went on to become the most successful placekicker in Bengals history and one of the most popular players in franchise history. In 13 seasons from 1980-1992 (tied for fourth all-time in most seasons as a Bengal), he is the team's all-time leading scorer with 1,151 points. And that's just the tip of the iceberg when it comes to Breech's impact not just on the team's success during his time in Cincinnati but on the Bengals record book as well.

Breech's footprints are stamped all over the Bengals' record book. In addition to the aforementioned career scoring mark, Breech is the team's leader in career point after touchdowns (PAT) made (476) and field goals made (225). Four of the top five seasons for made PATs belong to Breech, including 56 in 1988, the most in club history. His eight PATs on October 29, 1989 against Tampa Bay, is also a team single-game record.

His reputation as a reliable field goal kicker is evident in the team's record book as well. Breech's 13 consecutive field goals made in 1990 and his career field goal made percentage of 71.88 both rank fourth on the team's all-time list. While not known for kicking from distances beyond 50 yards, Breech was lethal from 30-39 yards, making 83.84% from that distance as a Bengal, third on the team's all-time list.

Making Breech's accomplishments even more striking is what can only be described as a very unique use of equipment. Breech, whose normal shoe size was a seven, wore a size five cleat on his right kicking foot. According to Breech, the smaller size show gave him more control and stability when he kicked. Say what you will about its quirkiness, the smaller shoe certainly gave Breech the ability to become a stalwart in Bengals history.

Unfortunately, despite his best efforts, the team's record in the regular season during Breech's tenure was below .500 (98-102, .490). That's not to say that Breech didn't do his best to make the Bengals more successful, though. In his 13 seasons, Breech was the team's leading scorer in 11 of them, including 1981 and 1987 when he was the AFC's leading scorer.

His contribution in 1981 (115 points) accounted for over 27 percent of the team's 421 points, a total that finished third overall in the NFL that season. His 89 points in 1988 helped the Bengals score an NFL leading 448, and the most points scored in a season by one team in team history.

Breech's 13 seasons in Cincinnati also marked a high point in the team's overall yearly NFL ranking in points scored and field goals made. Seven times during Breech's career with the Bengals (1981, 1982, 1984, 1985, 1987, 1991, and 1992), the team finished in the top half of the league in field goals made, highlighted by a fifth place finish in 1987. He was also an integral part of those eight Bengal teams that ended in the top half of the league in points scored, six of whom finished in the top-five (1981, 1982, 1985, 1986, 1988, and 1989).

Breech's performance even went beyond the Bengals' record book. His perfect nine field goals made in nine attempts during overtime is an NFL record. He also scored in 186 consecutive games, the third longest streak in NFL history.

As mentioned earlier, the Bengals did play below .500 during Breech's 13 seasons. The team did reach the post-season, however, four times from 1980-1992. And it was in those four playoff years that Breech cemented his credentials as a strong candidate for the team's Hall of Fame.

One of only seven players to be in a Bengals uniform for both of the team's Super Bowl appearances, Breech turned in his best work during the post-season. He is the team's all-time post-season leader in career points scored (52), career PATs (25), and PATs in a game (5, 1/6/1991 against Houston). Breech also holds the team record for most career post-season field goals made, converting on nine of 11 attempts (81.8%), including the most field goals made in a game (3) and the fifth longest successful field goal (43 yards) in team history.

Those last two records took place in Super Bowl XXIII against the San Francisco 49ers. While the game is most remembered for Joe Montana breaking the hearts of Bengals fans with his game-winning late fourth quarter touchdown drive, you might make the case that the only reason the Bengals were in position to win a championship was because of Breech's performance on the game's biggest stage.

Breech made all three field goals he attempted, including a 40-yarder that put the Bengals ahead 16-13 with 3:20 left to play. All told, Breech accounted for 10 of the team's 16 points in Super Bowl XXIII, allowing the underdog Bengals a chance at NFL immortality. Unfortunately, Montana and his magic intervened to spoil the coronation, leaving Breech, his teammates, and the team's fan base despondent. Breech would go onto play four more seasons for the Bengals, returning to the playoffs one final time in 1990 where he set the franchise record for most PATs in a post-season game.

In today's fantasy football-fueled NFL, Jim Breech would probably go undrafted or unnoticed by a legion of football fans. Fans of the Cincinnati Bengals, however, would warn you not to discount his value to your team—he was a reliable, productive, and clutch placekicker who was an integral part of two championship teams. And to think, Breech's storied history with the Bengals almost never happened. Instead, he could have very easily joined the Cleveland Browns in 1980 and quite possibly altered the events that led to the Bengals' two Super Bowl appearances. In the end, Breech hitched his size five kicking shoe to the Bengals wagon for the next thirteen seasons and went onto become a franchise fixture.

After examining the thirteen seasons Breech had with Cincinnati, it was a career personified by a quote made famous by the late John Lennon. "There's nowhere you can be," he once said, "that isn't where you're meant to be."

In other words, Jim Breech was destined to be a Cincinnati Bengals legend.

CHAPTER FOUR

BOOMER ESIASON

Captain of the U.S.S. Sugar

While defenses may win championships, today's NFL is dominated by those teams who have high-powered, quick-striking and efficient offenses. It's a trend that's been on the rise over the last two decades and there's no evidence or reason to believe it will slow down anytime soon. One of the key drives to this surge in offensive production has been the steady use by practically every NFL team of the "no huddle" or hurry-up offense.

Prior to the late 1980s, the only time a team implemented a no-huddle offense was in the last two minutes of each half in an effort to score either before the end of the first half or late in the fourth and final quarter. In fact during this era, it was more commonly referred to as The Two-Minute Offense, rather than the hurry-up offense as it is known today.

But all that changed, and with it, the way the NFL teams approached their offensive schemes, when the Bengals hired Sam Wyche as their head coach in 1984 to replace the departed Forrest Gregg.

Wyche was no stranger to the Bengals as he was a quarterback for the team from 1968-1970, starting nine games in his three seasons. After he retired from the NFL as a player, Wyche turned to coaching, eventually landing in San Francisco and working for Bill Walsh, his former quarterback coach in Cincinnati. From 1979-1982, Wyche directed the

49ers' passing game and was a member of the coaching staff that defeated the Bengals in Super Bowl XVI. It is there, in San Francisco, under the tutelage of Walsh, where Wyche developed the innovative philosophy that would transform how the rest of the NFL created their offensive schemes.

After spending one season in 1983 as the head football coach at Indiana University, Wyche was named as the Bengals' head man in 1984. His first four years in Cincinnati were hardly transformative. Those teams compiled a 29-34 record, coming close to reaching the post-season only one time. As the 1988 season approached, Wyche was clearly on the hot seat and nothing short of a playoff berth would ensure his continued employment.

Maybe it was in large part because he had nothing to lose, but Wyche decided in 1988 to radically change how his offense would look and perform. He decided to make the Two Minute or No Huddle offense as the team's standard or base offense. Wyche believed incorporating this offense full time would tire and confuse the opposing defense. He even went so far as to place 12 or more players in the huddle before deciding on the final set of personnel for each play (the NFL has since banned having more than 11 players in the huddle at any time).

Wyche called his new offensive scheme "Sugar" and while in theory it looked like it might work, he still needed a captain to steer this new concept through the choppy waters of infancy and to its ultimate journey, a spot in the NFL post-season.

Enter Norman Julius Esiason.

After watching and reviewing his play in 1988, it's hard to imagine anyone other than Esiason leaving Wyche's groundbreaking offensive philosophy. As a matter of fact, in the years that followed, Wyche never had a quarterback who executed his offense any better than the Long Island, New York native whose mother nicknamed him Boomer before he was born because of his constant kicking in the womb. But before he had his breakout season in 1988, Esiason had do some more kicking to ensure his place in Bengals history.

A three-sport star in football, basketball and baseball at East Islip High School, Esiason attended and played football at the University of Maryland. While at Maryland, Esiason benefitted from playing for two successful college football head coaches, Jerry Claiborne and Bobby Ross, and by having future college football head coach, Ralph Friedgen, as his offensive coordinator. Friedgen was responsible for not only developing Esisason at Maryland but future NFL quarterbacks Stan Gelbaugh and Frank Reich as well.

It is Esiason, however, who turned out to be Friedgen's most successful student. During his career as a Terrapin, Esiason completed 461 of his 850 passes (54.2 completion percentage) for 6,169 yards, 42 touchdowns and 27 interceptions. His performance was good enough for him to earn honorable mention All-American status in both 1982 and 1983, the latter in his senior season. As the 1984 NFL Draft approached, it seemed as if, based upon his college career and the players available in the draft, Esiason was a safe bet to be selected somewhere in the first round. Unfortunately for Esiason, the draft didn't unfold the way he or many had predicted.

For the first time in 10 years, the 1984 NFL Draft did not include a quarterback selected in the first round. Needless to say, being bypassed by every team with a first round pick didn't make Esiason a very happy camper. Rather, Esiason was beside himself. According to long time NFL Draft expert, Mel Kiper, Esiason was "going ballistic" when the first round ended and he had not yet been chosen by any NFL team.

Fortunately for the Bengals, when it came time for them to select a player in the second round, the left-handed quarterback from Long Island was available. As it turns out, even though he was the 39th overall pick in the draft, he was the first quarterback taken in the 1984 Draft. More importantly, as he embarked on his professional career, Esiason was headed to a franchise where he could learn from one of the league's best, the established veteran, Ken Anderson. Better yet, he was joining a team whose newly hired head coach, Sam Wyche, had developed a reputation as an offensive savant and a premier teacher of NFL quarterbacks.

On the surface, it appeared Esiason was being groomed long-term to become Anderson's successor. Those plans changed, however, in Week 6 of the 1984 season when Esiason started for an injured Anderson against the Houston Oilers. Esiason led the Bengals to a 13-3 win; his first career start that included his own three-yard touchdown run. Esiason went onto start three other games in 1984, finishing with a 3-1 record.

But despite Esiason's impressive four-game starting stint in his rookie season, Wyche installed Anderson as the team's starting quarterback when the 1985 season began. It was a decision that lasted only two games.

After opening the season 0-2, Wyche turned the reins of his offense over to Esiason in the third week of the season when the Bengals hosted the San Diego Chargers on September 22. Even though the Bengals lost to the Chargers that day, 44-41, the move to change quarterbacks set in motion a run of eight seasons in Cincinnati that catapulted the offense into the NFL elite and firmly established Esiason as one of the team's all-time greats.

Although the team finished 7-9 in 1985, it wasn't due to poor play by Esiason. He led an offense that scored, at the time, a club record 441 points while he personally completed 58.2% of his passes for 3,443 yards, 27 touchdowns and a 93.2 passer rating. It was a performance that would become a harbinger of things to come.

Over the next seven seasons with Esiason as the starting quarterback, the Bengals' offense finished in the top half of the NFL total offense rankings six times and the NFL passing rankings five times. The offense also finished in the top seven in points scored in four of those seasons, including team records that still stand for points scored in a game (61 on December 12, 1989 against the Houston Oilers) and touchdowns in a game (8 on October 29, 1989 against the Tampa Bay Buccaneers). Esiason also guided the offense to the top three seasons in club history in total net yards gained, highlighted by a club record 6,490 net yards in 1986. The top three games in Bengals history for net yards gained were also with Esiason under center, including a team record 621 net yards gained against the New York Jets on December 21, 1986.

Esiason personally excelled as well during those seven seasons. He still holds the team record for most passing yards in a game (490, October 7, 1990 at the Los Angeles Rams) and is tied for the most 300-passing yards in a game in a season (5, 1997). His five passing touchdowns in a game, a feat he accomplished twice, is tied for second in club history (December 21, 1986 against the New York Jets and October 29. 1989 against the Tampa Bay Buccaneers). The 1986 season in which he passed for 3,959 yards still ranks fifth on the team's all-time list.

But it is his 1988 season that places Esiason amongst the pantheon of all-time great Bengal players. By the time the 1988 season began, Esiason had become proficient in Wyche's No-Huddle, Hurry-Up or "Sugar" offense. As the season unfolded, Esiason became a full-fledged master.

The Bengals opened the season by winning their first six games, then cruised to a 12-4 regular season record and an AFC Central Division title. Even with a strong and deep pool of offensive talent, the key to what eventually resulted in the franchise's second ever Super Bowl berth, was the play of Esiason and his total command of Wyche's innovative offense.

Thanks to Esiason's leadership, the 1988 Bengals offense is arguably the best in the team's history, setting season team records for points scored (448) and touchdowns (59), numbers that contributed to the team leading the NFL in total offense and points scored. Those accomplishments were due in large part to the season Esiason had at the quarterback position.

Completing 57.5 percent of his passes (223-388) for 3,572 yards at 9.21 yards per pass attempt (second best in club history), Esiason threw for an AFC leading 28 touchdowns and finished with an NFL leading 97.4 quarterback passer rating. According to The Pro Football Historical Abstract, Esiason achieved a perfect 10.0 Q score and his 1,249.4 total adjusted yards led all players in 1988. Combining his individual performance with the fact the Bengals finished with best record in the AFC and home field advantage throughout the playoffs, and it's easy to see why Esiason was named first-team All-Pro and the NFL Most Valuable Player in 1988.

As the team prepared for the playoffs in 1988, the rest of the league, and specifically any future opponent of the Bengals, scrambled feverishly for a way to defend Esiason and the "Sugar" offense. The Bengals divisional round opponent, the Seattle Seahawks, believed the only way to curtail Esiason and his offense was to slow them down. In an effort to prevent the no-huddle offense from firing on all cylinders, the Seahawks feigned injuries while on defense, thereby forcing the game officials to stop the game, and more importantly, allowing Seattle to substitute players. Keeping the same defenders on the field was a key component to the "Sugar" scheme, so Seattle's ploy to force defensive substitutions stifled the Bengals offense.

Even though the Seahawks treachery held the Bengals offense to under their season average in points scored and yards gained, Cincinnati advanced to the AFC Championship game with a 21-13 win. Unfortunately, the damage to Esiason and the offense had been done. Wanting to ensure that no further controversy would transpire between opposing defenses and the Bengals offense, the NFL banned the use of the no-huddle offense in the AFC Championship game between Cincinnati and the Buffalo Bills. Although the Bengals went onto defeat the Bills, 21-10, and earn a trip to the Super Bowl, the offense was never the same. In the Super Bowl against the 49ers, Esiason threw for only 144 yards as the offense scored no touchdowns in a 20-16 loss.

Although Esiason and the offense returned to high-powered form in the four years that followed, neither did the team nor its quarterback recapture the magic of the 1988 season. The Bengals did return to the post-season in 1990 and even though they lost to the Los Angeles Raiders in the divisional round, that playoff season is best remembered for the team's and Esiason's performance against the Houston Oilers in the wild card round.

En route to a 41-7 victory over their AFC Central Division rival, the Bengals set team post-season records for points scored and touchdowns (5) in a game. Esiason set a post-season team record for the highest quarterback passer rating in a game (125.0) and tied a team record for most touchdown passes in a game (2). Little did anyone know at the time, but that victory over the Oilers still stands as the last playoff win in team history. It also marked the beginning of the end of the Esiason era.

At the end of the 1991 season, a year in which the Bengals finished a disappointing 3-13, the team fired Wyche, and in the 1992 NFL Draft that followed, chose David Klingler, the University of Houston quarterback, with the sixth overall pick. Once those events took place, Esiason clearly saw the handwriting on the wall and at the end of the 1992 season demanded a trade out of Cincinnati. On March 17, 1993, the team accommodated Esiason's request and traded him to the New York Jets for a third-round draft choice.

Over the next four seasons, Esiason played for both the Jets and the Arizona Cardinals, accumulating very pedestrian numbers while his teams compiled a 24-40 record and no post-season berths. As the 1997 season approached, it appeared Esiason's NFL career had come to a close as he contemplated retirement. But before he could call it quits, his old team, the Bengals, asked him to come back for one more go-round with the franchise. Esiason agreed to a one-year contract, even if it was in a back-up role to starter Jeff Blake.

Esiason's status as a back-up changed, however, when he became the starting quarterback after Blake started the 1997 season 3-8. In the final five games of the season, Esiason played some of the best football of his NFL career, throwing 13 touchdowns and only two interceptions while earning a 106.0 quarterback passer rating. The team finished 4-1 with Esiason under center, with the team scoring 30 or more points in four of those games. He impressed the Bengals so much that they offered him a two-year contract for the 1998 season. Esiason respectfully declined, and officially retired from the NFL after the 1997 season. Appropriately enough, he completed a 77-yard touchdown pass to Darnay Scott on the final play of his career.

From a wins and losses standpoint (73-86), Esiason's career with the Bengals was average at best. On the other hand, a .459 winning percentage while he was a Bengal and a 62-61 mark as the team's starting quarterback, does not define a career. The mark Esiason left on the franchise is indelible and goes far beyond the number of games he won or lost.

Esiason, a Pro Bowl selection in 1986, 1988 and 1989, is the team's all-time regular season leader in career average yards-per-pass attempt (7.62 yards) and 300-yard passing games (23). He also ranks second in career passing attempts (3,564), passing yards (27,148) and touchdown passes (187) and is third all-time in team history in career completions (2,015) and quarterback passer rating (83.1). He passed for 3,000 yards in a season in five out of the eight seasons he was a starter, and has three of the top five games in club history for most passing yards in a game. He also rushed for 1,598 yards on 447 attempts and seven touchdowns. The Pro Football Historical Abstract ranks him as the 73rd best quarterback in NFL history with a career Q score of 58.18 and 8,394.3 career adjusted yards.

Since his retirement, Esiason, who was named the NFL's Walter Payton Man of the Year in 1995 and selected to the Nassau County Sports Hall of Fame in 2004, has become a staple in the national spotlight. From 1998-2000, he was the color analyst for Monday Night Football. He then joined the Westwood One NFL radio broadcasts and has been the lead analyst for every one of their Super Bowl broadcasts since 2000. In 2002, he became a studio analyst for CBS on their The NFL Today pre-game show, a role he currently still holds. In 2007, he debuted with Craig Carton on WFAN in New York on the Boomer and Carton Show, a morning drive-time sports radio program. The show continues to air on WFAN and is currently simulcasted on the CBS Sports Network.

But in the hearts and minds of Bengals fans, Esiason will always be known as the blond, left-handed quarterback who during his ten seasons in Cincinnati led an offense that only the innovative and quirky mind of head coach Sam Wyche could create, a no-huddle scheme he called "Sugar."

For Bengal fans, nothing in team history has ever been so sweet.

CHAPTER FIVE

LEE JOHNSON

Thunderfoot

I t's not very often that a punter is considered one of an NFL team's all-time greatest players. In fact, it wasn't until 2014 that the first punter, Ray Guy, was inducted into the Pro Football Hall of Fame. Yet, when the history of the all-time Bengal greats is discussed, it must include a case for arguably the best punter in team history, Lee Johnson.

Born in Dallas, Texas, Johnson attended Brigham Young University and played for the legendary college football head coach, Lavell Edwards. While at BYU, Johnson kicked for 3,847 yards in his two seasons as the team's punter from 1983-1984, averaging a booming 46.9 yards per punt, a school record that still stands to this day. Johnson, nicknamed Thunderfoot by his teammates, still holds the school record for best punting average in a season (50.6 yards per punt in 1983) and the longest punt in a game, an 80-yarder against Wyoming on October 8, 1983. His 60.4 yard average per punt in that 1983 game against Wyoming is not only a school record but an NCAA record as well. His contributions on special teams helped lead BYU to the 1984 National Championship.

Thanks to his success at BYU, Johnson was chosen in the 1985 NFL Draft, uncommonly high for a punter or kicker when the Houston Oilers selected him in the fifth round with the 138th overall pick. Johnson spent the next two-plus seasons with the Oilers before joining the Cleveland

Browns for the last three games of the 1987 season. His stay in Cleveland was short-lived and led to his arrival in Cincinnati.

After playing three games for the Browns to open the 1988 season, Johnson joined the Bengals with 12 games remaining on the 1988 schedule. In the beginning, he was used exclusively for kickoffs and long field goal attempts. It wasn't until Week 14 on December 4 that Johnson became the regular punter, replacing Scott Fulhage in the game against the San Diego Chargers. Despite kicking for a pedestrian 39.0 average yard-per-punt on two attempts against the Chargers, the game marked the beginning of a 10-year run that resulted in Johnson becoming the most successful and prolific punter in team history.

Over the next 10 seasons, Johnson was the only punter the Bengals employed, amassing a list of records that solidifies his status as one of the team's historic players. Johnson ranks first in career total punts (746), punting yards (32,196) and punts inside the 20-yard line (186), and is third in career average yards per punt (43.16 yards). He stands second for most punting yards in a season (3,954 in 1993) and has the third highest punting yard average per team game (247.13 yards per game in 1993). Five times while Johnson was the team's punter, the Bengals ended the season in the top half of the NFL in punting, finishing second in 1993. Johnson holds several game records as well, including most punts in a game (11, November 2, 1997 against San Diego) and most punts inside the 20-yard line (6, November 2, 1997 against San Diego). He also ranks second in net yards per punt in a game (51.3 yards, November 6, 1994 at Seattle) and third in most punting yards in a game (474, November 2, 1997 against San Diego).

Johnson's performance in the post-season is just as impressive. He is the team's all-time post-season leader in career punts (25), punting yards (1,111) and punts inside the 20-yard line (8). He ranks second in career average yards per punt in the playoffs (44.44 yards) and net yards per punt (38.6 yards). He also holds the playoff game records for average yards per punt (51.6 yards, January 13, 1991 at Los Angeles Raiders) and punts inside the 20-yard line (3, January 8, 1989 against Buffalo and January 22, 1989 against San Francisco in Super Bowl XXIII). In addition to all of these post-season records, Johnson owns three of the four longest punts in a Bengals playoff game with his 64-yarder against the Raiders on January 13, 1991 being the longest in team post-season history.

If there is a dark cloud looming over Johnson's time in Cincinnati, it is the team's record while he was the primary punter. From 1989-1998, the Bengals were 56-104, appearing in the playoffs only one time (1990) and finishing .500 or better in only three seasons (1989, 1990 and 1996) when Johnson was the punter. Unfortunately, it was this lack of success that brought Johnson's career with the Bengals to an untimely end.

Following a 33-20 loss at home to Buffalo in Week 13 of the 1998 season, the Bengals' eighth consecutive loss to drop the team to 2-11, Johnson publicly criticized Cincinnati's management, particularly the owner and general manager, Mike Brown, and was specifically asked if he would pay to see the Bengals in person. His answer pulled no punches.

"No, no way," Johnson replied. "You're saying losing is OK. I guess if you've got nothing else to do. I'd sell my tickets."[8]

The Bengals' response was swift and defiant. Less than 24 hours later, despite playing in the most consecutive games in team history (169), the Bengals released Johnson, ending his 11-year association with the franchise. Much to his credit, Johnson never backed down from his comments and took release gracefully and pragmatically.

"I'm sure I was released because of what I said," Johnson said after he was cut. "I meant what I said, but I didn't think it was that incredible.

"The funk has been here since I've been here. I'm the last of the funk. Maybe now it will turn around."[9]

Johnson continued his NFL career for four more seasons, playing for the New England Patriots and the Minnesota Vikings, finally calling it quits with the Philadelphia Eagles in 2008. When all was said and done, Johnson played 18 NFL seasons, averaging 42.4 yards per punt for six different teams. His 1,226 career punts rank fourth in NFL history and his 51,979 career punting yards places him fifth on the league's all-time list. Amazingly, Johnson only had six punts blocked in his 259 games as an NFL punter.

These days, Johnson is an elite mountain cyclist. He has completed the Leadville 100, a 100-mile cycling event across the tough terrain of the Colorado Rocky Mountains, on nine different occasions. Given his past record of kicking for the Bengals over 11 tumultuous seasons for the equivalent of 18.29 miles, it seems only fitting that the next logical step for Johnson was to step on a bike and pedal miles over a rugged mountain surface.

Besides, it seems appropriate that anyone nicknamed "Thunderfoot" would transition from being an NFL team's all-time leading punter to using his feet to mountain cycle across the Rockies.

Better still, maybe, just maybe, all the biking will remove any existing funk Johnson might be carrying.

CHAPTER SIX

KEN RILEY

The Rattler

Once a year, in the week leading up to the Super Bowl, there's a vigorous debate about which inductees should be included in the Pro Football Hall of Fame. NFL insiders, media, and fans alike thrash it out until the names are announced the night before the Super Bowl. Over the past 25 years, most of those inducted were obvious choices and although they may not have succeeded on their first attempt, practically every player deemed worthy of inclusion eventually made it through and took their place in Canton, Ohio.

Strangely enough, despite the thorough and thoughtful discussion during this time, one name is conspicuously absent from the final list of candidates and is rarely even considered for Hall of Fame eligibility. He was nicknamed "The Rattler" and if you take a look at his NFL resume, maybe it's time to campaign for the Hall of Fame candidacy of Ken Riley, the great Cincinnati Bengal cornerback.

"You'll never find a bigger advocate of his making the Hall than me," former Bengals wide receiver and current NBC football analyst, Cris Collinsworth said. "I probably learned more football from Kenny Riley than from anyone I played for or against. Everything I did that worked against everybody else never worked against him. But as soon as he would pick off a pass on my route or beat me to a spot, he'd tell me why, explain what I'd done wrong. He wanted me to be better because that made the team better."[10]

A native of Bartow, Florida, Riley attended Florida A&M University and interestingly played quarterback, not cornerback, on the school's football team. After graduating from A&M as a Rhodes Scholar candidate, the Bengals selected Riley in the sixth round of the 1969 Common AFL/NFL Draft with the 135th overall choice. But when he arrived in Cincinnati, head coach Paul Brown had no intention of using him as a quarterback and instead converted him to cornerback.

In his rookie season, Riley made his Hall of Fame coach's decision look ingenious, tying for the team lead in interceptions with four and adding 334 kickoff return yards for a 23.9 yard return average. That 1969 season would mark the beginning of an NFL career spent entirely in Cincinnati, and as the numbers show, more than worthy of Hall of Fame consideration.

Over a career that spanned 15 seasons, the second most seasons played in team history, Riley was a key cog in a defense that finished in the top half of the NFL in points allowed 11 times, total defense 10 times and passing defense nine times. Riley never had a season in which he did not have an interception, leading the team or tying for the team lead in interceptions in seven seasons (1969, 1974, 1975, 1976, 1981, 1982 and 1983) and leading the AFC in interceptions three times (1976, 1982 and 1983). His nine interceptions in 1976 was a team record for most in a season for 30 years until Deltha O'Neill had 10 in 2005. Riley's 141 interception return yards in 1976 ranks third in team history and his two interception returns for a touchdown in 1983 is tied, with four others, for the most in a Bengals season. Remarkably, Riley was never named to a Pro Bowl team in any of his 15 seasons.

Riley's best season, however, was arguably 1983, a season that would turn out to be his last in the NFL. He contributed to a defense that finished first in the NFL in total defense, third in passing defense and sixth in points allowed by making 44 total tackles, intercepting eight passes, returning two of them for touchdowns. These accomplishments earned Riley his only first team All-Pro selection. More impressive, perhaps, is the fact that he did all of this at the age of 36.

Riley's career is also marked by several stand-out games. He participated in four games where the Bengals allowed the fewest net yards passing in team history, including the team record -35 yards against the Green Bay Packers on September 26, 1976. He set the team record for most interceptions in a game against the New York Jets on December 12, 1976 (a record he later tied on November 28, 1982 against the Los Angeles Raiders) when he picked off three passes, including two thrown by Joe Namath in his last game as a New York Jet.

As one of the team's starting cornerbacks from 1969-1983, the Bengals compiled a 110-104-1 record, qualifying for the playoffs in five of those 15 seasons. While the Bengals had a disappointing 2-5 record during those post-season appearances, Riley was a starting cornerback on the 1981 squad that appeared in the team's first-ever Super Bowl. Despite the team's poor won/lost record, Riley's efforts were clearly felt in those seven playoff games. He is tied for first in career post-season interceptions in team history (3) and ranks third in post-season career interception yards (34 yards). He also contributed to the defense that allowed only 16 yards net passing in a half against the San Francisco 49ers in Super Bowl XVI, the fewest in team post-season history, and only seven points against the San Diego Chargers in the 1981 AFC Championship game, the fewest points allowed in a Bengals playoff game.

By the time he retired after the 1983 season, Riley had established himself as not only one of the best to wear a Bengals uniform, but one of the premier cornerbacks in NFL history. Playing in 207 games as a Bengal, the most in team history, Riley finished with 316 total tackles, 98 passes defended and nine fumble recoveries. From 1970-1977, he teamed with Lemar Parrish to form the most successful cornerback pairing in team history and for those eight seasons, one of the top defensive secondaries in the NFL. Riley's 65 career interceptions, 596 career interception return yards and five interception returns for a touchdown are all Bengals team records. The Pro Football Historical Abstract ranked Riley as the 38th best cornerback in NFL history, finishing with a Q score of 236.63. Even his opponents deeply respected Riley and recognize him as one of the game's best.

"I always felt that he knew our system, our game plan, that he had viewed our films, that he knew our tendencies, my tendencies," recalled Hall of Fame wide receiver John Stallworth of the rival Pittsburgh Steelers. "From an intellectual standpoint, he was going to take away what I did well. He wasn't an in-your-face bumping guy, but he was going to be where he needed to be when he needed to be there. I knew he was going to challenge me every play."[11]

Yet despite all his impressive accomplishments, Riley has never been a finalist for the Pro Football Hall of Fame, and therefore his candidacy has never been discussed by the full selection committee. The fact he has been slighted for this honor is even more incredulous when you consider his 65 career interceptions ranks fifth in NFL history with the four players ahead of him on the list, Paul Krause, Emlen Tunnell, Rod Woodson and Dick "Night Train" Lane, all enshrined in the Hall of Fame. Most former players in a similar position would complain and make his case to anyone who would listen. But not Ken Riley.

"I'm not going to cry about it," Riley has said about his exclusion. "I think my numbers are deserving of the Hall of Fame. I've always been a modest and low-key type of guy. I've always thought your work would speak for you.

"It's like it's working against me now because the older you get and the longer you stay out of it, people forget who you are."[12]

Many people, however, have not forgotten about the 15-year NFL veteran who went back to his alma mater to become head football coach for eight seasons and then athletic director for 10 years thereafter. Riley has been inducted into six Halls of Fame (Florida Sports, Florida A&M, Polk County, Bartow, Florida, Tallahassee, Florida and Black College), named to the Florida High School Association's All-Century team that named the top-33 players in the 100-year history of Florida high school football, and selected to the All-1970s NFL second team by Pro Football Reference. As Riley so succinctly puts it, "I'm in every Hall of Fame but the big one."[13]

It's that big one, the Pro Football Hall of Fame, that has become Riley's Moby Dick. From a statistical standpoint there should be no question he deserves enshrinement. Whether or not he spent his whole career with a team that had a modicum of success that has stalled his candidacy is anybody's guess. What isn't a doubt is his place in Bengals history, arguably the best defensive back the team has ever had.

It's just a shame the rest of the NFL doesn't see it the same way.

CHAPTER SEVEN

KEN ANDERSON

Augustana's Finest

The *Augustana College website describes* its Rock Island, Illinois
campus as a "private, selective liberal arts college" and says its "visitors
comment on the beautiful wooden campus with its rolling, river valley
landscapes and winding pathways along the slough." It goes on to say,
"From the moment students set foot on campus, the college provides them
with the tools that will help them be successful here and in the future."

Given this description, it seems odd that when you Google, "Augustana
College notable alumni", the first image you encounter is that of an
American football player who hailed from a suburb of Chicago called
Batavia, Illinois.

But when that football player is Ken Anderson, it should come as no
surprise. For sixteen NFL seasons, Anderson was the model of consistency,
leading a then infant and undistinguished franchise in the Cincinnati
Bengals to national relevancy. While his season and career statistics look
non-descript compared to today's pass-happy offenses, Anderson's numbers,
upon reflection and the passage of time, were truly groundbreaking given
the NFL's environment in the late 1970s and early 1980s. Tutored by his
quarterback's coach when he first arrived in Cincinnati, the legendary Bill
Walsh, Anderson is considered by most observers as the first quarterback
to lead and execute the West Coast Offense. By the time he retired after

the 1986 season, Anderson had become the standard by which all other West Coast Offense quarterbacks were measured. But like any pioneer, the road to excellence, success and top of the mountain was filled with bumps and valleys that made the journey seem improbable at the outset yet, in the end, totally rewarding.

In early 1971, very few people, if anyone, who didn't attend Augustana College knew where the school was located. But if you were an NFL scout back then, you knew exactly how to find the private Lutheran university because of the play of their senior quarterback, Ken Anderson. As the 1971 Draft approached, teams were highly interested in the four-year letterman who was coming off his 1970 College Conference of Illinois and Wisconsin MVP season, and who, upon completing his senior season, held all 10 school passing records. Anderson had also finished his career fifth in NCAA history on the all-time list for career total offensive yardage (6,679 yards).

Unfortunately for Anderson, in the minds of many NFL decision makers, he wasn't regarded as a top tier selection in the 1971 NFL Draft because he played for a non-Division I or major college football program. Fortunately for the Bengals, when it was their turn to make the 67th overall pick in the third round, Anderson was still available and they jumped at the chance to add him to their roster.

In the beginning, Anderson was coming to a team fresh off their first ever division winning season in 1970, losing to the Baltimore Colts in the first round of the playoffs. He wasn't brought in to start at quarterback as the Bengals were comfortable with their incumbent at the position, Virgil Carter. Instead, they wanted Anderson to become the back-up, taking the spot that had been occupied the year before by future Bengals head coach, Sam Wyche.

As the 1971 season unfolded, it became apparent that the Bengals weren't going to repeat their 1970 performance. After winning the season opener, the team lost their next seven games, essentially ending any chance of repeating as AFC Central Division champions. Even though Carter led the NFL in completion percentage in 1971, Anderson was able to start four games that season, completing 55.0% of his passes for 777 yards and five touchdowns. Despite going 0-4 in those 1971 starting assignments, it was becoming obvious that Anderson was being groomed to become the starting quarterback sooner than anyone had anticipated.

When the 1972 season began, Anderson had officially wrestled the starting quarterback position away from Carter, guiding the Bengals to two, fourth quarter game winning drives en route to an 8-6 overall record. More importantly, it marked the beginning of Anderson's 13-year run as the team's starting quarterback and the start of a legacy that would define him as one of the most accurate and prolific quarterbacks of his generation. It's also a career resume that would and continues to spark debate about why he doesn't have a bust in the Pro Football Hall of Fame in Canton, Ohio.

If one characteristic defined Anderson's play on a yearly basis, it was his ability to make the vast majority of his pass attempts beneficial and efficient, hallmarks of what would make the West Coast Offense famous. Four times, Anderson had the league's highest passer rating (1974, 1975, 1981 and 1982) while leading the NFL three times in pass completion percentage (1974, 1982 and 1983 and fewest interceptions per pass attempts (1972, 1981 and 1982). Twice he led the league in yards passing (1974 and 1975), pass completions (1974 and 1982) and yards per pass attempts (1974 and 1975). He also was the NFL leader in passing touchdown percentage in 1981 and pass completions per game in 1982. His league-leading 70.6 completion percentage in 1982 stood as an NFL record for 27 years until Drew Brees set the new mark in 2009.

The Pro Football Historical Abstract also points out his excellence. Anderson had a Q rating of 8.8 or higher five times, including a perfect 10.0 in 1974, 1975 and 1981. According to the Abstract, Anderson was the yearly adjusted yards leader amongst NFL quarterbacks three times, accumulating 995.5 yards in 1974, 1,105.5 yards in 1975 and 1,662 yards in 1981.

This efficiency in the passing game helped the Bengals become a top-flight offense beginning in the mid-1970s. During Anderson's 13 years as the starter, the team finished in the top half of the NFL in passing 11 times, points scored 10 times, and total offense nine times. The offensive production during this time allowed Anderson to compile a 91-81 regular season record as a starter and earned him four Pro Bowl selections (1975, 1976, 1981 and 1982). More significantly, Anderson's stewardship of the offense was a key reason why the Bengals made the post-season four times during his tenure as the team's starting quarterback (1973, 1975, 1981 and 1982).

The year that Anderson is most famous for is the 1981 campaign, a season that resulted in the Bengals' first-ever Super Bowl appearance. It was a journey no one saw coming and one that was perilously close to taking place without Anderson as the starting quarterback.

The year before this, the Bengals finished a disappointing 6-10 under first year head coach Forrest Gregg, but did give the faithful some hope by winning three of their last four games. The offense, led by Anderson for the majority of the 1980 season, on the other hand, showed little promise, scoring only 244 points all season, the lowest in the AFC. Due to the lack of offensive production, Gregg began using 1979 first round draft choice, Jack Thompson, more often than not relegating Anderson to the bench. As the 1980 season came to a close there was a real possibility that Thompson would replace Anderson as the team's number one quarterback.

The one thing that definitely was changing for the franchise when the 1981 season began was the uniform they would wear. The Bengals debuted their new tiger-striped helmets, jerseys and pants that year and when the team opened the schedule at home against the Seattle Seahawks, it seemed Anderson had established himself as the team's number one quarterback. Unfortunately, after one half of play against the Seahawks in which Anderson threw two interceptions in route to a 21-0 halftime deficit, he was benched in favor of Turk Schonert and this time, the demotion looked to be permanent. Thanks to Schonert's efforts, the Bengals scored 27 unanswered points in the second half and defeated Seattle 27-21.

Immediately following the thrilling comeback against Seattle that would arguably save and make the season, controversy in the locker room was already brewing. Would Anderson retain his starting job despite a miserable opening week performance? Or would Schonert or Thompson, who was unable to play against Seattle due to an injury, start the following week on the road against the New York Jets? Gregg was apparently leaning towards going with either Schonert or Thompson until Anderson convinced his head coach he was the man for the job. Anderson rewarded Gregg's faith in him with a 22-34, 252 yard, two touchdown performance that led the Bengals to a 31-30 comeback victory over the Jets. The victory not only provided the team with a 2-0 start but it jump-started what would become a historic season for both the Bengals and Anderson.

Anderson finished the season with 300 completions on 479 attempts (62.6 completion percentage) for 3,754 yards, 29 touchdowns (third most in a season in team history), 10 interceptions, 1,348.7 adjusted passing yards according to The Pro Football Historical Abstract and an NFL leading 98.4 quarterback passer rating (second highest in team history). He led an offense that finished second in the NFL in total offense and third in passing offense and points scored. It was an individual performance that earned Anderson first team All-Pro selection and the 1981 NFL awards for Most Valuable Player and Comeback Player of the Year.

More importantly, Anderson's enormous success put the Bengals in a position to at least have a share of the lead in the AFC Central Division the entire 1981 season, culminating in the franchise's third-ever division title and a berth in the NFL playoffs. Once in the post-season, Anderson, who had been previously winless in two other playoff appearances, successfully navigated Cincinnati to wins over Buffalo in the divisional round and then San Diego in the AFC Championship in a game that would later be known as the Freezer Bowl. Playing in temperatures as low as nine degrees below zero with a wind chill factor of minus 59 degrees, Anderson—incredibly-- threw for 161 yards, two touchdowns and a 115.9 quarterback passer rating as the Bengals defeated the Chargers 27-7 and secured a spot in Super Bowl XVI in Pontiac, Michigan. While it seemed impossible to execute the offense with such efficiency in the brutal conditions both teams faced, Anderson was his usual modest self when describing his performance.

"We stayed with our short hand intermediate passing game," Anderson recalled. "We didn't throw the ball towards the sideline too many times. We kept it over the middle."[14]

While Anderson made it seem simple, his teammates believed his upbringing played a large part in his near perfect play in what was at the time, the coldest game in NFL history. "It was amazing," starting offensive guard Dave Lapham remembers. "Kenny Anderson from Batavia, Illinois, grew up in the cold. He knew what to do and how to handle it."[15]

The Bengals would face an equally surprising opponent in the Super Bowl, the San Francisco 49ers, led by their head coach, Anderson's former quarterback coach and mentor, Bill Walsh, and his newest West Coast Offense pupil, third-year quarterback Joe Montana.

In a virtual replay of their opening game of the season against Seattle, the Bengals played miserably in the first two quarters of Super Bowl XVI and trailed 21-0 at the half. This time, Gregg stuck with Anderson who then led a furious comeback, thanks to 17 first downs and 257 total net yards in the second half (both post-season team records). The Bengals climbed to within five points with 16 seconds left in the game, but when the ensuing onside kick failed, the 49ers won their franchise's first Super Bowl title 26-21. Even in defeat, Anderson accounted for himself quite well, finishing the game 25-34 for 300 yards and two touchdowns.

When the 1982 strike-shortened season opened, Anderson picked up where he had left off the year before. Despite playing only nine regular season games due to the players' strike, he was again masterful in leading the offense and the team to their first-ever consecutive playoff seasons. For the second consecutive year, Anderson had an outstanding record-breaking season. He set a club record 24.22 average completions per game and an NFL leading 70.55 completion percentage. His four 300-yard passing games in 1982 propelled him to a club record 277.22 average yards passing per game and an NFL leading 95.3 quarterback passer rating. His performance in a losing effort at San Diego, where he was 40-56, club records for completions and attempts in a game, for 416 yards, two passing touchdowns and one rushing touchdown, stood out.

Anderson's execution of the high powered Bengals offense contributed to the team finishing second in the NFL in total offense, third in passing offense and fourth in points scored. The 1982 Bengals offense also set a club record for average net yards per game with a 259.89 average per game. All of this production led to a 7-2 record and a berth in the AFC Playoffs.

Unfortunately, the Bengals couldn't duplicate the prior year's Super Bowl run, losing to the New York Jets at home, 44-17, in the first round of the AFC Playoffs. It was a stunning setback for a team considered at the time a favorite to repeat as AFC Champions. It sadly would also mark the last time Anderson would appear in the NFL playoffs. In what was his post-season curtain call, Anderson set playoff club records for completion percentage in a game (74.29), passing yards (354) and average yards per pass attempt (10.11). Despite the gaudy offensive numbers and team records, Anderson's three interceptions played a large part in keeping the Bengals from advancing to a second consecutive Super Bowl appearance.

Anderson went on to start for the Bengals for two more seasons after 1982 but neither he nor the team attained the success they had achieved in 1981 and 1982. Even though he opened the 1984 season with three consecutive 300-yard passing games, a club record for 29 years, it was apparent by the end of that season that the torch was being passed to Anderson's successor, Boomer Esiason. As the Bengals opened the 1985 season 0-2, the transfer of power was finalized when head coach Sam Wyche named Esiason his new starting quarterback. Anderson would never start another NFL game and at the end of the 1986 season, after playing 16 seasons and 192 games as a Cincinnati Bengal, both club records, he decided to retire from the game.

The final numbers for Anderson, the NFL's Man of the Year in 1975, are not only franchise Hall of Fame-worthy but Pro Football Hall of Fame-worthy as well. He is the Bengals career leader in passing attempts (4,475), completions (2,654), passing yards (32,838), touchdown passes (197), rushing yards by a quarterback (2,220) and rushing touchdowns by a quarterback (20). He ranks second in career average yards per pass attempt (7.34) and 300-yard passing games (19) and third in career completion percentage (59.31). He also holds the team record for the longest touchdown pass in team history, a 96-yarder to Billy Brooks on November 13, 1977 at Minnesota. His two 3,000-yard passing seasons in 1975 and 1981 are even more remarkable considering the era they occurred, when passing the football wasn't as dominant as it is in today's game.

Despite having a 2-4 record in the playoffs as a starting quarterback, Anderson holds virtually every post-season career passing record in team history. He is the career post-season leader in passing attempts (166), completions (110), completion percentage (66.27), passing yards (1,321), average yards per pass attempt (7.96), touchdown passes (9) and quarterback passer rating (93.5).

In retrospect, Anderson's NFL resume deserves consideration for induction into the Pro Football Hall of Fame. The Pro Football Historical Abstract ranks him as the 16th best quarterback in NFL history, due in large part to his traditional statistics and his career Q score of 127.08, his career-adjusted yards of 9,269 and his 15 net wins as a starting quarterback.[1] He has been a finalist twice for induction into the Hall of Fame (1996 and 1998) but both times, he has fallen short in his attempt to gain entry into Canton. In recent years, several football writers and bloggers have compiled lists of the Top 10 players who should be in the Hall of Fame and each list invariably includes Anderson. Whether or not he will eventually get in, only time will tell.

What is certain, however, is that when you Google, "notable Cincinnati Bengals alumni", a picture of Ken Anderson will be one of the first to appear.

And this time, it should come as no surprise.

---

[1] Of the 15 quarterbacks the Pro Football Historical Abstract ranked ahead of Anderson, only Peyton Manning and Steve McNair are not in the Pro Football Hall of Fame.

CHAPTER EIGHT

LEMAR PARRISH

The Dual Threat

In the early days of professional football, players played both offense and defense, making them the very definition of a two-way player. As the years passed and the game evolved, two-way players gave way to the dual threat player, the athlete who could start and play primarily on either offense or defense and then contribute on special teams by returning kickoffs and punts. By the beginning of the 1970s, dual threats like Bob Hayes of the Dallas Cowboys, Floyd Little of the Denver Broncos, and Gale Sayers of the Chicago Bears, were integral parts of a successful NFL team.

So when the Bengals used their seventh round pick in the 1970 NFL Draft on a running back out of the little-known Lincoln University of Missouri, you had to figure that the third-year franchise was hoping to find their own dual threat player in order to keep up with the rest of the Joneses in the NFL. Little did the Bengals know that when they chose Lemar Parrish with that 163rd overall pick, they would get in return, arguably the best all-around player in team history, a perennial Pro Bowl cornerback and premier kick and punt returner.

A standout football player at John F. Kennedy High School in Riviera Beach, Florida, Parrish attended the small college Lincoln University in Jefferson City, Missouri and made an immediate and long-lasting impact on the football program. A four-year letterman at Lincoln, Parrish's official position on the team roster was running back. It was on special teams, however, as a kick and punt returner, where he made his mark.

By the end of his senior season in 1969, Parrish had set the school records for longest punt return in a game (85 yards), total punt return yards in a game (129 yards) and highest average punt return yards in a game (43.0 yards), a season (16.8 yards in 1969 and a career (15.5 yards), all of which remain Lincoln University records to this day, nearly 50 years since they occurred. Parrish ended his career with an All-American selection in his senior year.

But despite the impressive college resume, Parrish went relatively unnoticed by NFL teams when it came time for the 1970 NFL Draft. Most teams believed they couldn't afford to use a draft pick, regardless of what round, on an unheralded running back from a beyond obscure college based solely on his talents as a kick returner. Fortunately for Parrish, not every NFL team felt that way. In fact, there was a team who had a blueprint for success in place for a player like Parrish and they had no qualms about using a late round selection to exercise their plan once again.

In the 1969 NFL Draft, Paul Brown and his Cincinnati Bengals surprised many by using their sixth round pick to select Ken Riley, at the time a quarterback from the small African-American college, Florida A&M. Upon arriving in Cincinnati, Brown immediately converted Riley to cornerback and inserted him in the starting lineup. By the end of his rookie season, Riley had tied for the team lead in interceptions while returning 14 kickoffs for an average of 23.9 yards per return. Brown apparently believed he could create the same magic with Parrish by converting an offensive player in college to a starting cornerback in the NFL, pairing him with the second-year Riley in the team's defensive backfield.

When the 1970 season began, "magic" was the last word people were using to describe Brown's project to draft two players, who had not been defensive players in college, and start them at the two cornerback positions. "Crazy" was the word heard more often than not. In the end, Brown's gamble was more than just magic. It was, much to the dismay of the Bengals opponents, a potent cornerback duo that stifled many NFL offenses for the next eight seasons.

From 1970-1977, the Bengals' defense consistently ranked in the upper echelon of the NFL. Six times during those eight years, the defense ranked in the top half of the league in total defense and pass defense, including the league's number one pass defense in 1975. Thanks in large part to a defense that finished in the top half of points allowed each season, and the efforts of Parrish and Riley manning the corners, the Bengals were 66-46 with only one losing season during that time, and appeared in the post season on three different occasions.

Parrish and Riley combined for 71 interceptions and six interception returns for touchdowns from 1970-1977, earning a league-wide reputation as one of the best cornerback duos in the game. Parrish accounted for 25 of those interceptions, the fourth most in team history, with four of them being returned for touchdowns, the second most in team history. Parrish set a team record when he returned two interceptions for a touchdown in a single game at Houston on December 17, 1972. He led the team in interceptions three times (1970-1972) and ranks third on the franchise's all-time career interception return yards with 354.

Parrish's performance at cornerback would probably be enough to earn him consideration as a Cincinnati Bengal great if that were his only contribution. It's when you add his talents and production as a kick and punt returner that he becomes a top-flight candidate for induction into the team's Hall of Fame.

Much like he had done in college, Parrish became a field position and scoring weapon, by returning kicks and punts as soon as he entered the NFL in 1970. In the November 8 game at Buffalo in his rookie season, Parrish returned a kickoff 95 yards for a touchdown and a blocked field goal 83 yards for another touchdown, helping the Bengals to a 43-14 victory. The convincing victory marked the first of seven straight wins for Cincinnati in 1970, propelling them to a surprising AFC Central Division championship and the franchise's first ever post-season appearance. All told that season, Parrish returned 25 punts for an 8.4 yard average and one touchdown and 16 kickoffs for a 30.1 yard average and one touchdown. As it turned out, Parrish's rookie season returning kicks was a harbinger of things to come.

In eight seasons as a Bengal, Parrish led the team in punt returns four times, none more impressive than his record-setting 1974 season. He returned 18 punts with only one fair catch that year for 338 yards, fourth on the team's all-time list for punt return yards in a season. His two punt return touchdowns in 1974 is also tied for the most in a season in team history. Parrish's average punt return of 18.8 yards not only remains a club record but led the NFL in 1974 as well. His standout 1974 season was exemplified by his performance against Washington on October 6 when he returned a punt 93 yards for a touchdown and returned a fumble 47 yards for another score in the Bengals 28-17 victory.

The only blemish on Parrish's resume with the Bengals is the team's performance in the playoffs during his tenure. Cincinnati qualified for the post-season three times from 1970-1977 (1970, 1973 and 1975) but failed to win any games. Like the rest of the team in those three playoff games, Parrish did little to make a significant impact. Parrish made 11 tackles with no interceptions and returned three punts for a total of 17 yards in those three playoff games. As the team's post-season failures mounted, frustration amongst some of the players became apparent.

Unfortunately for Bengals fans, Parrish was one of those players who found fault with the franchise. In particular, he was disappointed with the actions of head coach and team owner, Paul Brown. In an interview he did years later, Parrish claimed, "Paul (Brown) never showed any affection for the guys," and by the end of the 1977 season demanded a trade. Brown and the Bengals acquiesced to Parrish's wishes and sent him to the Washington Redskins prior to the 1978 season.

Parrish continued his high quality play after joining the Redskins, earning Pro Bowl honors in 1979 and 1980 and first team All-Pro status in 1979. He was also named by Pro Football Digest as the NFL's Defensive Back of the Year in 1979. After playing four seasons in Washington, Parrish brought his NFL career to an end with one final season in Buffalo in 1982. He finished his career with 13 return or recovery touchdowns (four interception returns, four punt returns, three fumble returns, one kickoff return and one blocked field goal return), a total that placed him fifth on the NFL's all-time list for non-offensive touchdowns. The Pro Football Historical Abstract placed an exclamation point on his career, naming him the 25th best defensive back in NFL history, finishing with a career score of 251.48.

For better or for worse, Parrish's career will forever be associated with the Bengals. In eight seasons as one of the team's starting cornerbacks, he was named to six Pro Bowls (1970-1971 and 1974-1977) and one of the leaders of a top-flight NFL defense. He very easily could have been named to these multiple Pro Bowls based on his kick and punt return numbers alone. He is the club leader in career punt returns for touchdowns (4) and is second in career punt returns (130), career punt return yards (1,201 yards) and career average yards per kickoff return (61 returns, 1,524 yards, 24.66 average per return).

Given that his defensive and special team numbers took place over 40 years ago, Parrish's legacy with the Bengals is firmly ensconced. He was a premier cornerback and kick returner in the 1970s. More importantly, he created the standard by which the future cornerbacks in team history, like Louis Breeden, Tory James, Leon Hall, and kick returners such as Mike Martin, Peter Warrick and Adam Jones would be measured.

And that seems appropriate when you discuss the impact Lemar Parrish had on the Bengals franchise. He was a dual threat as a player and is now a dual threat when determining the team's all-time greatest players.

CHAPTER NINE

JAMES BROOKS

The Straw That Stirred the Drink

When *future baseball Hall of* Famer, Reggie Jackson, arrived at the New York Yankees training camp in 1977, he was coming to a team that had fallen short of their ultimate goal the year before when they were swept by the Cincinnati Reds in the 1976 World Series. It was the Yankees' first appearance in the World Series since 1964 and their bombastic owner, George Steinbrenner, wasn't satisfied with second place, especially since he was intent on restoring the Yankee dynasty. Steinbrenner believed his team was merely one game-changing player away from once again ruling the baseball world, and he saw in Jackson the player who could fill that void. Consequently, Steinbrenner jumped at the chance in the winter of 1976 to sign the free agent Jackson, a key component in an Oakland A's team that won three consecutive world championships from 1972-1974.

In addition to his on-field talents, Steinbrenner believed Jackson would bring a swagger and proven winner's confidence to the Yankees clubhouse that would lead them to a World Series title. Jackson wasted little time in affirming his owner's beliefs when he was interviewed by Sport magazine during his first spring training wearing Yankee pinstripes.

"I'm the straw that stirs the drink," Jackson reportedly told writer Robert Ward before he had played one game for his new team.[16] And despite the fact that those comments were brash and considered by many disrespectful, it's worth noting that the Yankees went on to win the World Series in 1977, capped off by a three home run performance by Jackson himself in the series clinching Game 6.

While they certainly didn't have the tradition of the Yankees, the Bengals were at a similar crossroads at the end of their 1983 season that faced Steinbrenner and his team in the winter of 1976. The Bengals were two years removed from their Super Bowl appearance in 1981 and in the two seasons that followed, they failed to capitalize on the momentum of that championship season, losing in the first round of the playoffs in 1982 and finishing a disappointing 7-9 in 1983. To many fans and observers, the Bengals didn't have enough personnel pieces to return to the NFL's elite. On the surface, it appeared 1984 could be a season of change in Cincinnati. In reality, the facelift started just one week after the 1983 season ended.

On Christmas Eve 1983, seven days after the last game of the year, head coach Forrest Gregg announced his resignation in order to take the same position with the Green Bay Packers. Five days later, the Bengals hired former San Francisco 49er assistant, Sam Wyche, to replace Gregg and in essence to take the franchise in a new direction. Wyche, a quarterback for the Bengals from 1968-1970, brought with him the West Coast Offense, a system that emphasized short, horizontal passing instead of the traditional smash mouth, run-oriented offense favored by his predecessor. More importantly, Wyche's offense required more speed and less brawn from his running backs. It was a characteristic that the Bengals roster he was inheriting, severely lacked.

The prime example of Wyche's roster deficiency was Pete Johnson, the team's starting fullback since 1977. Despite gaining 5,421 yards and scoring 64 touchdowns over seven seasons, Johnson, a 252-pound, straight-ahead, plowing type of back, didn't fit Wyche's need for a fleet-footed, receiver out of the backfield, running back his offense required. Moving Johnson out of the starting lineup for 1984, however, seemed unlikely given the burly fullback's historically solid production and the lack of any other running back options on the roster.

Wyche's decision about what to do with Johnson was made easier thanks to Johnson himself. A year before, Johnson testified in court that he had purchased cocaine from a local dealer, prompting the NFL to suspend him for the first four games of the 1983 season. It was a black eye not only for Johnson but for the organization as well, something that did not sit well with their straight-laced and traditionalist owner, Paul Brown. Johnson didn't do himself any more favors when he demanded a new contract from the Bengals prior to the 1984 season. Not such a good idea when dealing with a team that at the time was notorious for having tight purse strings and a total disdain for renegotiating contracts. As expected, Johnson was making it easy for the Bengals to dismiss his past contributions.

Meanwhile, some 2,100 miles from Cincinnati, the San Diego Chargers were dealing with a disgruntled running back of their own. James Brooks had just finished his third season with San Diego in 1983 and even though he was a member of the high-flying Air Coryell offense that was responsible for two playoff appearances in three years, he was demanding a trade. Taken by the Chargers with the 24th overall pick in the 1981 NFL Draft out of Auburn University, Brooks felt he was under-utilized in his three seasons with San Diego and their high octane offense. Given what he had accomplished in college, Brooks had a point.

In his four years at Auburn, Brooks shared running back duties with future NFL players William Andrews and Joe Cribbs. Brooks was first in the Southeastern Conference (SEC) in total rushing yards (1,208 yards) and yards per rushing attempt (7.4 yards per carry) in his junior season in 1979 and was the team's leading rusher and scorer in this senior season in 1980. He finished his career at Auburn with 3,523 yards rushing (third best in school history) and the school's all-time leader in career kickoff return yards (68 returns, 1,726 yards, 25.4 yards per return) and all-purpose yards (5,596). He was also named to the All-SEC team in 1979 and 1980.

But despite his impressive college statistics, Brooks was relegated to a relatively part-time role in San Diego. In 38 games with the Chargers, Brooks started only seven games and accounted for only 12.2% of the team's total net yards. Instead of being a major contributor to San Diego's highly regarded and productive offense, Brooks, the NFL leader in all-purpose yards gained in 1981 and 1982, was used primarily as the team's kick and punt returner. Frustrated by his lack of significant playing time, Brooks asked for a trade out of San Diego.

Brooks' dissatisfaction, combined with his abilities as an all-purpose running back, was music to Sam Wyche's ears. Brooks was the perfect tailback for Wyche's West Coast Offense and with the team ready to rid themselves of an unhappy Pete Johnson, the Bengals believed they had found the perfect trade partner. On May 29, 1984, the two teams finalized the deal that exchanged their respective upset running backs. Little did either team know at the time, it was a trade that would send both franchises in opposite directions over the next eight years.

Johnson's career in San Diego lasted all of 13 games in 1984 before he was traded to Miami near the end of the season. The Chargers went on to have only one winning season between 1984 and 1991. Adding insult to injury, Johnson retired from the NFL at the end of the 1984 season.

Back in Cincinnati, Brooks became the straw that stirred the Bengals' drink.

Over the next eight seasons, his career flourished, as did the fortunes of his new team in Cincinnati. He became the lynchpin in an offense that became one of the league's elite, and was ahead of its time. In the eight seasons that Brooks was the starting running back (1984-1991), the Bengals' offense finished in the top half of the NFL in each of them, including 1986 and 1988 when they had the number one ranked offense in the league. They also finished in the top half of the NFL in points scored six times during that time as well, topped by a league high 448 points scored in 1988.

But it was in the running game where Brooks made his biggest impact. Contrary to popular belief, Wyche's "No-Huddle Offense" was more reliant on running the football than it was passing, and Brooks was the workhorse of a running game that finished in the top half of the NFL in rushing each year he played in Cincinnati, including 1988 and 1989 when the Bengals led the league in rushing offense.

The 1988 season in particular showcased how instrumental the running game was to the success of Wyche's offensive scheme. That offense set regular season Bengal team records for points scored (448), touchdowns (59), rushing touchdowns (27), net yards rushing (2,710 yards) and rushing attempts (563). For his part, Brooks contributed 1,218 yards from scrimmage and 14 touchdowns in 1988 as the Bengals rolled to the second Super Bowl appearance in team history.

While his 1988 statistics may seem minimal in the grand scheme of the entire season, it should, by no means, dismiss the career Brooks had while wearing Bengal stripes. Selected to four Pro Bowls while in Cincinnati (1986, 1988-1990), Brooks is the career team leader in average yards gained per rushing attempt (4.80 yards per attempt), third in career touchdowns (64) and 100-yard rushing games (17) and fourth or tied for fourth in career rushing attempts (1,344) and rushing touchdowns (37). He was also the team's yearly leading rusher four times (1985, 1986, 1989 and 1990) and rushed for 1,000 yards in a season three times (1,239 in 1989, 1,087 yards in 1986 and 1,004 yards in 1990).

Brooks' contributions have been validated by The Pro Football Historical Abstract, highlighted by his performance in both 1988 and 1989. In 1988, he finished with 1,073.9 adjusted rushing yards, 346.4 adjusted receiving yards and a Q score of 9.1. The following year, he ended the season with 1000.6 adjusted rushing yards, 111.4 adjusted receiving yards and a Q score of 7.8. It was two highlights in a career where the Abstract listed him as the 41st ranked running back in NFL history thanks to his player career score of 151.15 and career adjusted yards gained of 9,068.4

The diversity Brooks brought to Wyche's offense is clearly apparent in his career numbers as well. He is ranked second on the Bengals career leading rusher list (6,447 yards), ninth in points scored (384) and 14th in career receiving yards (297 receptions for 3,012 yards), the highest ranked running back on the team's all-time reception list. He also had three games where he had at least 100-yards receiving, the most of any running back in team history.

The Bengals reached the playoffs twice during Brooks' eight seasons with the team and he was a major contributor to their three victories in those two post-season appearances. He is ranked third in team history in career post-season rushing attempts (43) and average yards per rushing attempt (3.37 yards per carry) and fourth in career post-season rushing yards (145 yards).

Brooks' NFL career lasted only one more season after he left in Cincinnati in 1991, playing four games for Cleveland and two games for Tampa Bay in 1992. By that time, Brooks had been identified as one of the Bengals' all-time greats. Any doubts about his impact on the franchise should be erased when you consider that in his role as the

Bengals starting running back from 1984-1991, Brooks accounted for 20.8 percent of the team's total net yards and 13.0 percent of the Bengals' total points scored.

Any way you look at it, for eight seasons, that running back acquired from the San Diego Chargers was the straw that stirred the Bengals' drink.

CHAPTER TEN

CHIP MYERS

The Over-Achiever

he odds of making an NFL roster, even if you are a highly regarded college player, are difficult at best. According to NFLPA statistics, for every 100 college football players, only one will make an NFL roster. Those odds are increased significantly when an aspiring college athlete attends a school not known for producing NFL talent. Most scouts and football executives would probably advise those who play for those smaller colleges without the reputation for sending players to the NFL to consider another line of work.

Good thing former Bengal wide receiver Chip Myers didn't pay attention to either conventional wisdom or his critics.

Born Phillip Leon Myers in Panama City, Florida, Chip Myers attended the small college Northwestern Oklahoma State in Alva, Oklahoma. In most cases, his college career numbers of 109 receptions, 1,398 receiving yards, 16 touchdowns and two all-conference honors during the mid-1960s would equate to a mid-round selection in the NFL Draft. Unfortunately for Myers, when you play at a school no-one considers a professional football factory, like Northwestern Oklahoma State, your stock in the draft plummets like a balloon shot out of the air.

Unlike most players in his position, Myers at least got a chance to prove he could play in the NFL. With the 248th overall pick, the San Francisco

49ers selected Myers in the 10th round of the 1967 NFL Draft. He barely saw any action for the 49ers in his rookie year, catching only two passes for 13 yards the entire season. When the 49ers hired a new coaching staff after the 1967 season, led by new head coach Dick Nolan, the team cut ties with Myers.

Unable to find another NFL or AFL team willing to sign him for the 1968 season, Myers continued to pursue his quest of playing professionally by signing with the minor league football team, the Alabama Hawks. A member of the Continental Football League, the Hawks were considered the unofficial minor league affiliate of the Atlanta Falcons. It wasn't NFL caliber football but it did prove the extent of how badly Myers wanted to play the game at the highest level.

Myers' desire and tenaciousness paid off when the Bengals signed him for the 1969 season. In his first season in Cincinnati, he played in all 14 games and started five, catching 10 passes for 205 yards and two touchdowns. As the 1970 season began, and with the Bengals entering the NFL after two seasons in the AFL, Myers became a starting wide receiver for the offense, a role he assumed for the next four seasons. In his first year as a starter, he led the team in receiving yards (542) as Cincinnati made their first-ever post-season appearance. Although the Bengals lost in the first round of the playoffs to the Baltimore Colts, 17-0, Myers did have four receptions for 66 yards in the loss, an average of 16.5 yards per catch, and the third highest in team post-season history.

In 1971, Myers was beset by injuries, starting only seven games and catching 27 passes for 286 yards and one touchdown. He headed into 1972 with something to prove and with the newly installed starting quarterback, Ken Anderson, at the reins, Myers had his best season ever with the Bengals.

Starting in all 14 games of the 1972 season, Myers led the team in receptions (57) and receiving yards (792), numbers that placed him third and seventh respectively in the NFL. To go along with his three touchdown receptions, Myers' 56.6 yards receiving per game was also seventh best in the league in 1972. His performance earned him Pro Bowl honors for the only time in his career.

Myers was once again hampered by injuries in 1973 that limited his action to five games. As the 1974 season began, he had become a secondary receiver for Anderson and the Bengals offense. Despite losing his starting job, he became an invaluable possession receiver, leading the team in receptions in 1974 (32). He continued to excel as a secondary receiver in 1975 as his performance against the Buffalo Bills on Monday Night Football on November 17, 1975 clearly showed. His seven receptions for 108 yards was part of a then franchise record for yards passing and total offensive yards in a game as the Bengals won their first ever Monday Night game, 33-24. It was a role Myers embraced.

"The type of passes I catch don't make a lot of yards," Myers told Cincinnati magazine in August 1976.[17] He continued in his role as the grind-it-out type of receiver until 1976 when he retired at the end of the season.

After his playing career ended, Myers stayed active in the game he loved by becoming a coach; a journey he began at the University of Illinois as an assistant from 1980-1982. He then moved onto the NFL coaching ranks as a wide receiver coach with Tampa Bay (1983-1984), Indianapolis (1985-1988) and the New York Jets (1990-1993). He eventually found a coaching home in Minnesota, becoming their wide receiver coach from 1995-1997 and then their quarterbacks coach in 1998. It was in the latter role that Myers displayed his ability to teach and mentor at the highest level.

The quarterback for the Vikings in 1998 was Randall Cunningham and with Myers as his position coach he enjoyed the best season of his career, leading the Vikings to a 15-1 regular season record and a berth in the NFL Conference Championship. It was a season long performance, 3.407 passing yards and 34 touchdown passes with only 10 interceptions, which Cunningham credited Myers for helping to achieve.

"He gave me a very comfortable style of playing, where you just go and enjoy yourself," Cunningham recalled. "That's the kind of coach he was. I really respected him for that."[18]

More importantly, the Vikings also respected Myers' coaching style and the results he produced. After their offensive coordinator in 1998, Brian Billick, left to accept the head coaching position with the Baltimore Ravens on January 19, 1999, Minnesota promoted Myers, naming him the new offensive coordinator for the 1999 season. Just as he had done with his new role as a possession receiver in Cincinnati, Myers embraced the opportunity.

"I've been ready to do this for ten years," Myers said at the time. "I've just never (promoted) myself to do it, and I would never do that at all…A (job) title to me, it doesn't mean one thing. It never had, and hopefully it never will. I'm not comfortable even with (the coordinator) title. All I want is to be somewhere I can win."[19]

Sadly, Myers never got the chance to show what he could do as an offensive coordinator. On February 23, 1999, Myers suffered a fatal heart attack, tragically ending what had looked like a bright coaching career. While his death hit the Vikings organization hard, Myers left a lasting impact on those he worked with on a daily basis, a trait he carried over from his days as a Bengals wide receiver.

"I don't think there was anybody in this building who was more loved than he was," said Vikings defensive coordinator Foge Fazio shortly after Myers' death.[20]

His protégé in Minnesota, Cunningham, also paid tribute to the coach who brought him some of his greatest success as a professional.

"He was a big part of my success," Cunningham said about Myers before the start of the 1999 season. "I'll carry the teaching and things I've learned from him onto the field each game."[21]

His coaching accolades notwithstanding, it's Myers' contributions in eight seasons as a Bengal that provided the foundation for his future coaching successes and cemented his legacy as an all-time Cincinnati favorite. He was one of the catalysts of an offense at the beginning of the 1970s that transformed the future of the franchise and ushered in an era of potent offensive football for many years to come.

For four consecutive seasons from 1970-1973, the Bengals finished in the top half of the NFL in points scored and from 1971-1973, they finished no lower than ninth in the league in total offense. Myers was a large part of that success, finishing his career with 218 receptions for 3,079 yards and 12 touchdowns, good enough to place him 17th on the team's all-time reception list. All of this from a player nobody had given a chance to even sniff a play from scrimmage in the NFL.

"People always told me, 'you're too small, you're too slow,'" Myers said in his interview with Cincinnati magazine in 1976. "I knew with a deep down gut feeling that I wasn't going to stand still for people telling me I wasn't good enough."[22]

Forty years later, Bengals fans can testify that Myers' gut feeling was right—he was good enough. And then some.

CHAPTER ELEVEN

LOUIS BREEDEN

Filling Big Shoes

From *1970-1977, the Cincinnati Bengals* duo of Lemar Parrish and Ken Riley formed arguably the most productive pair of cornerbacks in the NFL. In eight seasons, the two combined for 61 interceptions and led a defense that finished in the top half of the NFL in total defense and pass defense six times. It looked like the Bengals were set at the cornerback position for many years to come. Then, suddenly, it all changed.

Believing the organization—especially owner and head coach Paul Brown--didn't appreciate his talents, Parrish demanded a trade after the 1977 season. Brown and the Bengals accommodated Parrish's request and traded him to the Washington Redskins prior to the start of the 1978 season. Parrish's absence in the defensive backfield created a void the Bengals were looking to fill as the 1978 season began.

Enter Louis Breeden.

Born in Hamlet, North Carolina, Breeden became a Bengal as the result of a very familiar and successful formula Brown had used in the past to fill his roster, particularly his defensive backfield. Like Riley and Parrish, Breeden played his college football at a small, historically African-American university, North Carolina Central University. Breeden was a four-year letterman from 1973-1976 for the football team at North Carolina Central, leading the team in interceptions three times (1974-1976) while being named to the All-Mid-Eastern Athletic Conference (MEAC) team twice (1975 and 1976). He was also a key member of the North Carolina Central defense that finished first in pass defense in Division II in 1976. His 17 career interceptions places him in a tie for fourth in the school's all-time interception list.

And also like Riley and Parrish, the Bengals selected Breeden in the later rounds of the draft, choosing him in the seventh round with the 187th overall pick of the 1977 NFL Draft. With Parrish still firmly ensconced in the starting lineup in 1977, Breeden's rookie year spent on injured reserve didn't curtail his growth or damage his chances of becoming an NFL starter. In fact, with the depth the Bengals had in the defensive secondary in 1977, his chances of being on the roster, let alone having any significant playing time, was remote at best. Being protected by the injured reserve list at least gave Breeden a chance to compete for a spot the following year, and to do so fully healthy.

That chance to start increased significantly after the Parrish trade and Breeden took full advantage of the opportunity. Breeden took over Parrish's left cornerback position and started all 16 games in 1978, making the transition seamless. Along with his three interceptions, Breeden led all defensive backs on the team in total tackles (69) and passes defended (12). After an injury-riddled 1979 season that limited his play, Breeden returned in 1980 to lead the team in interceptions with seven. His performance in 1980 marked the beginning of Breeden being an invaluable presence in the Bengals' defensive secondary.

In his ten seasons in Cincinnati, Breeden was a member of a defense that finished in the top half of the NFL in total defense six times (1978, 1980, 1981, 1983, 1984 and 1987), in pass defense five times (1978, 1980, 1983, 1986 and 1987) and points allowed four times (1978, 1980, 1981 and 1983). Personally, Breeden led the team in interceptions three times (1980, 1984 and 1986) and led all defensive backs in tackles (1978, 1981 and 1982) and passes defended (1978, 1985 and 1986) three seasons each as well.

Breeden, a primary starting cornerback in eight of his ten seasons in Cincinnati, set the club record for the longest interception return for a touchdown when he picked off Dan Fouts of the San Diego Chargers on November 8, 1981, and scored after a 102-yard return.[23] The following year, the 1982 strike shortened season, he was named first team All-Pro cornerback. He was a member of the franchise's first Super Bowl team and a starter on a defense that set the club's post-season record for fewest points allowed in a game (7 vs. San Diego on January 10, 1982 in the AFC Championship game), and the fewest net yards passing allowed in a half (16 vs. San Francisco in Super Bowl XVI).

Breeden retired after the 1987 season, spending his entire 10-year NFL career with Cincinnati. In his ten seasons as a Bengal, he intercepted 33 passes for 558 yards, both of which are the second most in team history. His 145 interception return yards in 1981 is also the second most in a Cincinnati Bengals season. His three interceptions against the Chicago Bears on December 14, 1980 is tied for most interceptions in a game in franchise history.

All in all it was a career that did more than just fill a giant pair of shoes; it was a career that created an even bigger pair of shoes to fill. Such was the hefty footprint left by Louis Breeden and his accomplishments over a position-defining ten-year career that helped define how future Bengal cornerbacks were measured.

CHAPTER TWELVE

GLENN CAMERON

Perry Mason in Cleats

You've probably heard the jokes a thousand times or more.
"What do you call a bus full of attorneys at the bottom of the ocean?"

"A good start."

"A lawyer is swimming in the water. A shark comes towards him and veers away. Why?"

"Professional courtesy."

Sometimes, however, the jokes don't quite fit. Sometimes, there's more to an attorney than just a person who spent years going to school in an attempt to earn a law degree and the spoils that go with it. Sometimes, it might just surprise you to learn of the journey some took to achieve their status as a practicing attorney-at-law.

All of these exceptions describe former Bengals linebacker Glenn Cameron.

To say Cameron does not fit the stereotypical profile of a practicing attorney and a partner in a major law firm is a huge understatement. Yes, he completed his law degree from the University of Florida in 1987 and yes, he has maintained a successful private practice, culminating in becoming a founding partner in the firm Cameron, Davis and Gonzalez in 1996. It's what Cameron did before he passed the bar that makes his life experiences unique and one of the Cincinnati Bengals all-time greats.

Born in Miami, Florida, Cameron attended the University of Florida and began playing football for Doug Dickey's Gators in 1971. Over the next four years, Cameron played a key role in the Florida defense. Unfortunately, there probably weren't very many people who knew he was a member of the Florida football team.

"We never had a team picture taken all four years I was at Florida, and I have no idea why," Cameron said in a 2010 interview. "That kind of sums up the '70s, maybe it was a time people wanted to forget, even though some good things were accomplished and great battles were won on the football field."[24]

Indeed there were, and Cameron was a large part of those accomplishments and battles. A three-year letterman from 1972-1974, he was a member of a Gator defense that allowed only 202.1 yards per game, the second lowest in school history, in his junior season in 1973. As a senior in 1974, Cameron's star rose dramatically. He led the team in tackles with 185 (third best in school history), earning him first team All-SEC linebacker and third team Associated Press All-American linebacker honors. He would later be inducted into the University of Florida Athletic Hall of Fame as a "Gator Great" in 1984 and ranked by The Gainesville Sun in 2006 as one of the 100 greatest Gators of the first century of University of Florida football.

More importantly, his overall play at Florida boosted his stock in the upcoming 1975 NFL Draft. When the Bengals' turn in the first round of the 1975 Draft came, they didn't hesitate to choose Cameron with the 14th overall pick of the draft. It was a first round selection the franchise wouldn't regret.

Over the next 11 seasons, Cameron was a steady presence in a defense that guided the Bengals to an 84-79 record from 1975-1985 and three post-season appearances, including the team's first-ever Super Bowl. Playing in 159 games as a Bengal and starting 102 of them primarily as a right inside linebacker, Cameron was part of a defense that finished in the top half of the NFL in pass defense five times (1975, 1976, 1978, 1980 and 1983), rushing defense (1976, 1977, 1980-1984) and total defense seven times (1975, 1976, 1978, 1980, 1981, 1983 and 1984) and points allowed eight times (1975-1977, 1979, 1981, 1982, 1984 and 1985). He started all 16 games in the 1983 season in which the Bengals finished with the NFL's number one ranked total defense. He was a contributor to the defense that holds the team records for fewest points allowed in nine games played (177 in 1982) and 14 games played (210 in 1976) as well as the defense that allowed the fewest total net yards allowed in a season in team history (2,893 yards in 1982).

The team's defensive captain in 1984 and 1985, Cameron led all linebackers in solo tackles twice (1980 and 1983) and total tackles (1983), passes defended (1981) and interceptions (1980) once. He also led the team in solo tackles (8) in the 1982 post-season. He finished his football career with 615 tackles, six sacks for 48 yards, 19 passes defended, seven forced fumbles and five interceptions.

With his football career over, Cameron directly began obtaining the skills and education he needed to pursue his new profession, that of becoming a licensed attorney. Immediately following his season with the Bengals in 1985, Cameron enrolled at the University of Florida Law School and earned his Juris Doctor degree in 1987. Upon his graduation, he began a private practice in West Palm Beach, Florida with the firm Ganster, Yoakley, Criser and Stewart.

In 1996, Cameron teamed up with his former Bengals teammate, Rick Davis, himself a private practicing attorney, to form their own law firm, Cameron, David, Gonzalez and Marroney in West Palm Beach. Since then, the firm, now known as Cameron, Gonzalez and Marroney has thrived, "recovering millions of dollars in awards and settlements for its clients", according to its own advertisements.

Cameron, himself, has prospered as well. Currently the head of the firm's litigation department, he is a board certified trial lawyer by the Florida Bar Board of Legal Specialization and Education. More importantly, he is a highly regarded and highly rated attorney.

"Glenn is an outstanding litigator who provides (us) with the much needed experience and knowledge that gives us the edge to compete in today's aggressive environment," states Bill Hodges, President of Arbor Land, Inc.

"Mr. Cameron's legal advice, understanding of the construction process and negotiating skills have been invaluable to our business," adds O'Neal Bates, President of B&B Properties.[25]

Lost in all of this recent professional success is Cameron's achievements as a Cincinnati Bengal on the football field. Even though his name isn't one of the first mentioned when the greatest ever Bengal players are discussed, there's no question Cameron made an impact on the success of the franchise. He became a starting linebacker at a time when the defense started to emerge as one of the NFL's best and was arguably the key factor in how the Bengals became a Super Bowl contender in the 1980s. Granted, he doesn't have the eye-popping statistics that make him stand out, but should that disqualify Cameron from being considered one of the team's all-time greats? The answer here is an unequivocal no.

Or to borrow from the vernacular from Cameron's current profession, case closed.

CHAPTER THIRTEEN

JAMES FRANCIS

The Forgotten Star

W*hen it comes to describing* the Cincinnati Bengals in the 1990s, not many positive words can be said. With the exception of the 1990 season when they won the AFC Central Division with a 9-7 record, the Bengals only had one other season in the 1990s where they finished with a .500 record or better (1996, 8-8). Overall, the team's record in the '90s was an NFL worst 52-108 (.325). It was a 10-year slog that created a malaise for the franchise that lasted beyond the decade, as it wasn't until 2005 that the Bengals finished above .500 and qualified for the playoffs.

In other words, the Bengals in the 1990s, were, to borrow a phrase from the NBA legend, Charles Barkley, "just turrible."

Lost in all of that misery was the play of a linebacker who, by all accounts, was the best defensive player for the Bengals in the 1990s. Had he played at any other time in the team's history, he would probably be considered one of the Bengals' all-time greats. Instead, James Francis has become a forgotten star of the franchise simply because he played during a low point in the team's narrative.

Francis, a native of Houston, Texas, attended Baylor University and was four-year football letterman from 1986-1989. A steady contributor in his first three seasons, Francis had a breakthrough season in his senior year in 1989, a season that established him as one of the school's all-time greats and more importantly, put him in a position to become a top pick in the 1990 NFL Draft.

By the end of Baylor's 1989 campaign, Francis led the team in tackles (129), tackles for loss (8) and sacks (6.0). He also blocked an NCAA record eight kicks that season as well. When it came time to hand out the post-season awards and honors, Francis brought in quite the haul. He was named to the first team of the AP All-American, American Football Coaches Association (AFCA), Football News, Sporting News and All-Southwestern Conference (SWC) squads. Additionally, The Houston Post named him the 1989 SWC Most Valuable Player.

Francis finished his career at Baylor with both feet firmly planted in the school's record book. His 334 tackles is sixth all-time in school history while his 198 solo tackles, 28 tackles for a loss and 13.5 sacks rank tied for eighth, tenth, and fourth respectively. His efforts earned him a spot on Baylor's All-Decade team for the 1980s alongside Pro Football Hall of Fame linebacker, Mike Singletary, and on the list of Baylor's 55 greatest players since 1953 by USA Today's 2010 College Football Encyclopedia. Based upon his collegiate performance, the Bengals used their first round pick to choose Francis with the 12th overall selection in the 1990 NFL Draft.

Francis made an immediate impact upon arriving in Cincinnati, and over the next four seasons was the most dominating force on the defensive side of the ball. From 1990-1993, Francis recorded 19 sacks, forced five fumbles, recovered four fumbles and intercepted seven passes, two of which he returned for touchdowns. He had a total of 224 tackles during those four seasons, leading the team in solo tackles, total tackles and sacks in 1990.

Unfortunately, the Bengals, as a team, couldn't match Francis's performance. Cincinnati's game on November 22 1992 against the Detroit Lions exemplified the stark contrast between Francis' play and the rest of his Bengals teammates. In the 19-13 defeat, the linebacker's two interceptions for a club record 107 interception return yards in a game and one touchdown accounted for more yards and touchdowns than the offense provided that day. The result against the Lions is a prime example of how Francis' efforts in his nine seasons as a Bengal were obscured by the lack of wins and poor overall record the team recorded during the same period of time.

In the five seasons beginning in 1994, Francis continued to exert his presence defensively. He led all linebackers on the team in fumbles recovered (1996) and interceptions (1997) one season each, sacks in two seasons (1994 and 1997) and passes defended (1994, 1995, 1997 and 1998) and forced fumbles (1994, 1996-1998) in four seasons.

Sadly, 1998 marked not only his worst season statistically but his last as a Bengal. Francis was waived by the team as one of the final cuts prior to the 1999 season and was signed by the Washington Redskins. After playing one season with the Redskins, Francis retired from the NFL at the conclusion of the 1999 season.

Because of the team's lack of success during his nine seasons in Cincinnati, Francis' imprint on the history of the franchise is clouded, if not totally hidden. But make no mistake about it, the left outside linebacker out of Baylor needs to be considered one of the team's best to wear the orange and black. That's because the numbers don't lie.

In the 133 games he played as a Bengal, 129 of which he started, Francis recorded 554 tackles and 33 sacks, most for any Bengals linebacker in the 1990s. He defended 60 passes, forced 14 fumbles and recovered eight fumbles. His 11 interceptions are third most by a linebacker in team history. He returned three of those interceptions for a touchdown, tied for third most in franchise history. In his lone post-season appearance for the Bengals in 1990, Francis led all linebackers in solo tackles (6) and total tackles (8). It's a resume that is certainly worthy of the team's Hall of Fame.

Unfortunately, Francis' accomplishments are compared with the time he played for the Bengals, a time many fans would like to soon forget. Given the miserable won-lost record, it's totally understandable. But before anyone completely erases the Bengals of the 1990s from their minds, they need to realize the entire decade wasn't a complete washout. Thanks to the play of James Francis, there's at least one bright star in the dark and ominous skies that was Bengals football in the 1990s.

And, please, don't you forget it.

CHAPTER FOURTEEN

BO HARRIS

Graduate of the Bengals Linebacker University

For years, *Penn State University* has been known as "Linebacker U" based upon its reputation for producing some of the greatest linebackers to play the game of football. Some of the elite linebackers to come from this storied college football program include Jack Ham, Matt Millen, Shane Conlan, LaVar Arrington and Cameron Wake to name but a few.

Although not at the level of Penn State, the Bengals of the 1970s had their own version of Linebacker U. Starting with the team's initial season in 1968 and lasting throughout the decade of the '70s, the Bengals had a steady line of high quality linebackers in their defensive lineup. All-time Bengal legends Ron Pritchard, Bill Bergey, Al Beauchamp, Jim LeClair, Glenn Cameron and Reggie Williams were all linebackers during this time in team history. Another linebacker of this era who doesn't necessarily get the attention the others previously mentioned have received, but certainly made his mark as a solid performer from 1975-1982 was Bo Harris.

Born Clint Lee Harris in Leesville, Louisiana, the future Bengals linebacker traveled only 250 miles from his high school in Shreveport to play college football and attend Louisiana State University (LSU) in 1971. A three-year letterman from 1972-1974, Harris helped LSU to a 23-10-2 overall record in those three seasons, including a berth in the 1973 Orange Bowl where the Tigers lost to the ninth-ranked Penn State Nittany Lions,

16-9. The 1973 season also marked the highlight of Harris' time in Baton Rouge as he was named All-SEC second team linebacker.

When the 1975 NFL Draft came to pass, the Bengals were searching for talent and depth at the linebacker position. They used their first round and 14th overall pick on University of Florida linebacker Glenn Cameron and then used a third round selection and the 77th overall to draft Harris. Choosing Harris, as it turns out, paid quality, long-term dividends.

Beginning with his rookie season in 1975, Harris played in 103 games as a Bengal over the next eight seasons, starting 74 of them as either a left inside or left outside linebacker. The Bengals were 62-53 (.539) during his tenure and he played a large part in the team's first ever post season victory and their debut Super Bowl appearance.

In the regular season, Harris was a starter on the 1982 defense that allowed the fewest total points in a season (177 points) and the fewest total net yards allowed in a season (2,893 yards) in team history and the 1976 defense that allowed the fewest points per game in a season (15.0 points allowed per game). When he was a usual starter, the team finished in the top half of the NFL in passing defense twice (1976 and 1980), points allowed and total defense three times (1976, 1980 and 1981) and rushing defense five times (1976, 1977, 1980-1982).

During his eight seasons in Cincinnati, Harris led or tied all linebackers on the team in interceptions (1976) and passes defended (1977) once, forced fumbles and fumble recoveries twice (1976 and 1980) and sacks three times (1977, 1979 and 1980). He had a career high with 89 tackles in 1981 and returned an interception for 62 yards for a touchdown against the San Diego Chargers on December 20, 1982.

Harris appeared in five playoff games as a Bengal, making his biggest post-season impact during the team's 1981 run to the Super Bowl. In that playoff season, Harris led all Bengal linebackers in solo tackles (13), sacks (1) and interceptions (1). His interception against Buffalo in the AFC divisional playoffs was one of two the Bengals recorded in the second half, a post-season team record that was matched a week later in the AFC Championship game against the San Diego Chargers.

At the end of the 1982 season, Harris retired from the Bengals and the NFL. He finished his regular season career with 404 total tackles, 15.5 sacks, 29 passes defended, seven forced fumbles, six fumble recoveries and seven interceptions. He also compiled 23 total tackles, one sack and one interception in the post-season as well.

More importantly, Harris was one of the many excellent linebackers who wore the Bengals uniform during the 1970s. And while he doesn't get the kind of recognition his peers like LeClair, Cameron and Williams receive, it would be a huge mistake to dismiss the contributions Harris made as a left side linebacker.

In fact, Harris was and should be considered an elite member of the 1970s class of Bengals Linebacker U.

CHAPTER FIFTEEN

BOB JOHNSON

The First Bengal

I*n the entire history of* the Cincinnati Bengals, there have been countless firsts and important decisions. These included the team's first win, their first playoff berth and their first Super Bowl appearance, as well as their replacement of legendary head coach Paul Brown. Other determinations, such as who the franchise would start at quarterback, and the building of their new stadium in the early 2000's are where and what their new stadium in the early 2000's would look like are but a few examples of how these two distinct properties have contributed to the franchise's ongoing saga and narrative.

On January 30, 1968, the Bengals encountered not only a first for a franchise but a tremendously important dilemma. It was the 1968 NFL/AFL Common Draft at the Belmont Plaza Hotel in New York City and it was the first draft for the AFL expansion franchise Bengals that would begin play in the fall of 1968. Even though, two weeks earlier, they had received 40 veteran players from eight other AFL teams in the league's Allocation Draft, the Bengals' first foray into the college draft process was more critical to their long-term success. In essence, the players they selected in New York City would provide the foundation and sustain the team for many years to come. To complicate matters, since it was the franchise's first ever draft, their first overall selection would receive more attention and face more scrutiny than usual.

The Bengals had the second overall pick in the 1968 NFL/AFL Draft thanks to an agreement between the NFL and the New York Giants, the team that held the number one selection as part of the compensation they received for allowing the New York Jets to take part in the future merger of the two leagues in 1970. The Giants traded their pick to the Minnesota Vikings who then selected future Pro Football Hall of Famer, Ron Yary, with their first overall choice.

That put the Bengals on the clock and under the gun. Arguably, no other future draft choice had more riding on it than the first one they would ever make. Needless to say, head coach and team owner, Paul Brown, needed to hit pay dirt with the selection.

Fortunately, they did that and more when they selected Bob Johnson as the first ever Cincinnati Bengal.

A native of Gary, Indiana, Johnson had already experienced first-hand, the pressure of being the first selection of a football program. After being named the head football coach at the University of Tennessee in 1964, legendary coach, Doug Dickey, made Johnson the first recruit he signed to play for the Volunteers. Beginning with his sophomore year in 1965, Johnson was Tennessee's starting center for the next three seasons, helping the Volunteers to a combined 25-6-2 record, including berths in the 1965 Bluebonnet Bowl and the 1966 Gator Bowl. In his junior season in 1966, Johnson was a Football News first-team All-American and a first team All-SEC selection. He was named to the 1966 SEC All-Academic team as well.

It was Johnson's senior season in 1967, though, that drew the attention of NFL executives and coaches. Team captain of a Tennessee squad that finished 9-2 and champions of the SEC for the first time since 1956, Johnson led the Volunteers to an Orange Bowl berth against Oklahoma. Despite losing to the Sooners 26-24, Tennessee finished second in the final AP and UPI polls. One of the highlights of that 1967 season for Tennessee was their 24-13 win in Birmingham against Alabama, handing Bear Bryant's team their only loss of the season and ending the Crimson Tide's 25-game unbeaten streak.

Another highlight of the 1967 season was the play of Johnson. Centering an offense that accumulated 196 first downs, 3,654 total yards and 259 points, Johnson was named to the first team of virtually every All-American team. Not only was he a consensus AP All-American, a first team All-SEC member and an Academic All-American, Johnson also received first team honors from UPI, the Newspapers Enterprise Association, the Football Writers Association of America, the American Football Coaches Association, Time Magazine, The Sporting News, The New York News and the NCAA.

And the accolades didn't end there. Johnson received the Jacobs Trophy as the SEC's best blocker and was named the conference's Most Valuable Offensive Lineman by The Birmingham Press. He finished sixth in the final Heisman Trophy voting, impressive for any player but even more so considering he was an offensive lineman. He finished his collegiate career by playing in the prestigious 1968 Senior Bowl and the 1968 Chicago Charities College All-Star game against the defending NFL champion, Green Bay Packers.

Johnson continued to receive honors for his play at Tennessee long after his college career was over. He was selected as one of the school's 55 best players since 1953 and its only center by the USA Today 2010-2011 College Football Encyclopedia and a member of the SEC's Quarter Century Team of 1950-1974. In 1989, Johnson, an all-time Academic All-American, was elected to the College Football Hall of Fame, and in 1993, received the NCAA Silver Anniversary Award for leading a distinguished professional career after college.

That distinguished professional career started with his time as a Cincinnati Bengal. Based upon his accomplishments at Tennessee, Johnson was obviously a highly sought-after player by every AFL and NFL franchise at the 1968 Draft. That the Bengals were seriously going to use their first ever draft pick and the second overall selection on an offensive lineman wasn't surprising. As it turned out, 10 of the 27 first round picks in the 1968 Draft were used on offensive linemen, including the first two and three out of the first four.

What was surprising was that the Bengals were using their draft pick on a center. There was no doubt Johnson was an NFL caliber player. But by choosing him with the second overall pick in the draft, Johnson became the second highest drafted center in NFL or AFL history. It was by all accounts a high risk move by the AFL's newest franchise but one that Paul

Brown, a strong proponent of the philosophy that the game was won on the front lines, believed would establish his new team with a long-term foundation up front and the centerpiece to his offensive line.

Twelve seasons later, Johnson proved Brown right. Just as he had done at Tennessee as Doug Dickey's first recruit, Johnson set the standard for current and future centers, this time for the professional franchise who chose him as their first ever draft choice.

Judging Johnson's impact during his 12 seasons as a Bengal, 10 as its starting center, using individual and traditional offensive statistics such as touchdowns and yards gained isn't possible or appropriate. This lack of quantitative numbers validates why no fantasy leagues require players to draft offensive linemen. Granted, the recent proliferation of advanced statistics, such as blown blocks on running plays, blown blocks that lead directly to a sack as well as the team's second level and open field yards gained, has created the ability to better-analyze a lineman's performance. It has also defined universal data points that evaluates a position's impact on a team's offense. Unfortunately, these statistics don't exist for the time 1968-1977 when Johnson was the Bengals' starting center.

On the other hand, even without these advanced metrics, there are traditional statistics that show the significant contribution Johnson made in the Bengals' early years. As the team's starting center, Johnson was part of an offense that finished in the top half of the NFL or AFL in rushing offense five times (1968, 1970, 1971, 1973 and 1974), passing offense (1972-1977) and total offense (1971-1975 and 1977) six times and points scored eight times (1970-1977). The 1975 season stands out in particular as the offense finished first in passing and second in total offense.

The best indication of how effective a center and his other linemen are to an offense is the performance of the team's running game. Using that theory to judge his impact, it's safe to say that Johnson was invaluable to the franchise's early and surprising success. In his 10 seasons from 1968-1977 as the team's starting center, and the unofficial captain of the offensive line, Johnson led an offense that averaged 139.5 yards rushing per game for an average of 4.2 yards per carry and 14.2 rushing touchdowns per season. In addition to running back Paul Robinson's 1,023 yard rushing season in 1968, the Bengals offense produced 21 100-yard rushing games in their first 10 seasons with Johnson at the center position. It was a running game that paved the way for the Bengals to record six winning seasons and three post-season berths in their first ten years of existence.

Due in large part to a good old-fashioned three yards and a cloud of dust offensive mentality, the Bengals amassed an unexpectedly successful 73-66-1 record in their first 10 seasons. Johnson and his teammates set several team records during this time including the most wins in a 14-game season (11 in 1975), the highest winning percentage in a season (.786 in 1975), the most consecutive games won (8, Games 8-14 in 1970 and Game 1 in 19741) and the second most consecutive games won in one season (7, Games 8-14 in 1970). They had also had two other six game winning streaks during this time (1973 and 1975) which are tied for the second most in club history.

The only blemish on Johnson's career with the Bengals was his record in the post-season. The Bengals lost all three games they played in the playoffs with Johnson at center by a combined score of 82-44, including a thrilling 31-28 on December 28, 1975 against the Oakland Raiders in which the offense scored a team post-season record 21 points and three touchdowns in the second half.

His post-season record notwithstanding, Johnson was recognized and highly regarded by the national media that covered the NFL for his contributions to the young franchise's early positive progress. He was named to his only Pro Bowl in his rookie season in 1968 and was a second team UPI All-AFC selection in 1970. In 1972, he began a streak of five consecutive seasons where he was named first or second team All-AFC or All-NFL, highlighted by his first team UPI All-AFC selection in 1972 and his first All-NFL selection in 1973 by the Newspaper Enterprise Association.

At the start of the 1978 season, Johnson was replaced in the starting lineup by rookie first round draft choice Blair Bush. When the 1978 season ended with a disappointing 4-12 record, Johnson thought he was leaving the game. However, he returned the next season for one final stint, playing five games for the injured Bush, serving as a long snapper on punts, field goals and extra points. After the 1979 season, Johnson officially retired from the NFL, becoming the last original Cincinnati Bengal to retire.

By that time, Johnson had cemented his legacy as one of the greatest Bengals of all-time. Despite playing a less glorified and publicized position like quarterback or wide receiver, Johnson is still considered, nearly 40 years later, one of the franchise's signature players. He remains the only Bengal to have his uniform number, 54, retired.

More significantly, many believe that without Johnson, the anchor of those first offensive lines in team history, the Bengals never would have attained their early success. Arguably, those first 10 seasons with Johnson starting at center were eventually parlayed into the team's first ever Super Bowl appearance a mere two seasons after he had retired. Frankly, that's a pretty far reaching dividend for a franchise-defining decision that was made 14 years earlier.

But when that decision was to make a player like Bob Johnson the first Cincinnati Bengal ever, getting rewarded many years later only proves that Paul Brown made the right choice all along.

CHAPTER SIXTEEN

JIM LeCLAIR

The Wrestler

Back in the winter of 1969-1970, there was a young man that dominated the junior college wrestling scene in the state of Minnesota. He compiled a 25-2 match record during that time as the number one-ranked wrestler in the state and the fourth-ranked junior college wrestler in the nation.

But instead of becoming the tag team partner of Ric Flair, a member of the illustrious Four Horsemen in the National Wrestling Alliance, the young wrestler followed a different path and passion. Little did anyone know that in the early months of 1970 the highly regarded wrestler from the Land of 10,000 Lakes named Jim LeClair would become one of, if not the best, middle linebackers in the history of the Cincinnati Bengals.

Like many who wore the Bengals uniform in the early years of the franchise, LeClair's road to becoming one of the team's legendary players did not take the traditional route of attending a high profile college football program and using it as a stepping stone to a career in the NFL. A native of St. Paul, Minnesota, LeClair's alternative journey started at Minnesota-Crookston Junior College in 1968, where, in addition to becoming a stand-out wrestler, he was a star on the football field as well. Enshrined in the school's Hall of Fame in 1999, he was a two-time National Junior

College Athletic Association All-Region first team linebacker and captain of the football team in 1969.

With his junior college eligibility completed, LeClair then attended the University of North Dakota beginning in 1970 and continued his excellence on the football field. A two-time All-North Central Conference linebacker, LeClair shone in his senior season in 1971. He amassed 187 tackles, three interceptions, four fumble recoveries and one forced fumble in 1971, a performance that earned him first-team honors as a linebacker on the AP Little All-American team and American Football Coaches Association teams. He was also named the 1971 North Central Conference's Most Valuable Defensive Lineman.

Despite playing only two seasons at North Dakota, LeClair forever left his mark on the school's football program. One of six linebackers named to the school's All-Century team in 1994, he was described in the university's 2015 football media guide as "one of the best linebackers ever to play at the University of North Dakota." More importantly, as LeClair prepared for a possible career in the NFL, his head coach at North Dakota gave him a ringing endorsement.

"Jim is a complete football player, one of the best I've ever coached," said Jerry Olson, North Dakota's head coach from 1968-1977, prior to the 1972 NFL Draft. "He is a very intelligent and dedicated athlete."[26]

But as the 1972 NFL Draft approached, LeClair had to deal with the all-too familiar dissent from pro football personnel. Prospective draft choices who'd played at smaller colleges before him, had heard ad nauseam that playing at Division II or III, even at an elite level, wasn't as worthy as playing at Division I and didn't adequately prepare you for life in the NFL. Fortunately for LeClair, the Bengals, who were ready to begin their fifth professional football season in 1972, didn't hold the same prejudices about drafting small college players as did the rest of the league.

In their previous four drafts, the Bengals selected no fewer than six players from non-Division I schools (Al Beauchamp, Essex Johnson, Ken Riley, Lemar Parrish, Vernon Holland and Ken Anderson) who went on to start and play significant roles in the team's surprisingly successful beginnings. That's why, in large part, the Bengals used their third round draft choice in 1972 and the 54th overall pick on a relatively unknown linebacker and wrestler from Minnesota and the University of North Dakota.

When he first arrived in Cincinnati for his rookie season in 1972, LeClair primarily served on special teams, playing only occasionally and in a reserve role on defense, thanks to the presence of Bill Bergey at the middle linebacker position. But when Bergey was traded to the Philadelphia Eagles at the end of the 1973 season, the opportunity to crack the starting lineup opened up for LeClair and he took full advantage. By the end of the 1974 season, LeClair became the team's starting middle linebacker, a spot he maintained until 1983.

Over the next 10 seasons, LeClair was the center of a defense that guided the franchise to some of its greatest successes, including its first ever Super Bowl appearance. Beginning in 1975 when he became captain of the defense, the Bengals finished in the top half of the NFL in total defense (1975, 1976, 1978, 1981-1983), rushing defense (1976, 1977, 1980-1983) and points allowed (1975, 1976, 1978, 1980, 1981 and 1983) and passing defense seven times (1975-1978 and 1981-1983). During the time LeClair was captain of the defense, the Bengals sported a 69-62 (.527) regular season record, and reached the post-season three times, including the magical Super Bowl ride in 1981.

Of those nine seasons, the 1976 defense in particular, stands out. During that season, the defense set club records for fewest total points allowed in a 14-game season (210), fewest points allowed per game in a season (15.11), most sacks per game in a season (3.29) and the single game record for most interceptions (6, December 12, 1976, at New York Jets) and fewest net yards passing allowed in a game (-35, September 26, 1976 vs. Green Bay). The 1976 defense also allowed the second fewest total net yards per game in a season (262.14 yards), the third fewest net yards allowed in a season (3,670) and accumulated the third most sacks in a season (46) in team history.

A major reason why the Bengals defense was so consistently solid during this time was the performance of LeClair at the middle linebacker position. Over the next eight seasons beginning in 1976, when full regular season defensive statistics were initially kept, LeClair led the team in total tackles five times (1976, 1978, 1979, 1980 and 1981) and solo tackles three times (1978-1980). He led all linebackers on the team in passes defended

(1979-1981) and interceptions (1975, 1978 and 1982) three times and total tackles in one season (1982). His performance on October 5, 1975 at Houston showcased his dominance. LeClair made four tackles on a goal line stand against the Oilers, preserving what would turn out to be a critical 21-19 victory on the team's march to a post-season appearance.

In that 1975 divisional Round Playoff matchup against the Oakland Raiders, LeClair made his presence felt. In the Bengals 31-28 loss, LeClair was one of the few bright spots, leading the team with 13 unassisted tackles and defending one pass. He ended his Bengals post-season career with 30 total tackles, four passes defended and one fumble recovery in six games.

After the 1983 season, LeClair, not unlike many other established NFL veterans at the time, was wooed by the big money contracts being offered by the owners of the newly formed United States Football League (USFL). In the case of LeClair, he was being courted by a New York real estate developer by the name of Donald Trump, the owner of the new league's New Jersey Generals. LeClair found the offer too good to pass up as he left the Bengals and played his final two years of professional football in 1984 and 1985 for Trump and the Generals.

His two-year stint in the USFL aside, LeClair is best remembered for being the lynchpin of the Bengals' defense for over 10 years. During his time in Cincinnati, LeClair averaged 79.5 solo tackles and 101 tackles per season[1] and added 8.5 total sacks. He also defended 30 passes, forced two fumbles, recovered six fumbles and intercepted 10 passes.

In retrospect, it's hard to imagine that back in the winter of 1969-1970 that a young Jim LeClair, who at the time was a top-flight amateur wrestler in the remote Greater Grand Forks of Minnesota and North Dakota, would over the next 16 years earn a reputation as one of the greatest middle linebackers in the history of the University of North Dakota and the NFL's Cincinnati Bengals. His career path when he attended the University of Minnesota-Crookston seemed to indicate he would become a "stylin' profilin', limousine riding, jet flying, kiss stealing, wheelin' n' dealin' son of a gun" member of the World Wrestling Federation. Instead, LeClair pursued a football career that earned him induction into the University

---

[1] Regular season solo and total tackles did not become official games statistics until 1976.

of North Dakota and the College Football Halls of Fame, a 1976 NFL Pro Bowl selection, a second team UPI All-AFC selection in 1982, an appearance in Super Bowl XVI and arguably the greatest middle linebacker in Cincinnati Bengals team history.

In the 2008 film, The Wrestler, Mickey Rourke plays Randy "The Ram" Robinson, an aging professional wrestler looking to recapture the fame he achieved over 20 years earlier. That character easily could have been the tale of Jim LeClair had he not chosen football over wrestling. Bengal fans, however, are eternally grateful that didn't occur.

And that's the bottom line, because Who Dey Nation said so.

CHAPTER SEVENTEEN

BRIAN SIMMONS

Well Worth the Wait

M*any people live their lives* by the old adage, "Good things come to those who wait." It's a philosophy, not only suitable for marketing beer and ketchup, but a way of life that emphasizes patience and endurance. No question, it's not a bad systematic view on how to spend your time and make your daily choices.

Unfortunately, for those who work in management, coaching and scouting of an NFL franchise, it's a philosophy they can't afford to practice. If there's one virtue that the owner of an NFL team and its fans both lack, it's patience. Neither one of them seems willing to wait a reasonable period of time for their team to experience any type of success. Anything short of a playoff berth with a two to three year time frame after acquiring a new breakthrough player or hiring a new coach, and both the owner and the fan base are calling for someone's head.

This pressure for immediate success is extremely high for general managers, coaches and scouts when it comes to the NFL Draft, especially when the franchise holds one of the top picks. In those instances, the team is more than likely coming off a very disappointing season, so it's not only important to draft for the future but to select a player who can make an immediate impact to alleviate the high expectations of a restless fan base and a demanding, results-oriented owner.

The Cincinnati Bengals found themselves in this exact situation at the 1994 NFL Draft. They held the number one overall pick thanks to their league worst record 3-13 record in 1993. Additionally, the pick was even more important considering the Bengals had a miserable 11-37 record in the three seasons since they had last appeared in the playoffs in 1990. While good things *may* come to those who wait, as preparations for the 1994 season began with the upcoming draft, owner and general manager, Mike Brown and the Bengal fan base were in no mood to exact any patience. Consequently, the pressure to deliver a game-changing player with the first overall selection in 1994 was at full throttle.

The Bengals faced an interesting decision with their number one overall pick. Among the college players eligible for the draft, five stood out as legitimate number one selections: Quarterbacks Heath Shuler and Trent Dilfer, running back Marshall Faulk, linebacker Willie McGinest and defensive lineman Dan Wilkinson.

Even though both sides of the ball desperately required help, on the surface, it appeared the Bengals offense was more in need of reinforcement and new blood than the defense. Statistically, the defense, while certainly deficient, had improved each year over the previous three seasons (28th, 26th and 16th respectively). Meanwhile, the offense performed worse each year during that same time frame (14th, 26th and 27th respectively). When you add in the fact that the Bengals had chosen 19 defensive players out of 35 selections in the previous three drafts, conventional wisdom seemed to indicate they would choose an offensive player with the coveted number one overall pick.

Since the Bengals had used their first round selection in 1992 on David Klinger, who was set to become the Bengals' starting quarterback in 1994, choosing Shuler or Dilfer was not an option.[1] That left Faulk, the running back from San Diego State University, who ended his collegiate career with 5,562 all-purpose yards and 62 touchdowns, finishing fourth

---

[1] Shuler would eventually be drafted third overall by the Washington Redskins while Dilfer was selected with the sixth overall selection by the Tampa Bay Buccaneers.

in 1993 and second in 1992 in balloting for the Heisman Trophy.[1] Most experts believed selecting Faulk was the prudent move for the Bengals and their moribund offense.

But in a move that would define his tenure in his early years as the owner and general manager of the team, Mike Brown, who had taken over the reins of the Bengals after his father Paul's death in August 1991, decided to go against the prevalent sentiment and decided to bypass Faulk and select a defensive player instead.[2] The choice, then, boiled down between McGinest from the University of Southern California and Wilkinson from nearby Ohio State University.

A look at the Bengals' roster at the time of the draft revealed adequate depth at linebacker and a lack of a pass rushing, run stuffing defensive lineman. The Bengals believed Wilkinson, a 6'4" 340-pound consensus All-American who was foregoing his senior year to enter the NFL Draft, would fill a void in their defense. With this backdrop, the Bengals selected Wilkinson with the first pick in the 1994 NFL Draft.

Over the next four seasons, Wilkinson started in 59 of the 64 games played but his impact on the defense and the defensive line was minimal at best, and certainly not at the level you would expect from an overall number one draft choice. It was becoming apparent that Wilkinson was slowly but surely turning into a bona-fide draft bust. To make matters worse for the Bengals brass, Wilkinson was making it known publicly that he wanted out of Cincinnati. After the Bengals placed the franchise tag on him at the end of the 1997 season, Wilkinson became dissatisfied with the franchise, going so far as to call Cincinnati "a racist city."[27]

Unwilling to allow a disgruntled player to potentially affect the locker room, the Bengals completed a trade in February 1998 that sent Wilkinson

---

[1] Many consider Faulk's second-place finish for the Heisman Trophy a travesty. Despite rushing for 1,530 yards and 21 touchdowns in 1972, Faulk lost to the more highly publicized and touted University of Miami quarterback, Gino Torretta.

[2] Faulk didn't have to wait long to become drafted. With the next pick, the second overall selection, the Indianapolis Colts chose the San Diego State running back. Twelve seasons, 19,155 total yards, 136 touchdowns and one Super Bowl ring later, Faulk was enshrined in the Pro Football Hall of Fame in 2011. Bengal fans can only speculate what might have been.

to the Washington Redskins in exchange for the 17th overall pick in the 1998 NFL Draft. Little did anyone fathom at the time of the trade, selecting Wilkinson four years earlier would soon pay immediate dividends for the Bengals when they selected linebacker Brian Simmons with the draft choice they received from the Redskins. After a solid nine-year career, Cincinnati fans could look upon Simmons as a classic case of good things coming to those who wait.

A four sport letterman in football, basketball, baseball and track at New Bern High School in North Carolina, Simmons played football beginning in 1994 at the University of North Carolina. An outside linebacker for the Tar Heels, he was a four-year letterman who impacted the program early and often. In his sophomore year in 1995, he led the team in interceptions and by the time he was a junior in 1996, Simmons was a nationally recognized top-flight linebacker.

As a junior, Simmons was named first-team All-ACC and second team All-American by the Associated Press and The Sporting News. His 85 tackles, 12 pressures, nine tackles for loss and two sacks was enough for Simmons to be named a semi-finalist for the Butkus Award given to the nation's best linebacker.

Simmons continued his stellar play as a senior in 1997. Ending the season with 119 tackles, 17 pressures, 13 tackles for loss and three sacks, Simmons was a consensus first team All-American as well as being named to the Associated Press, The Football News and The Walter Camp Foundation's first-team All-American rosters. Additionally, for the second consecutive year, he was a Butkus Award semi-finalist.

Simmons' play was also a catalyst for some of the greatest successes in the school's history. In the four seasons he played at North Carolina, the Tar Heels were 36-12, including a 3-1 record in bowl games. On two occasions during this time, the team finished the season in the top 10 in the Associated Press final poll (10th in 1996 and 6th in 1997).

When it came time to determine his draft stock in 1998, NFL teams only had to look at Simmons' four-year college resume to see he was first round material. A captain on defense his junior and senior years, Simmons ended his college career with 340 tackles (317 of them in his last three seasons), 35 pressures, 36 tackles for loss, 11 sacks, eight interceptions and one touchdown return.[1] He was a starting outside linebacker on a Tar Heel defense that led the ACC in total defense three times (1995-1997) and passing defense and scoring defense two times (1996 and 1997). Simmons also holds the school record for most interception return yards in a season when he returned four interceptions for 160 yards in 1996. It was a college career that eventually earned him a spot as one of North Carolina's 55 greatest players since 1953 by the 2010-2011 USA Today's College Football Encyclopedia and having his jersey number 41 honored by the school.

Given this impressive college career and armed with the 17th overall pick in the 1998 NFL Draft they received from the Redskins, the Bengals, by this time in desperate need of reinforcing their linebacker corps, didn't hesitate to select Simmons.[2] As it turned out, it was a very wise decision, even if it took over four years to transpire.

Simmons cracked the starting lineup in his rookie season in 1998 and immediately made a positive impact on the defense. His 78 total tackles trailed only fellow rookie Takeo Spikes for the team lead, while his three sacks, two passes defended, one forced fumble, one fumble recovery and one interception helped the Bengals finish with the 12th best passing defense in the NFL, an improvement of nine spots from the previous season. Simmons' advance defensive statistics in his rookie season, according to Football Outsiders, were also impressive. Of the 80 defensive plays involving Simmons in 1998, 52 resulted in a stop for a stop rate of 65.0 percent, while 12 ended in a defensive defeat. It was a performance that Simmons would repeat over the rest of his career as a Bengal.

Over the next eight seasons, Simmons was a mainstay of the Bengals defense. He led the team in solo and total tackles three times (1999, 2003 and 2004), forced fumbles twice (2003 and 2004) and fumble recoveries once (2003).[3] Simmons also led all-Bengal linebackers in interceptions four times (2002, 2003, 2004 and 2006), fumble recoveries (1998 and 2004) and passes defended (2002 and 2003) and sacks once (2002). From

---

[1] His lone interception return for a touchdown of 84 yards against Louisville in 1996 is the seventh longest in school history.

[2] The Bengals also had the 13th overall selection in the 1998 Draft. To validate how badly they needed linebackers, they chose linebacker Takeo Spikes from Auburn University with that 13th pick.

[3] His four fumble recoveries in 2003 was the fourth most in the NFL that season.

an advance statistics perspective, the 2002 season stands out. In addition to 20 defensive defeats, Simmons recorded 64 stops on the 91 defensive plays he was involved in for a career best 70.0 percent stop rate. Despite never being named to a Pro Bowl in his Bengal career, his play in Week 8 of the 2003 and Week 9 of the 2005 season did earn him AFC Defensive Player of the Week honors.

During Simmons' eight seasons as one of the team's starting outside linebackers, the Bengals' team defense had its moments of superb play. On December 12, 1999 against Cleveland, the defense held the Browns to 11 net yards rushing, the fewest in team history and their eight sacks against Jacksonville on December 9, 2001 is tied for the most in a single game. The 48 sacks recorded by the 2001 defense is the third most in a season in team history and the 31 interceptions by the 2005 defense is the second most. In Simmons' eight seasons as a starter, the defense finished in the top half of the NFL four times in passing defense (1998, 2001, 2002 and 2004) and points allowed (2003-2006), twice in rushing defense (2001 and 2006) and once in total defense (2001).

Simmons' excellent play, however, didn't equate to success for the franchise. The Bengals were a beyond disappointing 54-90 (.375) in the regular season during Simmons' nine years with the team, finishing above .500 in a season only once and shuffling through three head coaches (Bruce Coslet, Dick LeBeau and Marvin Lewis) and four defensive coordinators (LeBeau, Mark Dufner, Leslie Frazier and Chuck Bresnahan). The one winning year Simmons did experience was 2005, a season that saw the Bengals end a 15-year playoff drought when they won the AFC North Division with an 11-5 record. The post-season lasted only one game as the Bengals lost to the eventual Super Bowl champion Pittsburgh Steelers in the first round of the playoffs, 31-17, a game better known for the devastating knee injury suffered by quarterback Carson Palmer on the team's second offensive snap of the game.

Before the start of the 2007 season, the Bengals released Simmons and he immediately signed with the New Orleans Saints for the upcoming season. After playing one season with the Saints, Simmons retired from the NFL. By that time, the linebacker from New Bern, North Carolina, had established himself as one of the best players in Bengals history.

Simmons finished his Bengals career with 509 solo tackles and 722 total tackles, averaging 62.7 solo tackles and 89.1 total tackles a season as a starting outside linebacker. He totaled 23 sacks for a loss of 148 yards, 41 passes defended, 13 forced fumbles and eight fumble recoveries for 53 yards. His 11 career interceptions is tied for third most by a linebacker in team history. According to Football Outsiders, 57.0 percent of this 758 defensive plays as a Bengal resulted in a stop, with 138 ending in a defensive defeat.

Surely, the Bengals ownership and its fan base would have loved for Dan Wilkinson, the home-grown product out of Ohio State, to pan out as one of the team's best players to ever wear the orange and black. As it turned out, Wilkinson never materialized into the game changer the Bengals thought he would become and eventually became so dissatisfied with his time in Cincinnati that the team had no other choice but to trade their former number one overall draft choice. The trade landed them Brian Simmons and for the next nine seasons, he was a mainstay of the team's linebacker corps.

It was a move that Bengal fans and management can now attest that good things happen to those who wait.

CHAPTER EIGHTEEN

REGGIE WILLIAMS

The Councilman

T*he career path for many* students who attend an Ivy League institution is public service. Whether it is a position in the public sector or something as high profile as a political office, chances are the person in the job is an Ivy School graduate. In fact, 15 Presidents of the United States went to an Ivy League school for at least part of their education, including the last four.

It was this career road map that helped Reggie Williams, a 1976 graduate of Dartmouth College, land a seat on Cincinnati's City Council in 1988. On the surface, it doesn't appear that out of the ordinary for an Ivy League alumnus to attain essentially an entry level political office position a dozen years after graduating. It was what Williams did in the 12 years prior to his political appointment, however, which made his route to city government uniquely different than that of any other Ivy Leaguer serving as a public official. Instead of performing the usual clerking and staffing for a political candidate or organization before becoming a publicly elected official, Williams was a starting linebacker for the Cincinnati Bengals. And beginning in 1976, he made his mark as not only one of the greatest Bengals of all-time on the field, but off the field as well.

Born in Flint, Michigan, Williams' journey to success on the football field and in the public eye began with a major obstacle early on in life.

At the age of eight, he was diagnosed with a hearing disability and was referred to the Michigan School for the Deaf. For three years, he was required, according to a 1987 Sports Illustrated profile, to "relearn the mechanics of speech" before he returned to a more traditional school in the sixth grade. He went onto attend Flint Southwestern High School where he was a star on the wrestling and football teams.

Upon graduation, Williams accepted an academic scholarship to attend Dartmouth College in 1972 and while he continued his prowess on the wrestling mat by winning the Ivy League Heavyweight championship in 1975, it was his performance as a three-year letterman (1973-1975) for the Big Green football team that put Williams in position to pursue his personal and professional aspirations.

A three-time All-Ivy League first team linebacker, Williams helped Dartmouth to an Ivy League championship as a sophomore in 1973. As a junior, he accumulated 92 solo tackles and 143 total tackles, seventh most in school history for a single season. He capped off his career as a senior in 1975 by being named second team AP All-American and first team Football Coaches Association All-American. Williams finished his career at Dartmouth with 243 solo tackles and 370 total tackles, the second most in school history.

Despite having a solid college career, Williams' stock in the 1976 NFL Draft wasn't bullish. Due in large part to the fact that he played for an Ivy League school, he wasn't considered a very high draft choice, if one at all. Fortunately for Williams, the Cincinnati Bengals had a track record over their previous eight drafts to select a player from a low profile college and develop them into a highly proficient NFL starter. Bengal head coach and general manager, Paul Brown, once again decided to roll the dice and choose an unheralded college player when he used the 82nd overall pick in the third round of the 1976 NFL Draft to select Williams. It was a move some 14 seasons later that would prove Brown's unique ability to discover NFL talent in the most unlikely places.

Upon being drafted, Williams immediately became a starter on the Bengals defense as a right side linebacker, remaining a starter on the right side for the next 14 seasons. Needless to say, to remain a starter in the NFL for 14 years, a player has to perform at a highly proficient level, which Williams did--and then some. In his 14 seasons, he led the team in forced fumbles seven times (1977, 1979, 1981, 1983 and 1985-1987), fumble recoveries five times (1981-1983, 1985 and 1987), solo tackles four times (1976, 1977, 1981 and 1984), total tackles three times (1976, 1977 and 1984) and interceptions once (1977). He also led all Bengals linebackers in passes defended eight times (1976, 1978, 1979, 1982-1985 and 1988), sacks seven times (1976, 1978, 1982, 1983, 1985, 1986 and 1988), solo tackles (1986 and 1987) and interceptions (1981 and 1984) twice, and fumble recoveries (1979) and total tackles (1987) once.

Williams was a key member of several highly-ranked defenses in his time with the Bengals. From 1976 to 1989, the Cincinnati defense finished in the top half of the NFL in total defense (1976, 1978, 1980, 1981, 1983, 1984, 1987 and 1989) and passing defense (1976, 1978, 1980, 1983 and 1986-1989) eight times, rushing defense seven times (1976-1977 and 1980-1984) and points allowed six times (1976, 1978, 1980, 1981, 1983 and 1989). The 1983 defense was particularly exceptional, finishing first in total defense, tied for second in rushing defense, third in pass defense and sixth in points allowed.

Williams was also part of several record-setting defensive performances in Bengals team history. In his 1976 rookie season, Williams and his defensive teammates set the team record for fewest net yards passing allowed in a game (-35 yards) and fewest total net yards allowed in a game (36 yards) in a 28-7 Bengals victory over Green Bay on September 26. The 1976 defense also permeates the Bengals regular season record book. Their 26 interceptions are fourth most in team history while their 46 sacks and their 3,670 total net yards allowed ranks third all-time. The defense still holds the team record for fewest points allowed per game (15.00 points per game) and most sacks per game (3.29) and is ranked second in fewest total points allowed in a season (210) and fewest total net yards allowed per game in a season (262.14 net yards per game).

Williams' excellent play on the field resulted in some of the most successful seasons in team history. From 1976-1989, Cincinnati was 107-105 (.505) during the regular season but more importantly appeared in the post-season three times, two of which turned out to be the Bengals' two signature seasons. The 12 wins the franchise recorded in both 1981 and 1988 are tied for the most games won in a season in team history with the .750 winning percentage in both years ranking second in team history. The 1988 season marked the beginning of a 10-game winning streak at home, the second longest for consecutive games won at home in team history.

Even though Williams only participated in three post-seasons, he certainly made the most of the time he had in the playoffs. His three career sacks in the post-season is tied for the second most in team history and includes a sack in Super Bowl XXIII against San Francisco in which the team record for most sacks in a post-season game (4) was set. Williams, one of seven players to wear the Bengals uniform in both of their Super Bowl appearances, averaged 10.3 solo tackles and 14.3 total tackles per playoff season and led the team during the 1988 playoffs in solo tackles (13), total tackles (17) and sacks (3). It was part of a playoff performance that enabled the 1988 defense to set the post-season team records for fewest first downs allowed in a game (10, vs. Buffalo on January 6, 1989 in the AFC Championship game), fewest total net yards allowed in a game (181 vs. Buffalo on January 6, 1989) and fewest net yards rushing allowed in a game (22, vs. Seattle on December 31, 1988).

When all was said and done, Williams' career on the football field as a Cincinnati Bengal stacks up as one of the greatest in the team's history. His 14 seasons in a Bengals uniform and his 137 consecutive games played are the third most in team history respectively, while his 206 games played rank second all-time. In his career with the Bengals, Williams averaged 61.8 solo tackles and 83.1 total tackles per season and totaled 55 passes defended, 16 forced fumbles and 23 fumble recoveries. His 16 career interceptions, tied for eighth on the team's all-time interceptions list, is the most ever by a Bengals linebacker and his 62.5 sacks are the second most in team history.

Even though he was a solid performer year-after-year on the field, Williams was—inexplicably--never selected to a Pro Bowl or named to an All-Pro team. The only honor he received was being named to the 1976 NFL All-Rookie team. The lack of recognition for his play, though, was offset by the bounty of accolades and accomplishments Williams achieved for his actions off the football field.

In 1985, Williams received the Byron "Whizzer" White Award from the National Football Players Association (NFLPA) for humanitarian service, followed by being named the NFL's Walter Payton Man of the

Year in 1986. At the end of the 1987 season, Williams received even more national attention when he was one of seven professional athletes named as a Sports Illustrated Sportsman of the Year for his work with children in the Cincinnati area. In the magazine's profile of Williams, he was cited for increasing public awareness of communication problems and the programs of the Cincinnati Speech and Hearing Center, being an active member of Partners in Education with the Cincinnati Public Schools that recognized students for perfect attendance, and helped record, with 30 other teammates, a Bengals "Just Say No" song, with the proceeds going to the local Just Say No to Drugs foundation. All of the attention and recognition was a bit overwhelming for Williams.

"I still get embarrassed when attention is paid to what I do," Williams told Sports Illustrated. "But that makes every recognition a stronger mandate for future commitment. I'm committed for life."[28]

With his public off-the-field persona skyrocketing in 1988, it came as no surprise that when a seat opened up on Cincinnati's City Council, the local Charter Party appointed Williams to fill it. Despite being a key member of their eventual Super Bowl squad, the Bengals agreed to excuse Williams from practices on Wednesdays so he could attend weekly council meetings. The following year in 1989, Williams was elected to a second council term on the Charter Party ticket, receiving 42,645 votes, the fourth most of any candidate. Not surprisingly, holding a political office position while also playing linebacker on Sundays did pose for some interesting conversations on the football field.

"When I made a play that's a little more than my opponents like, I've heard comments like, 'Come on, you're a judge,' or 'Hey, you're an elected official, you're not supposed to be doing things like that,'" Williams said during the 1989 season.[29]

Playing aggressively while serving on a City Council wasn't the only criticism Williams received from his opponents and his peers. He controversially crossed the NFLPA's picket line during the 1987 NFL Players Strike, a difficult decision that Williams, in typical fashion, committed to one hundred percent.

"The reason I crossed the picket line is because I felt very strongly about how the players were about the strike," Williams recalled. "There were things being done that shouldn't have been. Sure, there was a lot of peer pressure, but sometimes you have to do what's right for you."[30]

At the end of the 1989 season, Williams believed it was right for him to retire from the NFL and in 1990 resigned from the City Council to start a new career as vice-president and general manager of the World League of American Football's (WLAF) New Jersey Knights. In later years, Williams would open the NFL's first Youth Education Town in Los Angeles, California and became the vice-president of Disney Sports Attractions in 1998. He also has endured 24 knee surgeries since his career ended, including having both knees replaced in 2005 so both would be compatible, and an additional eight operations in five months in 2008. The fragility of his knees has put Williams at risk of having his right leg amputated, and required both of his feet to be operated on because he had been trying to walk on one leg.

In the end, regardless of whether it's his football career, his work in the community, his public and private service or confronting surgery after surgery on his knees with the cloud of amputation hanging over him, Reggie Williams has written a history with the Cincinnati Bengals and personal legacy that is best described as excellent, reliable, professional, selfless and full of integrity.

What else would you expect from an Ivy League graduate?

CHAPTER NINETEEN

AL BEAUCHAMP

The Start of the Small College Pipeline

L*ike most teams who enter* a professional sports league as an expansion franchise, not much was expected from the Cincinnati Bengals in their early years. Many believed the best case scenario was for the Bengals to build for the long term, through the one-time 40-veteran player allocation draft and the traditional college draft. The most anyone could hope for was that in the first few seasons they would at least be competitive and not embarrass themselves or the league when the games were played.

What nobody expected was that in their third year as a team, and their first as part of the NFL, the Bengals would in the last seven games of the 1970 season, capture the newly-formed AFC Central Division and qualify for the post-season. It was a path to the playoffs by an expansion franchise that became the blueprint used by the Jacksonville Jaguars and the Carolina Panthers when they entered the NFL 25 years later and appeared in the playoffs in their second year in the league.

When the Bengals' quick personnel success was examined, the initial focus was on the players they chose in the allocation draft and the early rounds of the college draft. And while they were able to secure future franchise standouts like Bob Johnson, Paul Robinson, Greg Cook, Bill Bergey, Speedy Thomas and Mike Reid in the first three rounds of their first three college drafts, it was in the latter rounds of the draft where the

Bengals found the pieces that established the foundation not only early on but for future seasons. One of those late round pieces was linebacker Al Beauchamp.

A native of Baton Rouge, Louisiana, Beauchamp was taken in the fifth round and the 138th overall selection of the 1968 NFL/AFL Draft out of Southern University by the Bengals in their initial college draft. Choosing a player with Beauchamp's football background, playing for an under-publicized small Division II black college in Southern University was a formula that would benefit the Bengals greatly in their inaugural college draft and in successive drafts as well. In the years that followed they would select such future stars as Essex Johnson (1968, Round 6, Grambling University), Ken Riley (1969, Round 6, Florida A&M University), Lemar Parrish (1970, Round 7, Lincoln University) and Lenvil Elliott (1973, Round 10, Northeast Missouri State) in the later rounds on talent from the traditional Afro-American universities.

But it was a strategy that all began with the selection of Beauchamp. Given his play at Southern University, it's no surprise the Bengals wanted him as part of their inaugural team.

Beauchamp wasted little time making an impact for the Bengals as he became the usual starting left linebacker in his 1968 rookie season and immediately contributed to the defense's success. He finished his initial AFL season with two interceptions, including a 17-yard interception return for a touchdown against the Buffalo Bills in a 34-23 Cincinnati victory on September 22.[1] It was the first of three seasons that Beauchamp would lead all Bengal linebackers in interceptions (1968, 1971 and 1973). His six interceptions in 1971 were the ninth most by a player in the NFL that season.

Over eight seasons, Beauchamp was part of a defense that, despite its expansion roots, held its own against the rest of the AFL and NFL and still remains a leader in the team's record book over 40 years later. From 1968-1975, the Bengals' defense finished in the top half of the league in fewest points allowed six times (1970-1975), total defense and passing defense five times (1971-1975) and rushing defense four times (1970-1973).

---

[1] Additional regular season individual defensive statistics were not kept regularly until 1976.

During that same stretch, the Bengals' defense set the team record in 1972 for fewest total net yards allowed per game (253.71 yards per game) and in 1971 for most interceptions in a game (6, November 28 against San Diego). Their 16.36 points allowed per game and 3,552 total net yards allowed in 1972 are the second fewest in team history while their 229 points allowed in 1972 and 27 interceptions in 1971 rank third on the franchise's all-time list. Their efforts against the Pittsburgh Steelers on October 4, 1973 and against the Cleveland Browns on September 5, 1974 resulted in the second fewest first downs allowed in a game (6) and the third fewest net yards passing allowed in a game (3 yards) respectively.

Thanks to Beauchamp and his defensive teammates, the expansion Bengals far exceeded the expectations many had for them when they entered the league. The team had a more than respectable 55-56-1 record in their first eight seasons. But more impressive was their three appearances in the post-season (1970, 1973 and 1975) during that same time frame. Their 11-3 record in 1975 is the team record for the highest winning percentage in a season (.786) with the 11 victories tied for third for most wins in a season. During Beauchamp's time with the Bengals, the franchise had several record-winning streaks, including consecutive games won (8, 1970 Games 8-14 and 1971 Game 1)[1], consecutive games won in one season (7, 1970)[2] and consecutive home games won (9, 3 in 1975 and 6 in 1976).[3]

Unfortunately for Beauchamp, the team's regular season success did not translate into any post-season victories. The Bengals lost all three playoff games Beauchamp played in, despite his 18 solo tackles and 22 total tackles in his three post-season appearances. As it would turn out, Beauchamp would play for the last time as a Bengal in the 31-28 loss to the Oakland Raiders in the AFC divisional playoff game on December 28, 1975.

Prior to the 1976 season, the Bengals traded Beauchamp to the St. Louis Cardinals on June 21 for a fourth round draft choice where he played his ninth and final NFL season. In the end, though, Beauchamp will always be remembered as a Cincinnati Bengal and a significant contributor

---

[1] Currently tied for first all-time in franchise history.
[2] Currently second all-time in team history.
[3] Currently tied for third all-time in team history.

to the team's initial foray into professional football. In his 111 games played in Cincinnati, 83 of them as a starter, Beauchamp had 15 interceptions, tied for 10th in team history and the second most by a linebacker, returning two of them for touchdowns. He also recovered seven fumbles and returned them for a combined 63 yards.

More importantly, however, Beauchamp's selection by the Bengals in their initial college draft in 1968 became the model the franchise would use to unearth several overlooked and underpublicized college seniors, turn them into solid contributors and in some instances All-Pro NFL players. By scouring the Division II and III football programs for talent, particularly the predominantly black colleges of the South, the Bengals established a pipeline of small college football players that produced critical pieces of the foundation that became the formative and surprising successful years of a new NFL franchise.

Thanks to Al Beauchamp, the pipeline got off to a very prosperous start.

CHAPTER TWENTY

DAVE LAPHAM

The Voice of the Bengals

F*or the past 30 seasons,* the Cincinnati Bengals have had five coaches[1], and started nine different quarterbacks[2], 11 different halfbacks[3] and 16 different wide receivers.[4] Throughout all this change, there has stood one constant for the Bengals since 1986, even if it was an off-the-field position. For the past 30 seasons, former Bengals offensive lineman, Dave Lapham, has been the color analyst on the team's radio network. Thanks to his energetic and passionate pleas for the Bengals to succeed, Lapham has become a fixture to the legion of Cincinnati fans everywhere.

But before he became the undisputed "Voice of the Bengals", Lapham spent 10 seasons, eight as a starter, as a left and right guard on the Cincinnati

---

[1] Sam Wyche, David Shula, Bruce Coslet, Dick LeBeau and Marvin Lewis.

[2] Boomer Esiason, David Klingler, Jeff Blake, Neil O'Donnell, Akili Smith, Scott Mitchell, Jon Kitna, Carson Palmer and Andy Dalton.

[3] James Brooks, Harold Green, Garrison Hearst, Corey Dillon, Chris Perry, Rudi Johnson, Kenny Watson, Cedric Benson, BenJarvis Green-Ellis, Giovani Bernard and Jeremy Hill.

[4] Cris Collinsworth, Eddie Brown, Tim McGee, Carl Pickens, Jeff Query, Darnay Scott, Craig Yeast, Peter Warrick, Chad Johnson, T.J. Houshmandzadeh, Laveraneus Coles, Terrell Owens, Jerome Simpson, A.J. Green, Marvin Jones and Mohamed Sanu.

offensive line, making just as big an impression on the franchise's history for his on-the-field performance as he has in the radio booth.

Born in Melrose, Massachusetts, Lapham was a three-year letterman from 1971-1973 in football for Syracuse University. Even though the Orange went a sub-par 12-20-1 while he was a member of the football team, Lapham played well enough to gain the attention of NFL scouts and player personnel directors. After Lapham's senior season in 1973, in which he was a team captain, he was selected and participated in multiple major college football all-star games, including the East-West Shrine Game, the Blue-Gray Football Classic, the Hula Bowl and the prestigious Senior Bowl. His play in the practices leading up to the games and the games itself was good enough for the Bengals to select him in the third round of the 1974 NFL Draft with the 61st overall pick.

After playing in all 14 games of his 1974 rookie season, Lapham assumed the starting right guard position in 1975, a season that would become the most successful in team history up to that point and remains one of the best all-time for the Bengals. The team went 11-3, tied for third most wins and with a winning percentage (.786) that remains the highest in a season in team history, en route to a wild card berth in the NFL playoffs. During the regular season, Lapham was a key member of an offense that finished second in the league in total offense and was the NFL leader in pass offense. Several games that season stood out as well, including the 41 points scored in the second half against the San Diego Chargers on December 21 (second most in team history), the 34 first downs (tied for second in team history) and 441 net yards passing (third most in team history) against O.J. Simpson and the Buffalo Bills on November 17 in a 33-24 victory on Monday Night Football.

Lapham continued in his starting role at right guard for the next four seasons, unfortunately suffering through some of the worst seasons in Bengals history and dealing with three different head coaches.[1] After serving as a back-up in 1980, Lapham returned to the starting lineup the following year. Little did he know, nor anyone else for that matter, that the 1981 season would become legendary.

Coming off a 6-10 record in 1980 in Forrest Gregg's first year as head

---

[1] Bill Johnson, Homer Rice and Forrest Gregg.

coach, the 1981 Bengals, realistically, were just hoping to continue the road to respectability that they'd begun traveling the previous year. Instead, the dream season took place in 1981, culminating in the team's first ever Super Bowl appearance. A major reason why the 1981 season was so special was the play of Lapham and his teammates on offense.

The 1981 Bengals offense by almost any measure was not only one of the best in the team's history but in the entire NFL as well. Among the many team milestones achieved by the offense that year were most first downs in a season (361), the third most net yards passing (3,995 yards), the fourth most total net yards (5,968 yards), net yards passing per game (249.69 yards per game), and points scored (421) and the fifth most passing touchdowns (30) and total touchdowns scored (51) in a single season. The offense, led by league MVP Ken Anderson, finished second in the NFL in total offense and third in passing offense and points scored.

It was an offense that guided the Bengals to a club record 12 wins and the second highest winning percentage (.750) in team history. More importantly, it contributed to the team winning the AFC Central Division and a berth in the NFL post-season, a place where the Bengals had never won, losing the only three playoff games they had previously played. But 1981 was not like any other year in Bengals history as the magical ride that was the regular season continued into the post-season.

The Bengals won their first ever playoff game, a 28-21 victory against the Buffalo Bills on January 3, 1982 in the AFC divisional playoff round,[1] a breakthrough win due in large part to a solid running game established by Lapham and his offensive line teammates. The Bengals rushed for 136 yards at over four yards per carry and three touchdowns[2] in a victory that sent Cincinnati to the AFC Championship Game and one win away from an appearance in Super Bowl XVI. They would host the San Diego Chargers for the right to represent the AFC in the Super Bowl and in a season that was marked by the unexpected, not even the wildest of imaginations could have envisioned what would transpire when the two teams kicked off in the AFC title game.

The Chargers earned their berth in the AFC Championship the week

---

[1]   The game was also the first home playoff game in team history.

[2]   The three rushing touchdowns is tied for most rushing touchdowns in Bengals post-season history.

before by defeating the Miami Dolphins in the Orange Bowl, 41-38, a three-overtime marathon known as The Epic in Miami that many, to this day, consider the greatest playoff game ever played. The game was played in oppressively muggy and humid conditions that required many of the Chargers to receive IV's after the game. One of the most indelible images not only of the game but of NFL history was Charger tight end Kellen Winslow being helped off the field by his teammates, unable to return to the locker room on his own after suffering dehydration and severe cramps throughout the course of the game. Granted, the Chargers preferred playing for the Super Bowl in balmy San Diego but at least they could take comfort in knowing they wouldn't have to deal with hot, steamy and debilitating conditions in Cincinnati. As it turned out, the Chargers should have been more careful about what they asked for when it came to the weather on game day for the AFC title.

One can only imagine what was going on in the minds of the Chargers when they woke up in their hotel rooms the morning of the AFC Championship. What they knew was that the air temperature was −9 degrees and that, combined with the gusting winds, made it feel like it was anywhere between -37 degrees to -59 degrees below zero. What they couldn't have known was the impact of playing football in such sub-human conditions and a swing of 143 degrees from the week before in Miami.

"I went out with the first wave of guys because I returned kickoffs," recalled then-Charger special team captain, Hank Bauer, in a 2014 New York Daily News interview. "I walk out of the tunnel, ran right down the field to the other end and ran right back into the locker room. Everybody said, 'What are you doing, what's up?' And I told everybody, 'You know what? Take it all off. Number one, you're not going to be able to move with all this stuff on and number two, it ain't gonna help.' I was frozen by the time I got to the other end."[31]

Meanwhile, in the Bengals locker room, Lapham decided he and the rest of the offensive line would take a different approach to the brutal conditions. Acknowledging the fact it was "like Siberia" outside, Lapham convinced the rest of his linemen to play without sleeves on their arms.

"That was my idea," Lapham told the New York Daily News, explaining it was done for strategic as well as psychological reasons. "I had

Gary Johnson I was playing against and he was a grabber. On the pass rush, he'd try to swat and grab cloth and try to pull you off your shoes. I thought, 'Man, I don't want to have extra cloth on my arms.' I thought, 'I'm going to try to go out there and just regular.'

"John Woodcock [Chargers defensive end] and those guys came to the line of scrimmage the first time and they were like, 'What?' They had masks that had eye and nose holes, sweatshirts with pouches, all bundled up."

For Lapham and his teammates, it was a case of mind-over-matter, especially with a trip to the Super Bowl on the line. "It was a Darwinism game. You just went there and survived that sucker," Lapham recalled. And even though it was apparent the Bengals were winning the psychological war, Lapham admitted he and his teammates felt the physical toll of playing in sub-zero temperatures.

"I had to throw a forearm on the first play and I thought I had shattered my arm because it was just so brittle," Lapham said in 2014. "On that first drive when they had a TV timeout, I looked down at my arms and they looked like two lobster claws."[32]

Blocking with crustacean anatomy aside, Lapham and the rest of the offensive linemen dominated the Chargers defense en route to a 27-7 victory and a date in Super Bowl XVI against their former assistant, Bill Walsh and the San Francisco 49ers. Despite the arctic conditions, the Bengals totaled 318 yards, including 143 yards on the ground and one touchdown. Amazingly, Anderson threw for 175 yards and two touchdowns without being sacked, even though he played in winds that made it seem impossible to throw a spiral.

After the game, as everyone attempted to thaw out, many wondered what impact the weather had on the final outcome. In Lapham's mind it was a no-brainer—it was a non-factor. "We were the better team whether we played them in Antarctica or Hawaii," Lapham said 32 years later.[33]

Unfortunately, the Cinderella 1981 season ended in heartbreak as Walsh defeated his former employer behind future Hall of Fame quarterback, Joe Montana, 26-21. After spotting the 49ers a 20-0 halftime lead, the Bengals staged a furious second half comeback behind Lapham and the rest of the offensive line. In addition to scoring 21 points, the offense recorded 17 first downs and 257 net yards, both post-season club records. Sadly, it wasn't enough as the Bengals record-setting season ended on a sour note.

Lapham played two more seasons in Cincinnati, including the strike-shortened 1982 season when the offense finished second in the NFL in total offense, third in passing offense and fourth in points scored. After the 1983 season, Lapham joined several other NFL veterans who were lured by the seemingly infinitely-deep pockets of the owners of the new United States Football League (USFL), and jumped ship. In Lapham's case, he signed a 10-year guaranteed personal services contract with a then relatively unknown New York City real estate developer, Donald Trump, to play for Trump's New Jersey Generals. He played for the Generals for two seasons before retiring from professional football following knee surgery at the end of the 1985 season.

Today, most Bengal fans know Lapham as the team's radio announcer who unabashedly shares his joy over the air when the team plays well.[1] He punctuates the on-going play-by-play with such declarations as "Get him!", "There he is!" or "Got him!" Recognizing Lapham's contribution to the Bengals based solely on his radio work unjustly discounts his performance as a player for the franchise. In his 140 games played as a Bengal, 105 as a starter, Lapham played an integral part in making Cincinnati an offensive powerhouse in the NFL at the beginning of the 1980s and transforming the team into Super Bowl contenders.

During his time as a starting left and right guard, the Bengals were 76-69 during the regular season and qualified for the post-season three times, which included their first ever playoff victory and Super Bowl appearance. Lapham was part of an offensive line that assisted in 15 running backs rushing for 100 yards in a game and 15 quarterbacks passing for 300 yards in a game. He was part of the run blocking that allowed Pete Johnson to rush for 1,067 yards in 1981 and the pass protection that gave Ken Anderson the opportunity to throw for 3,169 yards in 1975 and 3,754 yards in 1981. In Lapham's eight years as a starter the Bengals finished in the top half of the NFL in passing offense seven times (1975-1978 and

---

[1] His commentary on A.J. Green's Hail Mary catch against the Baltimore Ravens on November 10, 2013 on the last play of the game is priceless and classic Lapham.

1981-1983), total offense (1975, 1977, 1978 and 1981-1983) and points scored (1975-1977, 1979, 1981 and 1982) six times and rushing offense twice (1979 and 1980)

In other words, it was a career that the current "Voice of the Bengals" would describe, very simply in his trademark enthusiastic tone as "Nice!"

CHAPTER TWENTY–ONE

JOE WALTER

The Good, The Bad and The Ugly

I n the 1966 classic spaghetti Western film and morality play, "The Good, The Bad and The Ugly", Clint Eastwood personifies The Good, Lee Van Cleef The Bad and Eli Wallach The Ugly in a conflict between three men competing to find a buried fortune amidst the American Civil War and the violence it created. Its themes of the daily hardships experienced by anyone during the war and the idea that a man is more defined by his actions than his words helped make the film an all-time classic.

Over 30 years later, the same allegorical characters and themes director Sergio Leone used in his epic film could describe the 13 years Joe Walter spent as an offensive tackle for the Cincinnati Bengals from 1985-1997: The Good, The Bad and The Ugly.

Born in Dallas, Texas, Walter was a four-year letterman in football at Texas Tech University. During his time at Texas Tech, the Red Raiders were members of the ultra-competitive, multi-talented and, as it turned out, highly unscrupulous Southwest Conference (SWC)[1]. On the one hand, facing the likes of perennial powerhouses at the time in Texas, Oklahoma, Texas A&M, Houston and SMU, every year didn't equate to a lot of wins for Walter and his Tech teammates. From 1981-1984, Texas Tech finished a combined 12-30-2.

On the other hand, competing week-in and week-out against such high quality competition allowed Walter to show NFL scouts he could play at the next level. While he wasn't considered a top tier draft choice, Walter apparently did enough to impress the Bengals talent evaluators as they selected him in the seventh round with the 181st overall pick in the 1985 NFL Draft. With that selection, Walter began his NFL odyssey that would compare favorably to one of Clint Eastwood's most memorable films.

The Good: 1985-1990. Although he didn't start any of the Bengals games in his 1985 rookie season, Walter did play in 14 of those 16 games as the team stumbled to a 7-9 record in Sam Wyche's second season as head coach. By the next season in 1986, Walter became the starting right tackle for what would become one of the most prolific offenses in team history and a stretch of winning football that made many of the players local and national celebrities. With the exception of the strike-shortened 1987 season, the Bengals competed for the post-season every year from 1986-1990, winning the AFC Central Division twice (1988 and 1990) and making their second Super Bowl appearance in team history. During those five years, Walter was a starting member of an offense that finished in the top half of the NFL each year in total offense and rushing offense and four out of five year in passing offense (1986-1989) and points scored (1986, 1988, 1989 and 1990).

It was the 1988 season, however, that is most fondly remembered by Walter and fans alike. Before losing to the San Francisco 49ers in Super Bowl XXIII, the Bengals were the most dominant offense in the NFL, leading the league in rushing offense, total offense and points scored. They

---

[1]   Due to the penchant of its member institutions to do anything to land a star recruit, the SWC became known as the "So you Wanna Car Conference". During the 1980's, the only programs in the conference not placed on NCAA probation were Arkansas, Baylor and Rice. The most notable school not to run afoul of the NCAA was SMU, who, because of repeated violations, received the Death Penalty, resulting in the cancellation of their entire 1987 and 1988 seasons.

still hold the team record for points scored (448), touchdowns (59), rushing touchdowns (27) and net yards rushing (2,710) in a season and remain second in first downs (351) and average yards per rushing attempt (4.813 yards per attempt) in a season in team history. Their 6,057 total net yards gained in 1988 ranks third in team history.

While quarterback Boomer Esiason is the player most identified as the key player to the offense's success in 1988, it was anchored by the greatest offensive line in team history and arguably one of the best in NFL history as well. With Walter manning the right tackle position, the rest of the offensive line consisted of Bruce Kozerski at center, Bruce Reimers at left guard, Max Montoya at right guard and Pro Football Hall of Famer, Anthony Muñoz, at left tackle. Add to the mix the offensive mind of Wyche and the tutelage of Jim McNally, one of the most respected offensive line coaches in NFL history, and you had an offense that made beautiful music together. According to Walter, there wasn't any big secret to why it all worked so well.

"Everybody kind of took care of each other, "Walter told the Cincinnati Enquirer's Scribe Series Podcast, citing Wyche's and McNally's work behind the scenes to insure all the gears of the machine ran smoothly and effectively. And despite losing to Joe Montana and his epic fourth quarter drive in the Super Bowl, Walter reflected fondly about the 1988 season and those Bengal teams in his early years with the franchise.

"Such a great team, a classic team," Walter told the Cincinnati Enquirer in 2002. "A heck of a ride for myself and the team."[34]

Unfortunately, things were about to go south for Walter and the entire Bengals franchise.

The Bad: 1991-1994. Coming off their second division title in three seasons the year before, the 1991 season appeared, on the surface, as another opportunity for the Bengals to make a post-season run. Beneath the exterior, however, imminent changes precipitated an eventual downward spiral for the Bengals that would last for the next 15 years.

The impending slide actually began the year before when Montoya became a free agent and signed with the Los Angeles Raiders prior to the start of the 1990 season. Montoya's departure raised a red flag when it came to the future of the team and their ability to sustain their recent success. Free agency had arrived in the NFL and it was no mystery that the Bengals, notorious at the time for their tight purse strings and reluctance to spend money, would not aggressively pursue any free agent. More importantly, given their fiscal past, it was highly unlikely owner/general manager Mike Brown and his family would keep any of their own free agents or match the contract offers a player would receive from another team.[1] With even more pending free agents on the 1991 Bengals roster, the prospects of keeping the core group of players together seemed highly unlikely.

Meanwhile, the relationship between Brown and his head coach Sam Wyche, despite the team's recent success, was deteriorating at an alarming rate. It was apparent to almost everyone in the locker room that the quirky, non-traditional approach espoused by Wyche, clashed with the straight-laced, conservative approach favored by Brown. That meant that any downturn in the performance on the field, no matter how slight or regardless of the reason, would cost the well-liked and well-respected by the players Wyche his job. It was, in retrospect, a perfect storm for disaster.

The Bengals went 3-13 in 1991 and as expected, Wyche was fired at the end of the season. As the 1992 season approached, what came next clearly surprised everyone. Muñoz and halfback James Brooks left the team, and, believing Esiason would soon leave via free agency, the Bengals used their first pick and the sixth overall in the 1992 NFL Draft to select David Klingler, a quarterback from the University of Houston. Add it all up, and the Bengals were a team on the brink of implosion.

"What just happened here?" Walter recalls thinking after the firing of Wyche and the roster upheaval. "We lost all our leadership."[35]

The situation didn't improve when Brown hired David Shula, the son of legendary NFL coach, Don Shula, to replace Wyche. Walter remembers thinking that when Shula was first named coach, it was "a cheap hire based on his dad's last name." His fears were confirmed on the first day Shula met with the team. According to Walter, Shula appeared visibly overwhelmed

---

[1] NFL free agency at the time was known as Plan B free agency. It was a system that allowed the NFL team to preserve limited rights of no more than 37 players per year. Those players became designated as Plan B free agents. A Plan B designee had to provide their current team an opportunity to resign them by matching their offer they had received from another team. A non-Plan B designee could sign with any team, leaving his current team with no chance to match any offer. In 1992, Plan B free agency was declared a violation of anti-trust laws and discontinued.

by the prospect of being an NFL head coach and unknowingly sent a message to the team that would doom his tenure in Cincinnati.

"He lost the team," Walter said when describing Shula's first interaction with the players and his staff. "There was no way he was going to win. He was done before he started."[36] Unfortunately for Bengals fans, Walter was right.

Over the next three season, the Bengals won a total of 11 games, setting records for futility in their wake. Between 1992-1994, Shula's teams set club records for most consecutive road games lost (15) and most consecutive games lost in one season (10, Games 1-10, 1993). After losing everyone except Walter and Kozerski, the once-potent Bengals offense went missing, finishing in the top half of any NFL offensive category just once (eighth in rushing offense in 1992). At the end of another 3-13 season in 1994, no one could imagine that the situation could get worse.

They were wrong.

The Ugly: 1995-1997. Even though he sported an 11-37 record in his three seasons as head coach, Shula returned for the 1995 season. It seemed as if Shula was about to right after going 7-9 in 1995, his best record in his four years in Cincinnati. But as the 1996 season began, Walter believed Shula was being "set up to fail" and that his days as the head coach were numbered.

"The coaching staff were doing whatever they could to get rid of Dave," Walter recalled. The turmoil between the coaches and players hit a breaking point after the Bengals blew a halftime lead to the San Francisco 49ers on October 20, 1996, losing 28-21 and sending Cincinnati to a 1-6 record. Shula was fired the next day and replaced by offensive coordinator Bruce Coslet, who immediately raised the ire of the players, according to Walter, by "accusing all of us of being out of shape."[37] Belittling comments aside, the Bengals reversed course by going 7-2 in their final nine games under Coslet, finishing the season 8-8. The offense was somewhat rejuvenated as well, ending 1996 ranked fifth in the NFL in points scored and 10th in total offense.

The Bengals had high hopes going into 1997 with Coslet returning for his first full season as head coach. Those aspirations quickly faded after they lost seven of their first eight games, finishing the year 7-9. By then, Walter had lost his starting job on the offensive line and was relegated to a reserve role. At the conclusion of the 1997 season and 13 seasons as a Bengal, Walter retired from the NFL.

In those 13 years as a Bengal, tied for fifth for most season played in team history, Walter played in 166 games, starting in 136 of them. He was part of an offensive line that created the holes for 25 running backs to rush for 100 yards in a game and five seasons where a running back gained at least 1,000 yards. As the team's right tackle, he was part of the pass protection that produced 29 300-yard passing games and eight 3,000 yard passing seasons from 1985-1997. Not bad for a guy who played for three different head coaches, three offensive coordinators, and two different offensive line coaches. More importantly, Walter did it without any regret.

"I was fortunate enough to play a kid's game until 1995," Walter said in 2002. "And I got paid on top of that."

CHAPTER TWENTY-TWO

BOBBIE WILLIAMS

Changing the Impression of the Franchise

You have to wonder why, in the spring of 2004, Bobbie Williams, a member of the Philadelphia Eagles for the previous four seasons and who had just finished the 2003 season as the team's starting right guard, decided to sign with the Cincinnati Bengals as an unrestricted free agent.

It wasn't because the Bengals were an offensive juggernaut. In the four season Williams played with the Eagles (2000-2003), Cincinnati's offense finished no better than 13th in the NFL in total offense and points scored (2003). By joining the Bengals in 2004, he would begin his career in Cincinnati by attempting to jump-start an offense with the daunting task of providing pass protection for Carson Palmer, the team's first round draft choice and the number one overall pick in the 2003 NFL Draft, who was beginning his first season as the team's starting quarterback.

Neither was it because the Bengals had a great winning tradition. When Williams arrived in 2004, Cincinnati had not been to the post-season since 1990, compiling a sad but true 63-145 record from 1991-2003, never once finishing a season above .500. Times were so bad during those 13 years that many NFL fans referred to the team as the Bungles. The only bright spot Williams could have possibly seen was that Marvin Lewis had become the head coach the year before and the team's 8-8 record in 2003, along with the fact that Palmer was waiting in the wings to become the franchise quarterback of the future. In fact, there was a small minority, which must have included Williams, who believed the Bengals were about to turn their fortunes around.

And it certainly wasn't because the Bengals were known at the time for paying top dollar for unrestricted free agents. In fact, not only did owner Mike Brown have a reputation for not paying for other team's free agents, he also failed to spend a lot of money to keep the talent he already had on his roster. The list of Bengals Brown allowed to leave via free agency or traded so he wouldn't have to pay what the market dictated, decimated what was a perennial playoff contending roster. Brown's tight purse strings led to a malaise that showed no end in sight and, worst of all, a franchise where seemingly no one in the NFL wanted to play.

But despite all the red flags that would indicate signing with the team was career suicide, on March 26, 2004, Williams joined the Bengals in hopes of earning a starting spot on the offensive line. While no one knew at the time just exactly why he chose his lot with Cincinnati, they also didn't know that Williams' decision to sign with the Bengals would mark a significant change in the fate of the franchise and transform it from the NFL's Black Hole to a place where players came to experience success.

A native of Jefferson, Texas, Williams was a four-year letterman from 1996-1999 on the football team at the University of Arkansas. Unlike the guard position he would play in the NFL, Williams played offensive tackle in college, earning a spot on the school's all-1990s team as one of two offensive tackles. In his junior year in 1998, Williams was part of an offense that racked up 2,668 passing yards, 26 touchdown passes and 390 total points, helping Arkansas become SEC West Co-Champions and finish the season ranked 16th in the final Associated Press poll and 17th in the USA Today Coaches poll.

In his senior season, the Razorbacks offense amassed 2,576 passing yards and 4,067 total yards en route to an 8-4 record that was culminated by a 27-6 victory over arch-rival Texas in the Cotton Bowl. Their Cotton Bowl win enabled them to finish ranked 17th in the final Associated Press poll and 19th in the USA Today Coaches poll. Personally, Williams had his best collegiate season, anchoring an offensive line that led the SEC in fewest sacks allowed (14). He was also named second team All-SEC and was selected to play in the 1999 Senior Bowl.

Based upon his senior year and his four year college career, the Philadelphia Eagles selected Williams in the second round with the 61st overall pick in the 2000 NFL Draft. Williams spent the entire 2000 season on the inactive list, forcing him to wait until 2001 to make his NFL debut where he played in just one game. By the time the 2002 season began, the Eagles had transitioned Williams from tackle to guard and in the process expanded his role in the team's offense. He played in every game in 2002 and when right guard Jermaine Newberry went down with an injury five games into the 2003 season, Williams entered the Eagles' starting lineup. With Mayberry set to return in 2004, the Eagles were not interested in signing the unrestricted free agent Williams.

As it turned out, Philadelphia's loss was Cincinnati's gain.

Beginning in 2004, over the next eight seasons, Williams became a fixture on the Bengals offensive line, missing only 10 games in that time while starting the remaining 118 games he played. His reliability began early on in his Bengals career when he played every offensive snap in 2004 and started every game from 2004 until he missed three games in 2006 due to an appendectomy.

More importantly, the arrival of Williams marked a revival of what had been a dormant offense and resuscitated a franchise that was in dire need of fresh air. From 2004-2011, Williams was part of an offensive line that produced six 1,000 yard rushing seasons (including the club record for most individual rushing yards in a season, 1,458 by Rudi Johnson in 2005), six 3,000 yard passing seasons, 19 300-yard passing games and 34 100-yard rushing games. In those eight seasons, the offense finished in the top half of the NFL in passing offense (2005, 2006, 2007 and 2010) and points scored (2004-2007) four times, total offense three times (2005-2007) and rushing offense twice (2005 and 2009). According to Football Focus, Williams played a significant role in that success as they selected him as one of the top six offensive guards in the NFL from 2008-2010.

The Bengals offense from 2004-2011 made its mark in the team record book as well. The 2005 offense allowed the second fewest sacks in team history (21), finished with the third most passing touchdowns in a season (32), completed the fourth most passes in a season (362) and scored the fifth most points in a season in team history (421). Meanwhile, the 2007 offense allowed the fewest sacks in a season in team history (17), completed the most passes in a season (373) and gained the third most net yards passing per game in a season in team history (250.75 yards per game).

Due in large part to the offensive renaissance, the Bengals ended their 15-year playoff drought when they won the 2005 AFC North Division. Unfortunately, the team lost to the eventual Super Bowl champions, the Pittsburgh Steelers, in the wild card Round.[1] That season did, however, mark a turning point in the future of the franchise. Since the 2005 season, the perception that Cincinnati was a perpetual loser not interested in doing the things necessary to build a sustainable winner has been erased. In fact, ten years later, the Bengals are considered by many a model NFL franchise.

By all accounts, Williams was a major reason for the transformation of the franchise. An established locker room leader, Williams was the team's 2009 Ed Block Courage Award winner. Given annually to a member of each NFL team based upon a vote of their teammates, the Ed Block Award, named in memory of the long-time trainer of the Baltimore Colts, is given to a player who serves as a role model of inspiration and "exemplifies commitment to the principles of sportsmanship and courage."

At the end of the 2011 season and their third consecutive playoff loss since 2005, the Bengals decided to part ways with their right guard and team leader for the past eight seasons. Williams signed a two-year contract with the Baltimore Ravens at the start of the 2012 season and retired from the NFL after one season.[2] Before he left Cincinnati, however, he made no secret of his feelings about the town that had been his home for the past eight years.

"To the people of Cincinnati, it has been an honor and a privilege," Williams said upon his departure in 2012. He also left a lasting impact on the future of the franchise when he put to rest any doubts whether another free agent should consider Cincinnati as a place to play.

---

[1] The Bengals' first playoff game in 15 years will forever be remembered for the horrible knee injury quarterback Carson Palmer sustained on the team's first offensive play of the game. Many argue Palmer was never the same in a Bengals uniform.

[2] In his lone season with Baltimore, Williams was a member of the Ravens Super Bowl XLVII winning team.

"Awesome organization and awesome people," Williams said about the Brown family. "Cincinnati treated me well my eight years there. I can't say one bad thing about it. Seriously."[38]

If you asked Bengals fans about Williams, they would say the same exact thing.

CHAPTER TWENTY-THREE

BRUCE KOZERSKI

Mr. Versatile

Every team, regardless of the sport, has a person on their roster that because of their athleticism and skill, or for the good of the team, is able or required to play multiple positions. More often than not, these players, like a utility player in baseball, aren't universally recognized as an all-star or a most valuable player. Yet without the contributions of these multi-talented players, their respective teams would be unlikely to achieve even a modicum of success.

Unlike baseball, where most teams employ a player who can play all three outfield positions or all four infield positions, finding a football roster that includes someone who can be used effectively in multiple positions is not as common. When it does occur, the increased expanse to the roster it creates, gives a team the freedom to add more players without exceeding the league mandated roster limits. It is a luxury every NFL team aspires to obtain.

Fortunately for the Bengals, they found their rare "Mr. Versatile" in the latter stages of the 1984 NFL Draft when they selected Bruce Kozerski in the ninth round with the 231st overall pick. Over the next 12 seasons, Kozerski played 172 games, starting 138 at center, left guard, right guard and right tackle on an offensive line that many regard as the best in team history.

A native of Plains, Pennsylvania, Kozerski attended and played football at the College of the Holy Cross in Worcester, Massachusetts. During his career as a Crusader, Kozerski was a standout center. In his junior year in 1982, he was named first team All-Eastern College Athletic Conference (ECAC) and third team All-New England. In his senior season the following year, he was selected first team All-ECAC, first team All-New England and first team All-American. Kozerski was also a 1983 first team Academic All-American, an NCAA Post Graduate scholar and was named the Davitt Award winner as the team's best offensive lineman.

Kozerski's arrival in Cincinnati coincided with Sam Wyche's first year as the Bengals' head coach, and as it turned out, their seasons together paralleled each other. While Wyche fought to return the Bengals to their Super Bowl heights of 1981 despite finishing 15-17 in his first two years as head coach, Kozerski struggled to establish himself as a dependable NFL offensive lineman, starting only one game in 1984 and 1985 combined.

By the time the 1986 season unfolded, both Kozerski and Wyche began to find their groove. Wyche guided Bengals to a 10-6 record in 1986, their first season above .500 since 1982. Meanwhile, Kozerski became the team's starting center in 1986. It was a relationship between player and coach that would last until Wyche was dismissed after the 1991 season. Their partnership over six seasons produced 48 regular season wins, two AFC Central Division titles, three playoff victories and a berth in Super Bowl XXIII. Wyche was hailed as an offensive genius and Kozerski was named a Pro Bowl alternate for three consecutive years (1988-1990). It was an experience Kozerski will never forget.

"In 1987, we did whatever it took to lose," Kozerski said in 1993 when describing how the Bengals went from laughing stock (4-11 in 1987) to Super Bowl finalist in one season. "The next year, we did whatever it took to win."[39]

With a change in head coach in 1992 came a change for Kozerski as well. Sam Wyche was out and David Shula was in. No longer was Kozerski the starting center, replaced by 1991 fifth round draft choice, Mike Arthur. Kozerski was moved to left guard in 1992 and over the following three seasons with Shula at the helm, started at center (1993), right tackle (1994) and right guard (1995).

Regardless of where Kozerski started on the offensive line, the Bengals offense flourished. In his nine seasons as a starting offensive lineman, the Bengals offense finished in the top half of the NFL in rushing offense six times (1986, 1988-1992) and total offense (1986, 1988-1991), passing offense (1986, 1988, 1989, 1991 and 1995) and points scored (1986, 1988-1990 and 1995) five times. Whether he played center, guard or tackle, Kozerski was part of an offensive line that helped produce five 1,000 yard rushing seasons, 29 100-yard rushing games, five 3,000 yard passing seasons and 16 300-yard passing games.

Of all the years during this offensive resurgence, three seasons stand out: 1986, 1989 and 1988. In 1986, the Bengals finished first in the NFL in total offense and holds the team record for total net yards in a season (6,490 net yards) and average yards per rushing attempt in a season (4.862 yards per rushing attempt). The 1986 offense also amassed the second most net yards rushing in a season (2,533 net yards) and the third most rushing touchdowns (24) and first downs (348) in a season in team history. The Bengals finished 10-6 in 1986, falling just short of making the NFL post-season.

Even though the 1989 Bengals finished with a disappointing 8-8 record, the offense did its part to keep the season from being a total disaster. The offense finished as the best rushing offense in the NFL and its 32 passing touchdowns and 6,101 total net yards are both the second most in team history for a single season. Their 348 first downs, 2,483 net yards rushing and a 4.694 yards per rushing attempt each rank as the third best in team history for a season.

But it is the 1988 offense that was the standard bearer for the Sam Wyche offensive laboratory. Led by NFL Most Valuable Player, Boomer Esiason, and an indomitable offensive line anchored by Kozerski at center, the 1988 offense led the NFL in rushing offense, total offense and points scored. Their 448 points scored, 59 touchdowns, 27 rushing touchdowns and 2,710 net yards rushing are all season best team records. They also hold the team record for second most first downs (351) and average yards per rushing attempt (4.813 yards per attempt) in a season and the 6,057 total net yards they gained is third best in team history.

It is no coincidence, then, that the 1988 Bengals won the AFC Central Division and advanced to Super Bowl XXIII, where they lost to the late game magic of Joe Montana and the San Francisco 49ers. On their journey to the Super Bowl, Kozerski and the offense set the team's post-season record for rushing touchdowns (3) and net yards rushing (254) in a playoff game in the AFC divisional round victory over the Seattle Seahawks on December 31, 1988. Two years later, the Bengals offense, with Kozerski still at center, exploded against the Houston Oilers in the AFC wild card playoff game on January 6, 1991, scoring 41 points and five touchdowns, both post-season team records.

Kozerski would never reach the post-season again following the 1990 season and after playing all 12 of his NFL seasons with the Bengals, he retired at the end of the 1995 season. And despite being a part of more teams that were unsuccessful than successful,[1] Kozerski cherished his time in Cincinnati.

"I wouldn't trade any of my years with the Bengals for anything," Kozerski told The Cincinnati Enquirer in December 2011. "They were a big part of my life."[40]

Kozerski's association with football did not end with his retirement from the NFL. In 1998, in addition to his duties as a geometry, pre-calculus and calculus teacher, Kozerski helped establish the football program at Holy Cross High School[2] in Covington, Kentucky, when he became an assistant coach. By 2011, he was the head coach, and led the school to its first state title. It was a feat so impressive that he received the 2011 Paul Brown Excellence in Coaching Award; an annual accolade for the Cincinnati region's top high school football coach. Pretty remarkable stuff for a high school math teacher until you realize it's not such a big surprise.

After all, Bruce Kozerski previously made his living as being "Mr. Versatile".

---

[1]   In Kozerski's 12 seasons in Cincinnati, the Bengals had a 79-112 regular season record.

[2]   The irony that he is teaching and coaching at a high school with the same name as his college alma mater isn't lost on Kozerski. "It makes a little bit easier to fill out a resume," Kozerski told The Cincinnati Enquirer in 2011.

CHAPTER TWENTY-FOUR

MAX MONTOYA

The Unlikely All Pro

I t's *highly unlikely that anyone* attending a Mt. San Antonio Community College football game in the suburbs of Los Angeles in 1975 believed they were watching a future NFL All-Pro offensive guard. As a matter of fact, even the player who would become that All-Pro probably would not have believed that some 15 years later, he would be considered one of the top offensive lineman in the NFL. So even though it may not have been evident or even conceivable in 1973 that Max Montoya was destined to become an NFL stalwart, the Cincinnati Bengals are sure glad his journey to the top of his profession included a prolonged stint on their offensive line in the 1980s.

Montoya's unexpected run to the NFL began at La Puente High School in La Puente, California, when in his senior year in 1973, he was unable to play football or basketball due to a heart murmur. Thankfully, Montoya's medical condition did not keep him from playing competitive sports permanently. But it did preclude Montoya from receiving any scholarship offers to play at the collegiate level once he graduated from high school. It was this landscape in the fall of 1974 that placed Montoya on the offensive line of a small community college in Walnut, California.

Montoya did not start in his freshman year at Mt. San Antonio College, but by his sophomore season, not only had he cracked the offensive line's starting lineup but his play was being noticed by several Division I head football coaches. One in particular, Terry Donahue at nearby UCLA, was extremely interested in making Montoya a Bruin and offered him a scholarship. Naturally, Montoya accepted and began his NCAA career in 1976.

As is commonplace at the Division I level, Montoya was redshirted in 1976. The following season, he became a starting offensive tackle as the Bruins finished 7-4. In his senior year in 1978, Montoya's play on the offensive line helped the UCLA offense gain 2,956 yards rushing (fifth best in school history) on 594 rushing plays (the most in school history). The ground and pound offense contributed to an 8-3-1 record for the Bruins and a berth in the Fiesta Bowl against Arkansas. They finished the season 12th in the final UPI poll and 14th in the final Associated Press poll.

As for Montoya, he was named to the West team in the 1979 Japan Bowl for collegiate all-starts but for some reason was not named first team All-Pac 10 conference. His failure to make the all-conference team wasn't due to a lack of talent or performance. It's just that for Montoya to earn first team All-Pac 10 honors when his cross town and conference rival, USC, had a guy named Anthony Muñoz playing the same position, made the job almost impossible. Interestingly enough, Montoya's and Muñoz's paths would merge later down the road.

Even though he wasn't recognized by the Pac-10 conference or any other post-season All-American teams after the 1978 season, Montoya was still considered a potential NFL prospect prior to the 1979 NFL Draft. Given their history in the previous 11 drafts of finding hidden gems in the late rounds and turning them into not just productive players, but, in many cases, Pro Bowl selections, having the Cincinnati Bengals choose Montoya in the seventh round with the 168th overall selection seemed only fitting. Like several other players drafted by the Bengals who preceded him, by the end of the 1980s, Montoya made the Bengals late round gamble pay off handsomely.

Although he started only one game at right guard in his rookie season, Montoya did play in 11 games in 1979 for a Bengals team that finished 4-12 for the second consecutive season. Whether or not Montoya would have earned more playing time or even started the following year, had team owner and general manager, Paul Brown, not decided to radically change the direction of the franchise, no one will ever know. But when Brown named Forrest Gregg the Bengals' new head coach prior to the 1980 season, the fortunes of Montoya and the rest of his teammates were changed forever.

For the Bengals, hiring Gregg was a breath of fresh air and an attitude adjustment for a team that had gone 26-34 in the four seasons since they last made the playoffs in 1975. For Montoya, Gregg's arrival not only meant a fresh start but more importantly the head coach brought with him the resume of an NFL Hall of Fame offensive lineman and the tutoring and mentoring the young California lineman desperately desired. In short, it all added up to magic on the football field.

Over the next 10 seasons, the Bengals became a perennial playoff contender, appearing in two Super Bowls while developing a dynamic offense that was the envy of the rest of the NFL. Along the way, Montoya established himself as one of the premier offensive guards in professional football. As the team's starting right guard, he was named to three Pro Bowls (1986, 1988 and 1989) and was named one of the guards on the Pro Football Focus first team All-1980s NFL team.

Much of the Bengals' accomplishments in the 1980s were attributable to the offense and Montoya, who started 143 of the team's 152 games during the decade, played a large role in that success. With either Ken Anderson or Boomer Esiason manning the quarterback position and Montoya joining up with Pac-10 rival Muñoz to anchor the offensive line, the Bengals finished in the top half of the NFL in rushing offense (1980, 1984-1989, including leading the league in 1988 and 1989) and points scored (1981, 1982, 1984-1986, 1988 and 1989, including a league leading 448 points in 1988) seven times and total offense and passing offense nine times.[1] The offense in 1986 and 1988 led the NFL in total offense while it finished second in 1981 and 1982 and third in 1985 and 1989.

With Montoya firmly ensconced at the right guard position, the Bengals had a player rush for 100 yards in a game 35 times and four players rush for 1,000 yards in a season (1981, 1986, 1988 and 1989), When he wasn't blocking for the running game, Montoya kept the pocket

---

[1] The only season in the 1980's that the Bengals failed to finish in the top half of the NFL in total offense and passing offense was 1980 itself, when they finished 6-10.

clean enough for Anderson and Esiason to pass for 300 yards in a game 31 times and finish the year with 3,000 or more passing yards in a season six times (1981, 1985-1989).

Given these impressive numbers, it is not surprising that the Bengals offenses of the 1980s dominate the team's record book. A Bengals offense from the 1980s holds the season team record for points scored (448 in 1988), touchdowns (59 in 1988), rushing touchdowns (27 in 1988), first downs (361 in 1981), total net yards (6,490 yards in 1986), net yards rushing (2,710 yards in 1988), average yards per rushing attempt (4.862 yards per attempt in 1986) and net yards passing per game (259.89 yards per game in 1982). They also hold the top five spots for first downs in a season[1] and total net yards passing in a season.[2]

Montoya also made a significant impact on the team's post-season history as well. He is one of six players to play for the Bengals in both of their Super Bowl appearances and started at right guard in four of the franchise's five playoff victories. Despite being on the losing end of both Super Bowl contests, Montoya was part of several post-season record-setting games. In the 1988 AFC divisional Round playoff game against the Seattle Seahawks on December 31, he and the rest of the offensive set the team's post-season record for net yards rushing in a game (254 yards) and tied the record for rushing touchdowns in a game (3), a record originally set when Montoya was the right guard in the 1981 AFC divisional game against the Buffalo Bills on January 4, 1982. He was also one of the Bengals' linemen who went without sleeves in the infamous AFC Championship "Freezer Bowl" game against the San Diego Chargers on January 10, 1982.

As the 1980s came to a close with the end of the 1989 season, the Bengals faced some very difficult personnel decisions thanks to the emergence of the NFL's Plan B free agency. In short, they didn't have the salary resources to keep the entire team together as they entered a new decade. Under the terms of Plan B free agency, the team could leave some of their eligible free agents unprotected, free to sign with any other NFL team without the chance to match another team's offer. The Bengals left some players unprotected simply because they had no interest in bringing

---

[1] 361 (1981), 351 (1988), 348 (1986), 348 (1989) and 341 (1985)
[2] 6,490 (1986), 6,101 (1989), 6,057 (1988), 5,968 (1981) and 5,900 (1985)

them back. Others were left unprotected on the belief the player would want to stay in Cincinnati at a lower price. Montoya was one of the players the Bengals were betting would stay.

"I think they were taking a calculated risk, knowing that I had a lot of ties in Cincinnati and had been there for a lot of years and was very comfortable with the situation," Montoya told The Los Angeles Times in July 1980. "They figured and I figured that I wasn't going to go anywhere.

"But I didn't think as many teams would come after me like they did and start swaying me with money."[41]

Montoya was obviously torn. On the one hand, he had established strong roots in Cincinnati, opening a successful Mexican restaurant in nearby Covington, Kentucky, in addition to being a lynchpin in the revival of the Bengals franchise.

On the other hand, by leaving him unprotected, the Bengals appeared to dare Montoya to leave, figuring he had too much at stake, both on and off the field, to leave town. They also thought no other team could lure him away financially. Worst of all, by not offering him a new contract, they appeared to dismiss his contributions of the past 10 seasons. In essence, Bengals management believed he would never leave.

They were wrong.

On March 4, 1990, Montoya exercised his right as a Plan B free agent and signed a two-year, $1.45 million contract with the Los Angeles Raiders, at the time, the most money paid to an offensive lineman in Raiders team history. He went onto play five seasons in Los Angeles, including three appearances in the post-season and one Pro Bowl selection in 1993. Meanwhile, the Bengals plunged into a sea of disarray and instability following Montoya's departure. After winning the AFC Central Division in the first season after Montoya left in 1990,[1] the Bengals went 15 seasons without a playoff appearance, compiling a 71-153 record from 1991-2004. And after having Montoya start all but three games during the 1980s, it took 12 seasons before the Bengals had the same player start every game

---

[1] Ironically, the Bengals were eliminated in the 1990 playoffs by Montoya and the Raiders in the AFC divisional round, 20-10, on January 13, 1991.

at right guard in consecutive seasons when Mike Goff started all 16 games at the position in 2000 and 2001.[1]

The divorce between himself and the Bengals aside, there's no question Montoya is one of the greatest, if not the best, offensive guard in team history. During his 11 seasons in Cincinnati, Montoya played in 157 games, starting in 144 of them. He was the starting right guard in the franchise's best decade and played a significant role in the offense that was the most productive and historic in team history.

Suffice to say Max Montoya had come a long way from the home field of Mt. San Antonio Community College in the 1970s. And chances are that those who saw him play back then can now tell anyone who will listen they were watching a future franchise great.

Even if they didn't know at the time.

---

[1]   Before Goff started every game in 2000 and 2001, the Bengals started 10 different players at right guard: Ken Moyer, Paul Jetton, Jon Melander, Tom Rayam, Bruce Kozerski, Todd Kalis, Ken Blackman, Scott Brumfield, Jay Leeuwenburg and Brian DeMarco.

CHAPTER TWENTY-FIVE

TIM KRUMRIE

The Bad Break

U nless you're a diehard Bengals fan, if you ask an avid NFL follower to describe the career of Tim Krumrie, invariably their first, and possibly only response is simply, "Super Bowl. Gruesome broken leg."

The fact is, most football fans only know about Krumrie because of a compound, segmented fracture of the leg he sustained on the game's biggest stage, Super Bowl XXIII against the San Francisco 49ers on January 22, 1989. It was a scene so graphic that Merlin Olsen, the analyst for the game's television broadcast, advised viewers after looking at the replay, "I don't think we want to see that one again."

But as Bengals fans, along with the most ardent followers of the NFL and the teams he played against, will attest, there was more to Krumrie's professional football career than just an ugly injury seen by more than 80 million people on national television. In fact, there was *much* more.

Before the achievements of today's players like Vince Wilfork, Ndamukong Suh, Dontari Poe and Haloti Ngata were heralded as superstars and their value recognized by the multi-million dollar contracts they received, those who played defensive nose tackle lived in regular anonymity and certainly didn't command a top-tier salary or a big-money contract. That all began to change when Krumrie entered the NFL in

1984; over the subsequent 12 seasons, he helped transform how the nose tackle position was played and perceived.

Krumrie was raised on a dairy farm near Mondovi, Wisconsin and attended Mondovi High School where he was a highly decorated athlete in two sports: wrestling, and football. As a wrestler, Krumrie won the Wisconsin state heavyweight title in his senior year in 1979. On the football field, he dominated the defensive side of the ball like no one before him. His play at Mondovi became the measuring stick for future Wisconsin high school defensive linemen. Established in 2009, the Wisconsin Sports Network and WisSports.net presents The Tim Krumrie Award, an honor given to the outstanding high school senior defensive lineman in the state of Wisconsin.

After graduating high school, Krumrie received a football scholarship to attend the University of Wisconsin. Recruited to play inside linebacker, Krumrie was moved to nose tackle, and as a result his future and his legacy were secured. A four-year letterman from 1979-1982, Krumrie started all 46 games in his career as a Badger and propelled the program to national recognition for the first time in 20 years. He led all defensive linemen on the team in tackles each of his four years[1] and was first team All-Big 10 for three consecutive seasons (1980-1982).

In Krumrie's first two years at Wisconsin, the Badgers went a combined 8-14 but began to show signs of a turnaround in 1980 when he led a defense that allowed only 117.5 rushing yards per game (10th best in school history) and 3.04 yards rushing per carry (7th best in school history). By the time the 1981 season ended, the Badgers' return to prominence had started, finishing the year 7-5 and appearing in their first bowl game in 20 years against Tennessee in the Garden State Bowl. The team's success coincided with the emergence of Krumrie as a collegiate standout on the defensive front line. His 135 tackles in 1981 remains the most tackles in a season by a defensive lineman in school history, launching Krumrie into the national spotlight. At the conclusion of the 1981 season, he was a first-team Associated Press, UPI, Walter Camp and Football News consensus All-American and a second team Newspaper Enterprise Association (NEA) All-American.

---

[1] He had 95 tackles in 1979, 105 in 1980, 135 in 1981 and 109 in 1982.

In his senior season in 1982, Krumrie, a team captain, was named to the Walter Camp first team All-American squad as well as being selected to play in the 1982 Hula Bowl post-season college all-star game. He capped his career as a Badger with a virtuoso performance in the 1982 Independence Bowl against Kansas State University. Krumrie's 13 tackles led a defense that held Kansas State to two yards rushing per carry and three points in a 14-3 Wisconsin victory. Krumrie's performance earned him the game's Defensive Most Valuable Player award.

Krumrie ended his career at Wisconsin as one of the best defensive linemen in school history. His 444 career total tackles is the most by a defensive lineman in school history and is the third highest by any defensive player in school history. His 276 solo tackles are the most in University of Wisconsin football history. He was named one of the 55 greatest University of Wisconsin football players since 1953 by the USA Today's 2010-2011 College Football Encyclopedia, selected to the school's Hall of Fame in 1999 and enshrined in the College Football Hall of Fame in 2016.

Krumrie's collegiate resume and talent had the look of a high to mid-level NFL draft choice in today's landscape. Unfortunately, in the early 1980s, NFL teams did not see the value in drafting a nose tackle with a high round draft choice. Nine rounds passed in the 1983 NFL Draft and despite a stellar collegiate career, Krumrie had yet to be chosen. With only three rounds left, it appeared Krumrie might go undrafted and he would have to pin his NFL hopes on making it as a free agent, a prospect that was, and is, slim at best.

But with the 10th round set to unfold, Krumrie's NFL fate was about to change. Given their history over their previous 15 college drafts of finding the future centerpieces of their team in the later rounds, the Bengals selecting Krumrie with the 276th overall pick seemed only logical if not destined to happen. What no one could have predicted, is the impact the nose tackle from Wisconsin would have on the Bengals, and to a certain extent, the NFL over the next 12 seasons.

Even though he started only twice in his 1983 rookie season, Krumrie did play in all 16 games and led all defensive linemen on the team in solo tackles (32) and total tackles (53). It was the beginning of an impressive streak that saw Krumrie led all defensive linemen on the team in solo and total tackles for 11 consecutive seasons (1983-1993).

Krumrie began an even more notable streak the following season, starting every game at nose tackle from 1984-1989. During that time, he played in 122 consecutive games, the fourth most in team history. In those six seasons, the Bengals finished in the top half of the NFL in total defense three times (1984, 1987 and 1989) and rushing defense (1984) and points allowed (1989) once.

It also marked the time when Krumrie had his most personal success. He led the team in total tackles four times (1985-1988) and solo tackles two times (1987 and 1988). In 1987, he was named second team UPI All-AFC and second team Associated Press All-NFL. In 1988, he was named first team All-AFC by Pro Football Weekly and first team All-NFL by Pro Football Weekly, the Pro Football Writers, the Associated Press and The Sporting News. He was selected to the Pro Bowl in 1987 and 1988 and was first team All-Pro in 1988, a season in which he also led the team in forced fumbles and fumble recoveries. After failing to start one game in 1990, Krumrie went onto start every game from 1991-1993.

One of the very few negatives in Krumrie's career was the Bengals regular season record in his 12 seasons, a sub-par 79-112 (.413). Even though he played at a high level in each of his 12 seasons, the team, at times, couldn't match Krumrie's success on the field. Six times, the Bengals ended the year with a sub-.500 record, including three seasons when they finished the year with a 3-13 record.

But amongst these dismal years was 1988, a season Bengal fans everywhere will not soon forget. Given the results of the prior year, a 4-11 record in a strike-shortened season that saw division within the team over players who crossed the picket line, expectations for the 1988 season were understandably low. As a matter of fact, many were surprised head coach Sam Wyche was returning and figured the best the Bengals could hope for was a season, unlike 1987, where they didn't embarrass themselves or the rest of the league. In other words, the outlook was bleak. Good thing for the Bengals, the forecasters were wrong.

Instead of experiencing a team implosion as many had predicted, the Bengals won their first six games en route to a 12-4 record, an AFC Central Division title and their first post-season berth since 1982. It truly was an unforgettable season for the team and their fans. As the playoffs unfolded it would be a memorable journey for Krumrie as well, but for all the wrong reasons.

The playoffs started off well for Krumrie, the defense and the rest of the team. In their 21-13 AFC divisional playoff victory over the Seattle Seahawks on December 31, 1988, Krumrie and the defense allowed a club post-season record low 22 net yards rushing. In the AFC Championship game against the Buffalo Bills on January 8, 1989, the defense limited quarterback Jim Kelly and his high-potent offense to a team post-season record low 10 first downs and 181 total net yards in a 21-10 win. Krumrie played a large part in the defense's performance, leading the defensive line with eight solo tackles, 13 total tackles and one forced fumble as the Bengals advanced to their second ever Super Bowl appearance to face the San Francisco 49ers.

It was the seventh snap of Super Bowl XVIII on January 22, 1989 when 49er quarterback Joe Montana handed the ball to running back Roger Craig on a simple running play near their own goal line. San Francisco center Randy Cross and guard Jesse Sapolu were responsible for blocking Krumrie on the play but they were unable to keep the Bengals' nose tackle from attempting to stop Craig for little or no gain. As Krumrie planted his left leg and foot to tackle Craig, the pressure his weight placed on his left ankle caused his lower leg to snap above the joint.

"Oh, blank, I really messed up," Krumrie told Sports Illustrated in January 2016 when recalling his initial reaction to the injury. "My left foot was facing the wrong way."[42]

After his leg was placed in an inflatable cast and he was carted off the field, doctors determined Krumrie had four breaks in his lower left leg, two in the tibia, one in the fibula and one in his ankle. It was a fracture so severe that his foot was attached only by his skin.

Incredibly, Krumrie refused transport to the hospital, demanding to stay in the locker room and watch the game on television. As he recalled later, Krumrie was gulping painkillers until late in the fourth quarter because, "I just wanted to remember the game."[43] Unfortunately, courage and fortitude weren't enough to inspire the Bengals to a victory as Montana's touchdown to John Taylor with 34 seconds remaining gave the 49ers a 20-16 victory. In the end, the Bengals could not overcome Krumrie's absence physically or emotionally.

In the weeks following the Super Bowl, Krumrie had a 15-inch steel rod implanted in his surgically-repaired left leg and, remarkably, was ready to play at the opening of the 1989 season, a mere seven months after his devastating injury. Even more impressive was his play post-surgery. Not only did Krumrie start every game in 1989, 1991, 1992 and 1993, he also led the team in sacks (4) in 1991 and total tackles (97) in 1992. His four sacks in 1992 contributed to the team's total of 45, the fourth most in team history.

And yet, when many football historians reflect on Krumrie, they always start with his Super Bowl injury. The fact is, Krumrie's career should not be defined by what took place at Joe Robbie Stadium on that fateful Sunday against the 49ers in football's biggest game. In his 12 NFL seasons, all with the Bengals, Krumrie made 700 solo tackles and 1,017 total tackles, an average of 58.3 solo tackles and 84.75 total tackles per year and 3.72 solo tackles and 5.40 total tackles per game. In the 188 games he played as a Bengal, the fourth most in team history, Krumrie had 34.5 sacks, 13 fumble recoveries, 11 passes defended and 11 forced fumbles.

It is a career that did not need a Super Bowl appearance or victory to justify it as top flight, especially considering the price Krumrie had to pay just to play for seven snaps. Instead, Krumrie should first be remembered for making the nose tackle position one of the premier defensive positions in the NFL. Nevertheless, the center and core of the Bengals' defensive front line from 1983-1994, has absolutely no regrets about what happened on Super Bowl Sunday and does not mind how his career is remembered.

"If you had told me, 'Tim, you're going to the Super Bowl and somewhere in that game you're going to break your leg,' I'd say, 'Break it.' It's that simple," Krumrie told Sports Illustrated. "I'm going to the Super Bowl. *I'm going.*"[44]

Looking back at his entire career, Krumrie is *also going* on the list as one of the greatest players in Cincinnati Bengals history.

CHAPTER TWENTY-SIX

RUFUS MAYES

The Great Trade Robbery

There's no doubt that on January 21, 1970, the Chicago Bears General Manager, George Halas Jr. and his Director of Player Personnel, Bobby Watson, believed their trade with the Cincinnati Bengals was good for their organization and would make them a better team. Even though they were sending their first round draft choice from the year before, offensive tackle Rufus Mayes, to the Bengals, they were receiving defensive linemen Bill Staley and Harry Gunner. The Bears were confident they were adding depth (and what they had hoped was a measure of improvement) to a defense that was 12ᵗʰ out of 16 NFL teams in points allowed in 1969, but finished with a dismal 1-13 record.

Besides, Mayes didn't start any of the 13 games he played in 1969 for a team that won only one game, so it seemed there was no place for him on their roster. On paper, it looked like a beneficial trade for the Bears in both the short and long term. In reality, the trade became a disaster for Halas Jr. and the Bears.

Once the NFL careers for all three players in the transaction were completed, The *Chicago Tribune*, in 2004, rated the trade as the sixth worst in Bears history. Staley played three seasons in Chicago, playing in only 26 games and starting 21.[45] Gunner's performance was even more disappointing. He played one season in Chicago and after the 1970 season, never played in the NFL again.

Meanwhile, over the next nine seasons starting in 1970, Mayes became a key piece of an offensive line that propelled the Bengals to unparalleled success for an expansion franchise. It was a trade so lopsided that it makes you wonder how bad the other five trades were that The Chicago Tribune rated worse than this one. Regardless of the Tribune's rankings, the Bengals robbed the Bears when they acquired Mayes, a player who set the franchise standard for excellence and consistency for play on the offensive line.

Raised in Toledo, Ohio, Mayes was a star player on the Toledo Macomber High football team. In his senior year, he started on the Macomber squad that won the 1964 City League Championship. But even before he helped lead Macomber to a title, Mayes was firmly on the radar of college recruiters everywhere. His high school coach, Steve Contos, recalls in particular how Hugh Hindman, the then Ohio State University offensive line coach, had his sights set on Mayes becoming a Buckeye.

"He said, 'I'll be back when he's a senior to get him,'" Contos told *The Toledo Blade* in January 1990 when remembering Hindman's recruitment of Mayes. "He told Rufus, 'You'll come to Ohio State, in your sophomore year you'll start for three years, you'll play on great teams, be an All-American and a professional player.'"[46]

Hindman proved prescient on one of his predictions when Mayes enrolled at Ohio State after graduating high school to play football for the legendary Woody Hayes. By the time he finished his college eligibility in 1968, Hindman's vision of Mayes' collegiate career came to fruition. A three-year letterman from 1966-1968, Mayes indeed started as a sophomore and in fact started in all 28 games the Buckeyes played over the next three seasons. In his first two years in Columbus, Mayes was a tight end as the Buckeyes struggled to reach .500 in 1966 and 1967. In his senior season, Hayes and Hindman switched Mayes from tight end to offensive tackle and the move paid immediate dividends. It also made Hindman's words four years earlier appear prophetic.

The Buckeyes were a great team in Mayes' senior year in 1968, finishing the season a perfect 10-0, winning the Big 10 title and eventually a national championship when they defeated USC 27-16 in the 1969 Rose Bowl. Mayes was a stand-out on the 1968 Buckeyes, earning first-team Big

10 honors as well as being selected to the second-team AP, Central Press Association, UPI, the Newspaper Enterprise Association All-American teams just as Hindman predicted. Mayes was also selected to the Time magazine and The Sporting News All-American teams as well. His play on the field impressed his irascible head coach, the iconic Hayes, a feat not easily accomplished.

"He was quicker than most of them (offensive linemen) and of course very powerful," Hayes said of Mayes, whose performance on the field earned him induction into the Ohio State's Men's Varsity "O" Hall of Fame in 1994.[47]

Not only did Mayes excite the hard-to-impress Hayes, but he had NFL scouts and executives vying for the opportunity to select him in the first round of the 1969 NFL/AFL Draft. When it came time for the Bears to make their first round selection, they chose Mayes with the 14th overall pick, certainly convinced at the time that they'd chosen their right tackle of the future. One year later, those plans changed.

Unlike his time in Chicago, once Mayes put on a Bengals uniform in 1970, he immediately assumed a starting role. Unfortunately, his presence at left guard did not produce any positive results early on, as the Bengals lost six of their first seven games to open the 1970 season. Their 43-14 victory, however, on November 8 against the Buffalo Bills started a streak of seven consecutive wins to end the season, giving them an 8-6 record and remarkably the inaugural AFC Central Division title, the franchise's first post-season berth in only their third year of existence.

The strong finish to the 1970 season also marked the first of six seasons in his eight with the team that the Bengals finished the year with a .500 record or better with Mayes in the starting lineup.[1] The 70-58 regular season record during this span also included three trips to the playoffs (1970, 1973 and 1975) and two AFC Central Division titles (1970 and 1973). Even more significant were Mayes' contributions to the offense and his play between 1970-1978 that created the legacy and standard for the franchise at the offensive tackle position.

With Mayes anchoring the left side of the line, the Bengals offense

---

[1] Even though the Bengals finished 8-6 in 1972, Mayes only played in six games that season. Consequently, that season was not included in this statistic.

finished in the top half of the NFL in points scored seven times (1970-1971 and 1973-1977), total offense (1971, 1973, 1974, 1975, 1977 and 1978) and passing offense (1973-1978) six times and rushing offense four times (1970, 1971, 1973 and 1974). In 1975, they had the NFL's top ranked passing offense thanks to quarterback Ken Anderson's 3,169 passing yards and 21 touchdown passes. During Mayes's eight seasons as a starter, the Bengals had a quarterback pass for 300 yards in a game five times and a running back rush for a 100 yards or more in a game 14 times. He was also part of an offensive line that only 24 sacks in 1973, tied for fourth fewest sacks allowed in a season in team history. These accomplishments look even more impressive when you consider that in the 1970s the NFL was not the offensive happy league that it is now.

The team's success in the regular season during these years did not, unfortunately, carry over into the three post-season appearances they made in 1970, 1973 and 1975. Mayes and the Bengals went winless in three road playoff games, losing by a total combined score of 82-44 to the likes of the Baltimore Colts, the Miami Dolphins and the Oakland Raiders. Their most competitive performance was the 1975 AFC divisional playoff game against the Raiders on December 28. Despite losing 31-28, the Bengals offense established team post-season records for points scored in a half (21), touchdowns in a half (2) and passing touchdowns in a game (2).

At the end of the 1978 season, Mayes did not receive a qualifying contract offer from the Bengals and immediately became a free agent. On June 22, 1979, he signed three one-year contracts with the Philadelphia Eagles, signaling an end to his career in Cincinnati. Due to the circumstances of his departure, the Bengals found themselves in an eerily familiar position. Since they received no compensation from the Eagles because they did not make a qualifying offer, the Bengals faced the possibility of being the team that was robbed when dealing with Mayes' services. As it turned out, they made the right decision. Mayes played only one season in Philadelphia without starting a game and retired from the NFL following the 1979 season.

In his post-NFL life, Mayes began a career as a family man and a marketing representative for Hewlett-Packard in Bellevue, Washington. Sadly, on January 9, 1990, he passed away due to bacterial meningitis at the age of 42. His death shocked and stunned his family, friends and former teammates who remembered him as more than just a football player.

"He was the nicest person you'd ever want to meet," Dave Witkowski, a high school teammate of Mayes, told The Toledo Blade on January 11, 1990. "He was a top notch individual as a friend, and a decent person."[48]

Mayes's untimely passing gave Contos, his high school football coach, a chance to recollect the foresight of Ohio State's offensive line coach Hugh Hindman when he came to recruit his team's all-star lineman. "All he predicted came true," Contos recalled.[49]

In retrospect, Mayes' lasting impact on the history of the Bengals is not solely defined by the team's regular season success or the offense's production during his tenure as a starting left tackle. His eight seasons as the primary left tackle for the Bengals began a franchise tradition, still in effect today, of having offensive tackles known for their skill, consistency and longevity. Bengal legends such as Mike Wilson, Joe Walter, Willie Anderson, Levi Jones, Andrew Whitworth and Pro Football Hall of Famer, Anthony Muñoz, all followed in the footsteps of Mayes and carried on the high standard of play he originated at the tackle position in the formative years of the Bengals franchise.

Considering how Mayes' career ultimately turned out, it is a good thing the Chicago Bears cannot charge the Bengals with first degree trade robbery.

CHAPTER TWENTY-SEVEN

WILLIE ANDERSON

Getting One Right

For a period of five years from 1991-1995, the Cincinnati Bengals experienced some of their most disappointing seasons in team history, compiling a 21-59 (.262) regular season record in those five seasons. To make matters worse, many of the games played in those five seasons were not very competitive--as evidenced by the fact that the Bengals were outscored 1,898-1,349 or by an average of nearly seven points per game (6.86 points per game). The good news--if you want to call it that--for Bengals fans after each of these discouraging seasons, was that it earned the team a high draft choice in the upcoming NFL Draft each year, providing the Bengals organization the opportunity to find a game-changing player to satisfy their win-starved fan base.

Sadly, the only thing more miserable in those five seasons for a Bengals fan to watch than a game on a Sunday afternoon was Day 1 of the NFL Draft when the team made their first round draft choice. Instead of witnessing the selection of the player that would turn the fortunes of the team around, Bengals fans were subjected, year after year, to a first-round selection, which included the number one overall pick in back-to-back years in 1994 and 1995 that either barely made the starting lineup or simply never made an impact on Sunday afternoons. The roll call of

136

Cincinnati's first round draft choices from 1991-1995 make the most ardent of Bengals supporters, even to this day, shudder in disbelief:

1991	Alfred Williams	Linebacker	18th overall pick
1992	David Klingler	Quarterback	6th overall pick
1993	John Copeland	Defensive End	5th overall pick
1994	Dan Wilkinson	Defensive Tackle	1st overall pick
1995	Ki-Jana Carter	Running Back	1st overall pick

Those five draft choices combined to play 24 seasons in Cincinnati, an average of 4.8 years, without any fanfare or remarkable play. More importantly, they all failed to improve a team desperate to return to respectability in the NFL.

So, you can imagine when the Bengals came to the 1996 NFL Draft after another disheartening 7-9 season in 1995, expectations of selecting a franchise changing player with the 10th overall pick were tempered severely by the team's track record in the previous five drafts. When NFL commissioner Paul Tagliabue announced the Bengals had selected Auburn offensive lineman Willie Anderson with their first pick in the 1996 Draft, the overall mood of Bengals supporters remained ambivalent, fearful that Anderson, like the previous five first-round draft choices, would never materialize into a player who would change the fate of the franchise.

Twelve NFL seasons later, Anderson proved to the Bengals and their fans that his selection was one of the best first-round draft choices the team ever made.

A graduate of Vigor High School in Prichard, Alabama, where he was named a USA Today High School All-American in 1992, Anderson was a three-year letterman at Auburn University from 1993-1995 and a starter at offensive tackle in each of his three years. He was named an All-SEC offensive tackle in his sophomore season in 1994 and in his junior season the following year, the 1995 Tigers offense was one of the most prolific in school history. With Anderson starting at offensive tackle, the 1995 Auburn offense set 10 offensive records that rank in the top seven in school history, including two records, 135 passing first downs and 233 pass completions that remain the most in a season in Auburn football history.[1] The team's 3,438 yards rushing and 312.5 yards rushing per game led the SEC in 1995 and helped Auburn reach its first post-season bowl game since 1990 where they lost to Penn State in the Outback Bowl, 43-14. Thanks to these types of offensive numbers, The Birmingham Post-Herald named Anderson a member of the offensive line on Auburn's All-1990s team.

Anderson elected to forego his senior season at Auburn and declare for the NFL Draft in 1996 which made him available for the Bengals to select him with the 10th overall pick. Anderson immediately dispelled the notion he was another in a recent trend of the team's first-round draft busts when he started 10 games at left tackle in his rookie season for an offense that finished fifth in the NFL in points scored and 10th in total offense. The improved performance of the offense helped the Bengals finish the year 8-8, their first season at or above .500 since 1990.

The good news for the Bengals and their fans as the 1997 season unfolded, was that it marked the beginning of a 10-year stretch in which Anderson started every game for the franchise. During that time, he continued to justify his first round draft selection by being named to four consecutive Pro Bowls (2003-2006) and being named first-team All-Pro three consecutive years (2004-2006), one of only two Bengals to earn first-team All-Pro three times or more. He was also honored by the Pro Football Reference as a second-team offensive tackle on their All-2000's decade team.

The bad news, though, was that same 10-year span featured some, if not the most, disappointing seasons in Bengals team history. From 1997-2006, the Bengals finished last in the AFC Central or North Division three times and posted only one winning season, compiling a less than stellar 61-99 (.381) regular season record in those 10 seasons. The worst stretch of football in that span was 1998-2002 when the Bengals were an embarrassing 19-61 (.237) during the regular season. The low mark of those five years was the 2002 season that ended with 14 losses, a .125 winning percentage and seven consecutive losses at home, all team records

---

[1] The remaining top 10 records are rushing touchdowns, passing yards, points scored, total offensive yards, total yards per game, completion percentage and passing touchdowns.

for futility in a season. It was a time in Anderson's career with the Bengals that he soon rather forget.

"Some of the worst football ever," Anderson remembers. So bad, in fact, that those Bengals teams played from behind so often that Anderson recalls having "to pass block the entire second half." In later years, he was told by a number of ESPN NFL analysts that they were encouraged to make fun of the team, using such references as the "Bungles" and the "fumbling, bumbling, Bengals" on air to describe the team's performance. Anderson was more direct when describing those lean seasons: "It was bad, bad, bad."[50]

The team's fortunes changed, however, thanks in large part to the abysmal 2002 season. Their 2-14 record was the league's worst that year so the Bengals received the first overall selection in the 2003 NFL Draft which they used to choose the reigning Heisman Trophy winner, USC quarterback Carson Palmer. Seemingly overnight, the drafting of Palmer, combined with the addition of several other key draft selections such as wide receivers Chad Johnson, T.J. Houshmandzadeh and Chris Henry, and running back Rudi Johnson, the Bengals, who had back-to-back 8-8 seasons in 2004 and 2004, were ready to break through in 2005.

"We had three potential 1,000-yard receivers, a franchise quarterback and an offensive line that opened up big holes in the running game," Anderson said when reflecting upon the 2005 Bengals. "And we had a defense that turned it over and gave the ball to the offense in great field position."[51]

Anderson and the many offensive weapons on the 2005 squad didn't waste the opportunities the defense gave them and did some major work of their own as well, finishing the year fourth in points scored, fifth in passing offense, sixth in total offense and 11th in rushing offense in the NFL. Palmer, Anderson and the rest of the offense contributed to the 421 points scored in 2005, the fifth most in team history and their 32 passing touchdowns and 362 pass completions ranked third and fourth respectively in team history. Meanwhile, Anderson and his offensive line teammates allowed only 21 sacks the entire season, the second fewest in club history. All of this offensive proficiency helped lead the Bengals to an 11-5 record, the AFC North Division title and their first trip to the post-season since 1990.

The Bengals entered the 2005 playoffs confident they would make a deep run and with the strong belief they could bring Cincinnati its first NFL championship. Their first opponent in their quest for a Super Bowl was their division and arch rival, the Pittsburgh Steelers. Five weeks earlier, the Bengals had defeated the Steelers in Pittsburgh, 38-31, to essentially clinch the AFC North Division, so playing them at Paul Brown Stadium in the wild card round of the playoffs didn't bother Anderson and his teammates one iota. In fact, they relished the challenge, firmly believing they were the better team.

And after the Bengals' first pass play of the game, it appeared their confidence was well-founded. Palmer completed a 66-yard pass to Henry, the longest pass completion in the team's playoff history. It gave the Bengals a first down deep in Steelers territory, and best of all, the early upper hand in what many felt was a battle between the two best teams in the AFC.

But instead of celebrating the fact they were about to draw first blood against their most bitter rival, the eyes of every Bengals player and their fans turned towards the commotion behind the previous line of scrimmage. There they saw their third-year quarterback, Palmer, lying in a heap, writhing in pain. While practically everyone was following the flight of Palmer's perfect pass to Henry, very few had noticed the Steelers' defensive tackle and former Bengal, Kimo von Oelhoffen's tackle on the Bengals quarterback. If they had, they would have witnessed von Oelhoffen diving low into Palmer's left knee, tearing both the anterior cruciate and medial collateral ligaments as well as causing additional cartilage and meniscus damage.[1] Needless to say, Palmer was done for the day.[2]

Palmer's injury totally deflated the Bengals that day as they eventually lost to the Steelers 31-17. To add insult to injury, Pittsburgh used the win over Cincinnati to capture their fifth Super Bowl title. More significantly, the injury to Palmer, in Anderson's opinion, went beyond just one playoff loss. It marked the beginning of the end of what he and many of his

---

[1] Because of von Oelhoffen's tackle, the NFL adopted the "Carson Palmer Rule" the following season. The rule requires that defenders, unless blocked into the quarterback, must avoid hitting at or below the knees when the quarterback looks to throw with both feet on the ground and in a defenseless position.

[2] Adding salt to the wound, Henry was also injured on the play and missed the rest of the game.

teammates had believed would be a bright and successful future for the Bengals over the next several seasons.

"We were a young team and we knew Carson was going to get better, but that game signaled the downfall of that team," Anderson sadly remembers. "The next five years weren't kind to us. That game started it all."[52]

Palmer did return to open the 2006 season, but in many respects, was never the same. The Bengals went 8-8 in 2006 and failed to achieve another winning season until 2009. By then, Anderson and many of the other key components of the 2005 offense were gone. Before the start of the 2008 season, management asked Anderson, who had become the highest-paid offensive lineman in team history, to take a pay cut. Even though he sincerely wanted to play his entire career and retire as a Cincinnati Bengal, Anderson refused to accept a pay reduction and asked the team on August 30, 2008 to release him so he could pursue employment with another NFL franchise. The Bengals accommodated Anderson's request and on September 5, he agreed to terms with the Baltimore Ravens. Despite signing a three-year contract with the Ravens, Anderson retired from the NFL after one season.

During their history, the Bengals have become known for having, at different periods, some of the best offensive linemen in the NFL. If the team were to construct their own Mt. Rushmore of Offensive Linemen, there's no question one of the four faces prominently featured would include Willie Anderson. Despite rarely being considered for enshrinement in the Pro Football Hall of Fame, Anderson's performance in his 12 seasons in Cincinnati clearly merits some serious discussion. From 1996-2007, a period in which he started 173 games, Anderson was the linchpin in an offensive line that helped nine running backs rush for 1,000 or more yards in a season, including the top six in franchise history, and 50 occasions when a Bengals running back rushed for 100 or more yards in a game. Wielding a steady influence at the left tackle position, Anderson's pass protection prowess produced seven seasons where a Bengals quarterback passed for 3,000 or more yards and 24 games where either Boomer Esiason (1), Neil O'Donnell (1), Jeff Blake (5), Jon Kitna (5) or Carson Palmer (12) passed for 300 or more yards in a game.

Yet when Anderson's legacy is debated, it's unfairly judged by the

Bengals record during his time in Cincinnati. While there's no escaping the fact that the team was 76-116 (.395) in his 12 seasons, what's also inescapable is the performance of the Bengals offense, even during those lean years of the late 1990s and early 2000's, with Anderson in the starting lineup. The Cincinnati offense finished in the top half of the NFL in total offense (1996, 1997, 1999, 2003 and 2005-2007), passing offense (1996, 1997, 2002, 2003 and 2005-2007) and points scored (1996, 1997, 2003-2007) seven times and rushing offense six times (1996, 1997, 1999, 2000, 2003 and 2005). Not bad for a franchise that was ridiculed by the national media seemingly every Sunday afternoon.

A major reason why the Bengals had to deal with the weekly derision from the national media was because of their poor record when selecting a player in the first round of the NFL Draft. For a period of five years from 1991-1995, the Bengals failed to produce a first-round draft choice who made any significant impact. In many respects, the annual missteps the team made during these drafts exacerbated the downward spiral the Bengals encountered at the end of the 1990s.

But that all stopped when the Bengals chose Willie Anderson with their first round pick in the 1996 NFL Draft. Selecting Anderson marked the end of first-round busts and the beginning of the team's transformation from the Bungles to what many consider today the model others should follow when rebuilding their own consistently successful NFL franchise.

And that may be the lasting legacy Willie Anderson leaves behind.

CHAPTER TWENTY–EIGHT

HOWARD FEST

The Perfect Name

S ometimes *you notice someone with* a name that fits his or her
profession or occupation to perfection. Hulk Hogan could be nothing
but a larger-than-life professional wrestler. Even before he tried his first
case, F. Lee Bailey already had the persona of a take-no-prisoners attorney
based on his name alone. And, demonstrating nominative determinism
at its finest, what other job could Larry Speakes possibly have had than
White House spokesperson?

A name like Howard Fest practically begged for him to engage in a
physical and hard-nosed occupation. Born in San Antonio, Texas, Fest
would stay true to his name and become a very successful and rugged
offensive lineman in the NFL. More importantly, he spent the vast majority
of his professional football career as an indispensable offensive guard and
tackle for the Cincinnati Bengals, playing and starting on the franchise's
first team in the AFL and then the NFL two seasons later.

After graduating from Thomas Edison High School in San Antonio,
Fest attended the University of Texas and played football for the legendary
college football head coach, Darrell Royal. As a sophomore in 1965, Fest
was a little-used tight end, catching one pass for nine yards. At the start of
his junior season, Royal moved Fest to offensive tackle where he remained
and became a starter for the following two seasons. The Longhorns were

13-8 in those two seasons, highlighted by a 19-0 victory over Mississippi in the 1966 Bluebonnet Bowl.

Despite not being named to any post-season all-star rosters or earning a spot on any all-conference or All-American teams, the Bengals thought enough of Fest's ability to select him in the sixth round with the 139th overall pick in the 1968 AFL/NFL Draft, their first ever college draft. As the team assembled their roster for the inaugural season in the AFL, Fest not only became an original Bengal but he impressed the coaching staff so much that he was the starting right tackle for the 1968 season, playing in all of the team's 14 games. His ability to play in every game during those first few years would make Fest one of the early legendary Bengals in team history.

In his eight seasons in Cincinnati, Fest never missed any of the 112 games the Bengals played from 1968-1975 and was the primary starter at right offensive tackle in 1968 and 1969 and at left guard from 1971-1975. He made a significant contribution in the franchise's surprising success in their early years in the AFL and NFL, an uncommon feat since most expansion franchises in any professional sport struggle mightily in their first few seasons, rarely finishing with a winning record for the year, much less a berth in the post-season.

But the Bengals were the exception to the expansion rule in Fest's eight seasons. From 1968-1975, Cincinnati had a combined 55-56-1 regular season record, a respectable record for any NFL team, and even more impressive considering it was their first eight years in the league. Among the notable achievements during this time were the 11 wins the team amassed in 1975, the fourth most victories in a season in team history and the most in a 14-game season, as well as their eight consecutive wins from the end of the 1970 season and beginning of the 1971 season, tied for the most all-time in team history. Additionally, their .786 winning percentage in 1975 remains the team record for highest winning percentage in a season.

Adding to the Bengals' unexpected good fortune in their early years were their three post-season appearances that included two AFC Central Division championships, one in 1970 and the other in 1973. Unfortunately, Fest and the Bengals didn't win a playoff game in those three appearances, falling woefully short against the Baltimore Colts and the Miami Dolphins by a combined score of 51-16 in their first two games, before gamely battling the playoff-tested Oakland Raiders in 1975. Despite losing 31-28, the Bengals gave the Raiders all they could handle, scoring 21 points in the second half, and a team record for most post-season points scored in a half that still stands today.

While it's difficult to quantify the impact Fest had on the Bengals' success in their first eight seasons, there's no debating how important the offense's performance from 1968-1975--bolstered by Fest and the rest of the offensive line--was to the team's surprising start in the NFL. In their initial eight years, the Bengals finished in the top of the AFL or NFL in points scored six times (1970-1975), total offense (1971-1975) and rushing offense (1968, 1970, 1971, 1973 and 1974) five times and passing offense four times (1972-1975). Some of the highlights the offense produced included the 61 points they scored at Houston on December 17, 1972 (tied for the most points scored in a game in team history), their 34 first downs against Buffalo on November 17, 1975 and at Philadelphia on December 7, 1975 (tied for second most in team history) and the 441 net yards passing against Buffalo on November 17, 1975 (third most in team history).

Fest and the offensive line played a major role in Paul Robinson's 1,023 yards rushing in 1968 and Ken Anderson's 3,169 yards passing in 1975, the first time each of those achievements occurred in team history. They also played a key part in helping 18 running backs rush for 100 yards in a game and four quarterbacks pass for 300 yards in a game. The most impressive effort by Fest and the rest of the linemen, however, was the 24 sacks they allowed in 1972 and 1973 respectively, the fourth fewest in team history. Given their strong performance in 1975, the Bengals were ready to take the next step in their NFL evolution. Sadly, Fest wouldn't have a chance to contribute.

Before the start of the 1976 season, the NFL held an expansion draft for the two new teams that would begin play in 1976, the Tampa Bay Buccaneers and the Seattle Seahawks. Per NFL rules, the existing 26 NFL franchises were allowed to protect 29 players from their rosters, with the remaining players eligible for either Tampa Bay or Seattle to select them for their own inaugural roster. After the first player was selected from their roster, the existing 26 teams were allowed to protect two additional players. The draft continued until the Buccaneers and the Seahawks had each chosen 39 players, or three from each team.

The Bengals elected to leave Fest unprotected in the 1976 NFL Expansion Draft and eventually Tampa Bay selected him, effectively ending his eight year tenure in Cincinnati. Fest started in all of the Buccaneers' 14 games in 1976 and after playing in only five games in 1977, he retired from the NFL. Whether or not Fest's retirement was hastened by the fact that Tampa Bay lost their first 26 games in the NFL is anybody's guess.

Meanwhile, the Bengals didn't fare much better following Fest's departure. Over the next five seasons, the Bengals went a combined 32-44, failing to make the playoffs in each of those years. It wasn't until 1981, when they assembled a new dominating offensive line led by Anthony Muñoz and Max Montoya that Cincinnati returned to NFL prominence and the post-season.

But before Muñoz and Montoya helped lead the Bengals to success in their second decade of existence, the blueprint for an impactful offensive line was led by the original Bengals who manned the center, guard and tackle positions when the team began play in 1968. Of all the players to line up and block for those early Cincinnati offenses, no one could have guessed that a former tight end from the University of Texas who caught one pass in his Longhorn career would become a staple on those lines, developing a reputation as a hard-nosed, ever-dependable right tackle and left guard for the team's first eight seasons in the AFL and NFL.

But with a name like Howard Fest, it makes perfect sense.

CHAPTER TWENTY–NINE

EDDIE EDWARDS

The Sack Man

Let me tell you how it will be
There's one for you, nineteen for me
Cos I'm the taxman, yeah I'm the taxman

Weird Al Yankovic has made a career out of parodying many of the songs in music history. He took Michael Jackson's "Beat It" and made it into "Eat It". He turned Madonna's "Like a Virgin" into "Like a Sturgeon". While Coolio had a mega-hit with the single, "Gangsta's Paradise", Weird Al had his own hit with the parody, "Amish Paradise". Yankovic's discography is prolific and successful, earning him four gold and six platinum records in the United States alone.

But with all due respect to Yankovic and his many achievements, including four Grammy awards and a further 11 nominations, he missed an opportunity to cross over into the world of the NFL by not converting The Beatles hit, "Taxman" into an homage to the Cincinnati Bengals defensive lineman of the 1970s and 1980s, Eddie Edwards. In fact, had he just tweaked the opening lyrics, Yankovic would have been well on his way to penning the parody, "Sackman"; an extremely appropriate tribute to the Bengals' all-time quarterback sack leader.

Let me tell you how it will be
There's one play for you, nineteen for me
Cos I'm the sackman, yeah, I'm the sackman

Born in South Carolina and raised in Fort Pierce, Florida, Edwards' prowess on the football field at Fort Pierce Central High School caught the eye of the coaching staff at the University of Miami (FL). At the time of his recruitment in 1972, Miami had yet to become known as the "U" and were not the national powerhouse they would become by the 1980s. Nevertheless, Edwards accepted a scholarship to play for the Hurricanes and was a two-time time letterman when he entered his senior season in 1976.

Should five yards lost appear too small
Be thankful I don't take it all
Cos I'm the sackman, yeah, I'm the sackman

In his final collegiate season, Edwards became a bona-fide star, averaging 13 tackles per game and leading the team in quarterback sacks with 11. His senior year performance earned his first-team consensus All-American honors and spots in the 1977 Hula Bowl and Japan Bowl all-star games. He also received the Jack Harding Memorial Award given to the Hurricane's most valuable player as selected by the team's players and coaches. More importantly, thanks in large part to his senior season, Edwards skyrocketed to the top of many NFL teams' draft boards.

"Eddie just had it all," Miami coach Hal Allen said when describing Edwards' talents. "Great size, speed, quickness and a hard-working attitude that you rarely see in a player of his pure natural ability."[53]

One of those teams who agreed with Allen and had Edwards high on their own draft board, was the Bengals. So when it was their turn to make the third overall pick in the 1977 NFL Draft, the Bengals didn't hesitate to select him with their first round draft choice.

If you make a pass, I'll sack your cleats
If you try to duck, I'll sack your seat
If you use two men, I'll sack your fleet

If you move aside, I'll sack your feet
Sackman!
Cos I'm the sackman, yeah, I'm the sackman

Edwards started at left defensive tackle for Cincinnati in his rookie season in 1977 and made an immediate impact, leading all defensive linemen on the team in solo tackles (60) and total tackles (71) while adding four quarterback sacks. He continued to start every game he played over the next two seasons (30) at either left or right defensive tackle, accumulating another 10 quarterback sacks. Then in 1980, the Bengals moved Edwards to left defensive end where over the next eight seasons, he developed his sackman persona.

During the years 1980-1987, Edwards was credited with 69.5 sacks, including 13 in 1983 and 12 in 1980, good enough for the second and fourth most sacks in a season in team history respectively. He led the team in sacks five times (1980, 1982, 1983, 1985 and 1986) and all defensive linemen two additional seasons (1981 and 1984). His most memorable performance was in the last game of the year on December 21 1980, when he sacked Cleveland Browns quarterback, Brian Sipe, five times, a team record for sacks in a game. According to Edwards, his record setting performance was more a combination of technique, skill and the immediate desire to go to where the weather was considerably warmer.

"To tell you the truth, I wanted to hurry up and play the game and get back to Florida. It was just too cold, "Edwards later recalled. "Everything I did that day worked. That day everything our line coach (Dick Modzelewski) told me worked."[54]

Edwards and his sacks played a significant part in the Bengals finishing in the top half of the NFL in total defense (1978, 1980, 1981, 1983, 1984 and 1987) and rushing defense (1977, 1980 and 1981-1984) six times, and points allowed four times (1978, 1980, 1981 and 1983) in the eleven years he was a starting defensive lineman (1977-1987). He also started on the Bengals defense that allowed the fifth fewest points in a season (255 points in 1977), the fourth fewest points per game in a season (16.79 points per game in 1977) and the fourth fewest net yards allowed per game in a season (270.44 yards per game in 1983) in team history.

Don't ask me why I want your shirt (Aaah, Mr. Bradshaw)
If you don't want to eat some dirt (Aaah, Mr. Sipe)
Cos I'm the sackman, yeah, I'm the sackman

In his twelve seasons with the Bengals, Edwards experienced some of the team's most successful seasons and some of their most disappointing. From 1977-1988, the Bengals compiled an 89-93 (.489) regular season record which included six seasons where the team finished below .500 (1978, 1979, 1980, 1983, 1985 and 1987). On the other hand, Edwards was part of three teams to qualify for the post-season, including the franchise's two Super Bowl appearances in 1981 and 1988, making him one of only seven players to appear in uniform for both of the Bengals Super Bowl matchups and only one of six Bengals to play a snap in both games. Edwards made a total of seven solo tackles, 10 total tackles and one sack in his NFL playoff career.

By the time Edwards suited up for Super Bowl XXIII in his college hometown of Miami, against the San Francisco 49ers on January 22, 1989, he knew his time in the NFL was coming to an end. In fact, Edwards "begged" Bengals head coach, Sam Wyche, to let him be in uniform for the game with his family and friends in attendance "because I had a pretty good idea this was it."[55] With the Bengals heartbreaking loss to the 49ers, Edwards' instincts were proven correct and he retired from the NFL shortly thereafter.

Now my advice for those who block
I'm on my way to clean your clock
Cos I'm the sackman, yeah, I'm the sackman

Unlike many of today's impact players, Edwards played his entire NFL career with only one team, the Bengals. In the 170 games he played, of which he started 158, Edwards made 426 solo tackles, an average of 35.5 per year, 544 total tackles for an average of 45.3 per season, recovered 17 fumbles and forced nine fumbles. He scored one touchdown in his NFL career, a fumble recovery in the end zone against the Seattle Seahawks on November 16, 1986.

But it was his ability to sack the quarterback that places Edwards on the list of all-time Bengals greats. He is the team's all-time leader in sacks, with 83.5,[1] an average of 6.96 sacks per year. The 83.5 sacks resulted in 674.5 yards lost, an average of 8.1 yards lost per sack. It was a career, had it occurred in a larger media market, that would have garnered Edwards national acclaim. Thankfully for Bengals fans, Edwards had and continues to have no regrets about playing his entire career in Cincinnati.

"Not many guys played with the same team for 12 years and I'm proud I got to play in two Super Bowls," Edwards said after his career was over. "A lot of guys never played in any."[56]

And a lot of guys were never responsible for 83.5 sacks. Despite playing in small market Cincinnati, Edwards played well enough to have his career immortalized in song.

> *And you're working for no one but me*
> *Sackman!*

Too bad Weird Al Yankovic never thought to make it happen.

---

[1]   According to the NFL statistics, only 47.5 of his sacks are considered official since they did not recognize sacks as an official statistic until 1982.

CHAPTER THIRTY

RICH BRAHAM

Mr. Indestructible

If you had to guess how many seasons and games someone in the NFL played after sustaining two sprained ankles, a herniated neck disc, a broken toe, and undergoing four arthroscopic knee surgeries, chances are your estimate would fall somewhere between three and five seasons and no more than 50 to 60 games played. The odds anyone could overcome those kinds of significant injuries are highly unlikely and practically impossible. But to then go on to have a long, fruitful career as well as making a significant impact on the history and the future of a franchise, a player would have to be pretty indestructible.

For Bengals fans, it's a good thing then that Rich Braham defied the improbable and become one of the longest tenured and highly successful offensive linemen in team history, despite being more likely to have an ongoing role as a patient on Grey's Anatomy.

Braham began his football odyssey, and in turn, his medical voyage, in Morgantown, West Virginia, where he attended University High School. He decided to stay home to continue his football career when he enrolled at West Virginia University despite not being offered a scholarship. He successfully walked-on to the team in 1989 but was red-shirted and did not play. In 1990, his freshman year of eligibility, he started the last three games of the season at left tackle, a preview of what was to come over the next three seasons.

In his sophomore season in 1991, Braham became a full-time starter and by his junior year in 1992 he started every game, earning the Whitey Gwynne Award as West Virginia's unsung hero on offense. As he entered his senior season in 1993, Braham and the Mountaineers were prepared for a breakthrough year. They did not disappoint.

The 1993 Mountaineers finished the regular season a perfect 11-0, captured the school's first Big East Championship and earned a spot in the Sugar Bowl against the Florida Gators on January 1, 1994. The offense was manned and captained at left tackle, as it had for 37 consecutive games, by Braham, who, along with his West Virginia teammates, broke through on the national stage. He earned All-Big East honors in 1993 and was named first team Kodak and UPI All-American and second team AP All-American that year as well. His teammates and coaches recognized his contributions in his senior season by presenting him with the 1993 Ira E. Rodgers Award for outstanding leadership, academic and football achievement.

Braham finished his college career as a four-year letterman (1990-1993) and was named by the 2010-2011 USA Today College Football Encyclopedia as one of four offensive tackles on West Virginia's 55 greatest players team since 1953. Fourteen years later, the university would recognize his career achievements by inducting Braham into the West Virginia Sports Hall of Fame. More importantly, his college career established him as a potential NFL offensive lineman.

One of the teams who believed Braham had NFL talent were the Phoenix Cardinals. They showed their faith in his ability by choosing him in the third round of the 1994 NFL Draft with the 76th overall pick. Unfortunately, the Cardinals lost their confidence in their newly acquired offensive lineman midway through the 1994 season and placed him on waivers. Shortly thereafter, he was picked up by the Bengals and so began a 13-year career in Cincinnati which, while it included several surgeries and injuries, is recognized more for its production and for Braham's key role in the renaissance of a once moribund franchise. By the time he had retired after the 2006 season, not only were the Bengals once again relevant but

Braham had set the standard for excellence for the team's future offensive centers as well.

Braham's first two seasons in Cincinnati were far from memorable. During the 1994 and 1995 seasons, Braham played in only three games, suffering an ankle injury in the 1995 pre-season that forced him to miss the entire season while he sat on injured reserve. Fully recovered from his ankle injury, Braham began the 1996 season as the Bengals left guard and started all 16 games, the last three at center after Darrick Brilz was injured. It also marked the start of Braham's legacy and longevity as he would play and start in 141 of the team's 160 games from 1996-2005.

Sadly, while Braham impressed his teammates and coaches with his play and his toughness at left guard and center from 1996-2004, the team did very little to create a positive impression throughout the league. In those nine seasons, the Bengals never finished a season above .500, posting a dismal 50-94 record during that time frame. On occasion, Braham and the offense showed glimpses of excellence as evidenced by their 4.640 average yards per rushing attempt and their 350 pass completions in 2002, both of which rank fifth in team history.

During these nine seasons, the offense's output in 2000 stands out in particular, finishing with a 4.675 average yards per rushing attempt (fourth best in team history) and 2,314 net yards rushing (fifth best in team history). The highlight of the 2000 season was the Bengals 31-21 upset victory over the Denver Broncos on October 22, a game that saw Corey Dillon set the team record for yards rushing in a game (278 yards) and the team record for net yards rushing in a game (407 yards). Later in the year, Braham and the offense gained 292 net yards rushing against the Arizona Cardinals on December 3, the third best in team history. By the end of the season, the Bengals finished second in rushing offense in the entire NFL.

For the most part, though, the Bengals were an afterthought and mainly a laughing stock between the years 1996-2004. Those teams set several dubious team records for futility, including the most games lost in a season (14 in 2002), the lowest winning percentage in a season (.125 in 2002) and the most consecutive home games lost (11, 5 in 1998 and 6 in 1999). In 2002, the Bengals lost seven consecutive home games and in 1998 lost nine consecutive overall games. In those nine seasons, the best record the team could muster was 8-8, something they did in consecutive years in 2003 and 2004.

Throughout all of this misery, Braham became the leader of the offensive line. His role as captain of the line was accelerated in 1999 when he was moved to center even though he had little or no prior experience playing the position. Not only did Braham succeed at his new position despite his lack of having game experience at center, he became the blueprint and model that all future Bengals centers are measured against.

And he accomplished all of this while seemingly always battling an injury or undergoing one surgery after another. During his 98 starts at center, Braham dealt with four arthroscopic knee surgeries, two sprained ankles, a herniated neck disc and a broken toe. Amazingly, even with all of these maladies, he only missed 15 games in seven seasons as the team's number one center.

The only thing missing from Braham's resume after the 2004 season was a winning season. As the Bengals entered the 2005 season, the idea of a winning record and a trip to the playoffs seemed plausible. Due in part to those back-to-back 8-8 seasons in 2003 and 2004, and the emergence of quarterback Carson Palmer as the face of the franchise, Braham and the rest of his teammates believed 2005 was the year they would become a significant force in the NFL. When the dust settled, their beliefs were confirmed.

The 2005 Bengals finished the regular season 11-5, capturing the AFC North Division title and qualifying for the playoffs for the first time since 1990. Much of the success of that season was attributed to the performance of Braham and the rest of the offense. Led by Braham at center and Palmer at quarterback, the offense scored 421 points (tied for fourth in team history) and completed 362 passes (fourth best in team history) for 32 touchdowns (tied for second most in team history).

The offensive line, anchored by Braham at center, played a critical role in the success of the offense, paving the way for running back Rudi Johnson to rush for a team record 1,458 yards and giving Palmer the protection to throw for a team record 3,836 yards. They allowed only 21 quarterback sacks the entire season for an average of 1.31 sacks per game, the second fewest in team history. Even though the season ended abruptly against the Pittsburgh Steelers in the first round of the playoffs, the Bengals ended the year fourth in the NFL in points scored, fifth in passing offense, sixth in total offense and 11th in rushing offense.

Braham and the rest of the Bengals had high hopes for the 2006 season. But he suffered a tibia plateau fracture in their Week Two game against the Cleveland Browns and unlike the other injuries he had sustained in the past, Braham was unable to return and missed the rest of the season. Not surprisingly, the Bengals couldn't overcome this injury and finished the year 8-8. More importantly, the severity of the injury led to Braham's retirement from the NFL at the end of the 2006 season.

In his 13 seasons as a Bengal, tied for fourth-most seasons played in team history, Braham established himself as the standard for all future Bengals centers and the reputation for playing at a high level while contending with his injuries. Whether starting at left guard or center, Braham was a member of an offensive line that created the holes for a running back to gain 1,000 or more yards in a season eight times, including the top-five rushing seasons in team history. From 1996-2005 when Braham was a usual starter, the Bengals had 42 single game 100-yard rushing performances. On the passing side, the team with Braham anchoring the line had five seasons with a 3,000 yard passer and 17 single game 300-yard passing performances. It was a career worthy of placing Braham on the short list of the greatest Bengals of all-time.

Or at the very least, on the short list of leading candidates of the NFL's all-time walking wounded.

CHAPTER THIRTY-ONE

BRUCE REIMERS

Sunday Afternoon Dreams

G rowing up in Humboldt, Iowa, a small town 120 miles north of Des Moines and less than 30 miles from the Minnesota border, a young Bruce Reimers had a single mission in the early to mid-1970s after his family attended Sunday morning church services.

"I wanted to watch [pro] football on Sundays," Reimers recalls.[57]

It was with this backdrop that Reimers began to foster the idea that one day, others in Humboldt would turn on their television on Sundays and see him playing in an NFL game. It was, and always will be, a long shot for any young man to take a snap in an NFL uniform. But with a lot of hard work and talent Reimers became a fixture for 10 seasons. His offensive line coach in the pros, Jim McNally called him one of the toughest players he ever coached, and Reimers played the first eight seasons from 1984-1991 as an offensive lineman for the Cincinnati Bengals, shown on Sunday afternoon television sets all across the nation.

Reimers' road to starring on Sunday afternoon television began at Humboldt High School where he became an All-State first team defensive tackle.[1] By the time he was a senior in 1978, college football coaches all

---

[1] Reimers was so dominant as a high school defensive tackle that in 1998 he was inducted into the Iowa High School Athletic Association Hall of Fame.

across the Midwest were working on signing him to a football scholarship. Interested in playing close to home when Iowa State head coach Earle Bruce offered him an opportunity to play defensive tackle for the Cyclones, Reimers jumped at the chance. He saw limited action in his freshman year in 1979 and in 1980 he was red-shirted for medical reasons. By then, Bruce had left to become the head coach at Ohio State University and Iowa State's new head coach, Donnie Duncan had a different plan for Reimers when he returned to action in 1981. Duncan believed Reimers was a better fit on the offensive line and inserted him as the starting left guard when the season began. Little did Reimers know that Duncan's personnel decision would pave the way for him to become a starter in the National Football League.

Reimers started all 11 games at guard in 1981 and in his junior year in 1982. At the beginning of his senior season in 1983, he missed the first four games due to torn scar tissue on his knee and stretched ligaments he suffered in the off-season and spring practice. When he returned to the starting lineup, Reimers didn't miss a beat, earning first-team All-Big 8 honors as the Cyclones amassed 2,783 yards passing for 19 touchdowns, marks that remain the fifth best in school history. At the end of the year, Reamers' play merited him invites to the 1983 Blue-Gray and Senior Bowl post-season all-star games and the respect of his teammates and coaches as he was named the recipient of Iowa State's Arthur Floyd Scott Award given to the team's best offensive lineman.

Reimers finished his collegiate career at the other side of the spectrum from where it started. Initially brought into play defense, Reimers, a four-year letterman, was moved to the other side of the football where he became one of six guards on Iowa State's 55 Greatest Players Since 1953 according to the USA Today's 2010-2011 College Football Encyclopedia. In 2009, he would also be inducted into the school's athletic Hall of Fame for his performance. Incredibly, he accomplished all of this success despite undergoing four knee operations during his time at Iowa State. More importantly, Reimers' play in his four years as a Cyclone gave him the opportunity to play at the next level, the NFL.

Sometimes, a player is one component of an NFL's team's epic college draft. Sometimes, a player finds himself selected by a team that provides the perfect learning environment. Rarely does a player get chosen by a team who can offer both of these opportunities. Fortunately for Reimers, when the Bengals selected him in the eighth round of the 1984 NFL Draft with the 204th overall pick, he, by chance, began his NFL career as a rare exception to the NFL Draft rules.

Reimers was part of a Bengals draft class that included Ricky Hunley, Boomer Esiason, Stanford Jennings, Barney Bussey and Leo Barker, players who would directly or indirectly led the team and their new head coach, Sam Wyche, to the franchise's second ever Super Bowl appearance four years later. Additionally, the Bengals drafted two other offensive linemen in 1984, Brian Blados and Bruce Kozerski, and together with Reimers, they all would make significant contributions to a revolutionary offense that would transform how the game was played.

Reimers and the two other rookie offensive linemen developed into significant impact performers so quickly because they came to an offensive line fully loaded with top-notch experience. This included perennial All-Pro's Anthony Muñoz and Max Montoya and seasoned veterans Dave Rimington and Mike Wilson. Better yet, the offensive line was under the direction of Jim McNally, arguably the best offensive line coach in NFL history. For a rookie trying to forge an NFL career like Reimers', who had only been an offensive guard for three collegiate seasons, being coached by McNally and tutored by such greats like Muñoz and Montoya, being chosen by the Bengals was like manna from heaven.

According to Reimers, McNally was "always the teacher", leaving no stone unturned in an effort to find an advantage against their opponents and "never letting somebody out-prepare his boys." Reimers learned very early that McNally, who is due some credit as the leading innovator of the zone blocking scheme, held the key to his future success. "If he told something," Reimers recalls, "he was right."[58]

Reimers obviously paid attention to what McNally and his veteran teammates told him early on in his Bengals career. After playing mainly a reserve role in his first three seasons, (45 games played, five games started), he became the team's starting left guard in the 1987 season. What should have been a special season for Reimers turned sour when an ankle injury cut short his playing time (10 games played, eight games started) and an NFL player strike divided the Bengals locker room so badly that the team finished 4-11 and on the brink of implosion.

But as the Bengals began their preparation for 1988, the coaches and players believed the upcoming season had the chance to be special. Reimers, in particular, sensed in training camp that "you just knew something was going to happen." By the time the 1988 season came to a close, Reimers' instincts were proven right. Or as he put it years later, "it was magic."[59]

The Bengals finished the regular season 12-4, champions of the AFC Central Division and participants in the post-season for the first time since 1982. Cincinnati's sudden success was due in large part to the innovative no-huddle offense introduced by Wyche. Reimers believed Wyche, who he considers "an awesome coach" and "way ahead of his time",[60] created an offense that definitely gave the Bengals an edge over their opponents in 1988. When the dust settled, Reimers was proven right. The 1988 Bengals offense truly was something special.

With Reimers starting all 16 games at left guard and led by Esiason at quarterback, running back Ickey Woods and wide receiver Eddie Brown, the Bengals offense scored 448 points, 59 total touchdowns, 27 rushing touchdowns and 2,710 net yards rushing on 563 attempts, all of which remain team records for a single season. The 351 first downs and their 4.813 yards per rushing attempt are the second best in team history while their 6,057 total net yards ranks as the third best season in team history.

The 1988 Bengals offense also featured some outstanding individual performances. Esiason threw for 3,572 yards, Woods ran for 1,066 yards and Brown caught 53 passes for 1,273 yards and nine touchdowns. Esiason had three games with over 300 yards passing while Woods and Brown each had five games where they had 100 yards rushing and 100 yards receiving respectively.

None of this offensive outburst would have happened without the stellar play of Reimers at left guard, Muñoz at left tackle, Kozerski at center, Montoya at right guard and Joe Walter at right tackle. Arguably the best offensive line in team history, Reimers and the rest of the offensive front paved the way for the Bengals to finish the season atop the NFL in total offense, rushing offense and points scored and 11th in passing offense. Their efforts guided the Bengals to Super Bowl XXIII where they lost in heartbreaking fashion to Joe Montana and the San Francisco 49ers, 20-16. The last-minute loss in the Super Bowl was so devastating that to this day, Reimers has never watched a replay of the game.

After the 1988 season, Reimers continued his strong play at left guard for another three seasons. But at the end of the 1991 season, the Bengals traded Reimers to the Tampa Bay Buccaneers, making him the second member of the Bengals vaunted 1988 offensive line following Montoya's departure to the Los Angeles Raiders after the 1989 season to leave McNally and his inner circle. The parting of both Montoya and Reimers marked the beginning of the dismantling of the 1988 championship team and in retrospect the beginning of the rebuilding of the Bengals franchise. Reimers went on to play two seasons in Tampa before retiring at the end of the 1993 season.

When great Bengal offensive linemen are discussed, Bruce Reimers is rarely mentioned, probably due in part to the fact he only started in 64 games in his eight seasons in Cincinnati. Passing judgment, though, on Reimers' impact based solely on the number of games he started is short-sighted and frankly, unfair. In the five seasons he was the usual starting left guard, the Bengals finished in the top half of the NFL in total offense and rushing offense all five years, in passing offense four times and points scored three times. With Reimers manning the left guard spot, the Bengals had three running backs rush for 1,000 or more yards in a season and 21 backs rush for 100 or more yards in a game. Meanwhile, the quarterback in his tenure, Esiason, threw for 3,000 or more yards in a season four times and had 15 games in which he passed for 300 or more yards.

Today, Reimers looks back at his ten-year NFL career and can hardly believe it all started in the small town of Humboldt, Iowa by watching football after church, and ended with such accomplishments as playing on one of the best offensive lines in NFL history for one of the greatest offensive line coaches, culminating with playing in the ultimate game, the Super Bowl. "I got to live my dreams," Reimers simply recalls.[61]

Thankfully for Bengals fans, his dream came true while wearing a Cincinnati uniform.

CHAPTER THIRTY-TWO

VERNON HOLLAND

The Sharply-Dressed Man

There once was a time when the Baby Boomers began striking out on their own and Generation X was deciding who to take to prom, a time that every professional working man wore clothes from Hart, Schaffner & Marx, and carried a briefcase to work. Today's professionals of grown up Gen X's and their millennial counterparts, on the other hand, wear their Levi jeans to work with a backpack or laptop case slung over their shoulder. The only time someone in the 1970s wore blue jeans and carried a backpack was if they were going on a camping trip, not spending a day at the office.

So in 1971, when Vernon Holland started his professional career wearing expensive clothes and toting a briefcase to work, it didn't seem out of the ordinary. Problem was, Holland's first job out of college was with the Cincinnati Bengals as a member of their offensive line, not the type of occupation one usually associates with Armani suits and Halliburton briefcases. By the end of the decade, however, those who went to work against Holland on a weekly basis wished he played in a designer three-piece suit instead of his Bengals uniform every Sunday afternoon.

Born in San Antonio, and raised in Sherman, Texas, Holland played his college football at the historically black college, Tennessee State University in Nashville. A steady presence on the offensive line at right tackle in his sophomore season in 1968, NFL scouts began to take notice of Holland's play during his 1969 junior year, a season in which Tennessee State scored 28 rushing touchdowns, the second most in school history, en route to a 7-1 record. For his efforts, Holland was named to The Pittsburgh Courier's All-American team. It was all a prelude, though, to the team's and Holland's breakthrough season in 1970.

The Tigers finished the 1970 season undefeated at 11-0 and won the Black College National Championship with a 26-25 victory over Southwest Louisiana in the Grantland Rice Bowl. Holland was the mainstay of an offense and its front line that produced a total of 51 touchdowns in 1970, 26 via the rushing game. Both the total touchdowns in a season (tied for ninth) and rushing touchdowns in a season (fifth) remain in the top ten in school history. It also marked the season where Holland received serious national acclaim for his performance and serious consideration as an early round selection in the upcoming 1971 NFL Draft. He was named to the All-American teams of The Associated Press, Time Magazine, Kodak, The Sporting News and The Pittsburgh Courier in 1970 and had put himself in a position to continue his football career at the professional level.

Despite playing collegiately at a smaller school and without the national exposure afforded to those who played at the Division I level, Holland was still considered a top prospect in the 1971 NFL Draft. Most draft observers believed it wasn't a matter of if he would be drafted but rather a question of who would select him and when. Had those experts done their homework, they would have known exactly where Holland would happen upon his landing spot.

In their previous three NFL Drafts, the Cincinnati Bengals had drafted 18 players from historically black colleges, a group which included future franchise stand-outs Al Beauchamp, Essex Johnson, Ken Riley and Lemar Parrish. It seemed only logical that head coach and general manager Paul Brown would once again defy the critics and use of one of his draft picks on a player from a university not known for producing a long line of NFL talent. What made this choice so risky in the eyes of other NFL executives was the belief Brown would draft Holland in the early rounds when he would probably be available in the later rounds.

Undeterred, Brown and the Bengals used their first round draft choice and the 15th overall pick in the 1971 Draft to select Holland. Brown took his faith in his new offensive tackle even further by making him the starting right tackle in Game 1 of Holland's rookie season in 1971. By the end of the 1979 season, Holland repaid Brown's faith and then some, becoming the unquestioned leader of the offensive line throughout the decade, and the model the franchise used to develop their future right tackles.

In his nine seasons in a Bengals uniform, from the moment he dropped off his briefcase in his locker and exchanged his suit and tie for a helmet and shoulder pads, Holland became known for his reliability and strength. In the 130 games the Bengals played from 1971-1979, Holland missed only 11 games and started at right tackle in 118 of the 119 he played. In fact, with the exception of the 1974 season, Holland played and started every game from 1971-1979.

As for his strength, it was obvious to Holland's teammates that he was someone special. "He didn't have weight room strength," recalls Dave Lapham, who played alongside Holland on the offensive line from 1975-1979. "He had natural body strength."[62]

The combination of his dependability and toughness not only made Holland the anchor of the Bengals offensive line throughout the 1970s but it propelled the young franchise into the upper tier of the NFL. With Holland stationed at right tackle, the Bengals finished a season with an above .500 record five times during Holland's tenure, qualifying for the playoffs in 1973 thanks to their winning the AFC Central Division championship and in 1975 as a wild card entrant. Needless to say, for a franchise that began play in 1968, those types of seasons were unexpected and required the rest of the league to take notice of the magic Paul Brown was conducting in Cincinnati.

The 1975 season was especially impressive for a franchise playing in only their eighth AFL or NFL season. Competing in the same division as the Pittsburgh Steelers, a team that won four Super Bowls from 1974-1979, the Bengals finished the season 11-3, and a .786 winning percentage, the highest in team history. The success of the 1975 Bengals was largely attributable to the performance of Holland and the rest of the offense. With Holland anchoring the offensive line and Ken Anderson coming into his own as the team's quarterback, the Bengals finished 1975 with the NFL's number one ranked passing offense, the second best total offense and ninth in points scored. Anderson ended the year with 3,169 yards passing, the first time a Bengals quarterback threw for 3,000 or more yards in a season while Holland was named second team All-AFC by the United Press International (UPI). Unfortunately, the Bengals' first-round playoff opponent, the Oakland Raiders, were arguably the second-best team in the AFC behind the Steelers during the 1970s. The Bengals lost 31-28 at Oakland in a hard fought divisional round playoff game in what many still consider one of the best playoff games ever.

While 1975 does stand out, Holland's career is not defined by just one season. In 1972 and 1973, Holland, (nicknamed "Suki" by his teammates), and the rest of the offensive line allowed only 24 quarterback sacks each year, the fourth fewest in team history. In 1979, the Bengals rushed for 2,329 net yards and 23 rushing touchdowns, both marked the fourth best in team history. In Holland's eight full seasons as the starting right tackle, the Bengals finished in the top half of the NFL in total points scored seven times, total offense and passing offense six times and rushing offense three times. He also played a pivotal role in the six games that Anderson threw for more than 300 yards and the 16 occasions when a running back rushed for 100 or more yards in a game.

In many ways, football is a cruel sport and an even crueler business. When Holland answered the bell practically every Sunday for nine seasons, the Bengals hailed him as the cornerstone of their offensive line. They also realized, however, that all of those games produce an enormous amount of wear and tear on the human body. Imagine trying to drive a car on one set of tires for over 100,000 miles without even once rotating them and you get a sense of how a right tackle would perform under a similar amount of use.

So despite having an established and model right tackle in Holland already on their roster, the Bengals front office used their first round selection and the third overall pick in the 1980 NFL Draft to choose the player practically everyone considered the best offensive lineman in the draft, Anthony Muñoz. With their selection, the Bengals replaced their long-standing right tackle, Holland, with the unproven Muñoz, even though it appeared Holland still had the ability to make an impact on a weekly basis. Given the circumstances facing Holland, most NFL veterans would have caused a scene, or at the very least, used the press to vent his frustrations. But in a reflection of the way he arrived for work each day, Holland was the consummate professional after being cut by the Bengals prior to the 1980 season.

"He was very gracious about it," the Bengals' then-assistant general manager, Mike Brown, remembers. "He said good-bye and thanked us."[63]

Holland signed with the Detroit Lions after being cut by the Bengals but played in only two games and after four weeks into the 1980 season, was released. He then signed with the New York Giants prior to Week 7 of the season and played the remaining 10 games, starting in five of them. At the end of the 1980 season, Holland retired from the NFL after a successful 10-year career.

On April 21, 1998, Holland died suddenly of a heart attack in Nashville, Tennessee at the age of 49. Since his death, the Ohio Valley Conference, the conference that Holland's alma mater, Tennessee State University is currently a member of, has established the Vernon Holland Scholarship to honor the former Tiger tackle. The scholarship promotes graduate level studies and is awarded to former Ohio Valley Conference student athletes interested in a career associated with sports. Given how he conducted himself and his business in the NFL, it's a fitting tribute to a man who always believed just because he played football for a living it didn't mean he couldn't come to work dressed for success.

In the end, Vernon Holland proved a sharply-dressed man could also become a sharp-as-nails NFL offensive tackle.

CHAPTER THIRTY–THREE

MIKE WILSON

Moon Pie

On April 29, 1917, the Chattanooga Bakery in Chattanooga, Tennessee created a snack consisting of two round graham cracker cookies with marshmallow filling in the center and chocolate coating, in an effort to satisfy the post-lunch cravings of Kentucky coal miners. The bakery called the concoction a Moon Pie and it immediately became, and still remains today, a staple of American South cuisine. By the 1950's, many Southerners started to accompany their Moon Pie with a RC Cola, a pairing that inspired Big Bill Lister to record the hit single, "Gimme an RC Cola and a Moon Pie".

Given this culinary history, it's not hard to imagine the Cincinnati Bengals thinking about the Big Bill Lister tune when it came time to make their fourth round selection and the 103rd overall pick in the 1978 NFL Draft. In fact, you can close your eyes and picture owner and general manager Paul Brown giving his fourth round selection instructions to the team's representatives at the draft by singing, "Gimme a starting right tackle and a Moon Pie."

In this case, Brown wasn't asking for a snack to go along with his new draft pick but instead he was drafting an impressive offensive lineman from the University of Georgia by the name of Mike Wilson who received the nickname "Moon Pie" from his college teammates during his freshman year. Why they gave him this nickname is unclear because unlike the snack, "Moon Pie" Wilson didn't crumble like a graham cracker or have a marshmallow center during his eight seasons in Cincinnati as a starter on the offensive line.

Born in Norfolk, Virginia, Wilson attended Johnson High School in Gainesville, Georgia. While he lettered in track at Johnson High, it was his play on the football field that established him as a statewide phenom and caught the eye of college recruiters as he earned the school's offensive lineman of the year in both his junior and senior seasons in 1971 and 1972. Wilson, who had his jersey number 77 retired by the school in 1991 and was inducted into the State of Georgia Sports Hall of Fame in 2001, was so dominant that Johnson High had a single game plan each week, according to his coach, Phil Carpenter. "We just ran behind him," Carpenter said about Wilson. "We never passed the ball."[64]

When it came time to choose where he would play college football, Wilson's decision was relatively easy, accepting a scholarship from the University of Georgia, a mere 42 miles from his hometown of Gainesville. What wasn't easy was his transition from high school to college, a situation exacerbated by the fact that the coaches at Georgia had him playing defensive tackle instead of on the offensive line. Wilson became so upset he quit five times during the first quarter of his freshman year on 1973. Although he returned to the team each time, it was a conversation with legendary head coach Vince Dooley that convinced Wilson to remain a Bulldog.

"He (Dooley) said, 'I really have confidence in what you can do. Just give it this year and I guarantee you, you'll see a difference,'" Wilson remembered. "So I stuck it out and it did get better."[65] Even though he did stick it out through his freshman season, Wilson still found himself playing defense as a sophomore in 1976, starting on the defensive line for a Georgia squad that finished 6-6 and a berth in the Tangerine Bowl.

With his junior season set to start, those words of encouragement and patience Dooley uttered two years before, proved prophetic when Wilson was moved to the offense in 1975. Inserted as the team's starting left tackle, Wilson helped the Bulldogs to a 9-3 record and berth in the Cotton Bowl against Arkansas. More importantly, not only did Wilson flourish in his new role on the offense but his future career as a professional football player began to evolve and take shape. In his first year at left tackle, Wilson was named second team All-SEC by the Associated Press after a season in which Georgia rushed for 3,267 yards, the third most in school history, for an average of 297.0 yards rushing per game, the second best average in school history.

With one year under his belt at left tackle, Georgia expected more out of Wilson and the rest of his teammates at the start of the 1976 season. Neither Wilson nor the rest of the Bulldogs disappointed Dooley or the rest of the coaching staff. The Bulldogs finished 10-2 and champions of the SEC and received an invitation to the Sugar Bowl against the University of Pittsburgh. The offense played a significant role in the breakthrough season, rushing for 3,075 yards for an average of 279.5 yards per game, marks that remain the fifth best in school history.

As for Wilson, he played a large part in the team's success and was recognized nationally for his contribution. He was named first team offensive All-SEC offensive tackle by both the AP and the UPI, first team All-American by the AP and the Newspaper Enterprise Association and SEC Co-Lineman of the Year by The Atlanta Constitution. His coaches at Georgia recognized his importance by presenting him with the J.B. Whitworth Award as the team's lineman of the year. Wilson's collegiate career ended with an invitation to the prestigious post-season college football All-Star game, the Senior Bowl, in January 1977.

Although his time at Georgia started on shaky ground, Wilson finished it as a three-year letterman and as a member of the University of Georgia's 1970s Team of the Decade. He was also selected by the USA Today's 2010-2011 College Football Encyclopedia as one of five offensive tackles on Georgia's 55 Greatest Players Since 1953, a prospect unimaginable when he first arrived in Athens. Wilson's performance the last two years at left tackle put him in a position to be selected in the 1978 NFL Draft, a career he was anxious to pursue.

In the 1970s, the NFL usually held its annual college draft during the early parts of the month of April. In 1977, though, those plans changed, thanks to a court decision that ruled it was against the U.S. Constitution to restrict an individual player to a single team, thereby raising doubts about whether or not the NFL Draft was a viable and legal procedure. It took months before the NFL was satisfied that their draft complied with the law, and as a result, it was pushed back to May 3-4, 1977.

Unsure of when or if the NFL Draft would occur, and unsure about his status within it, Wilson opted for what he did know. The Toronto Argonauts of the Canadian Football League (CFL) offered him a contract for the 1977 season and a chance to immediately begin playing professional football. So, instead of waiting for the NFL to decide on the status of their draft, Wilson signed with the Argonauts and began play as a starting left tackle in July 1977. Undeterred by his declaration to play in the CFL, the Bengals selected Wilson in the fourth round of the 1977 NFL Draft.

Upon arriving in Toronto, Wilson experienced immediate success. He was named a CFL East All-Star and a CFL All-Star at the offensive tackle position. He was also awarded the Leo Dandurand Trophy as the Most Outstanding Lineman in the CFL's Eastern Division. It seemed the Bengals had wasted a draft pick on the Georgia offensive tackle because based upon his performance in his rookie season, both Toronto and Wilson were looking forward to the 1978 season. Then, fate intervened.

In the Argonauts second pre-season game of the 1978 season, Wilson suffered a knee injury and shockingly, Toronto quickly released him. Without a job and seemingly with no immediate prospects for employment, Wilson was unsure of what would happen next. Enter the Bengals, who still owned the draft rights to Wilson and in need, it appeared, of a Moon Pie snack and an offensive tackle.

"Three days after I got out of the hospital, Mike Brown, the owner of the Bengals, flew up and started working a deal with them (Toronto) to buy my contract up," Wilson recalls. "I ended up playing the last nine games of the Bengals that season."[66]

It made sense for the Bengals to sign a proven lineman like Wilson considering the new landscape in the NFL. In 1977, NFL teams averaged an anemic 17.2 points per game, the lowest offensive output since 1942. The 1977 season marked the end of an eight year period known as The Dead Ball Era when defenses in the NFL overpowered the offenses. Bowing to public pressure to increase scoring and to open up the passing game, the league in 1978 instituted a series of major rule changes such as prohibiting defensive backs from making contact with wide receivers five yards beyond the line of scrimmage before the ball is thrown, and permitting offensive linemen to extend their arms and open their hands in an effort to extend and relax the pass blocking rules. Given this new environment, adding proven and talented offensive linemen seemed a prudent move for the Bengals if they had any hopes of competing for division titles and championships.

After playing in the last nine games, eight of which he started, in 1978, Wilson immediately made Brown's trip to Toronto appear prescient when he became the Bengals' starting left tackle at the start of the 1979 season. Even more impressive than his ascension into the starting lineup was the fact that Wilson did not miss a game over the next seven seasons, starting all but one of those 105 games. The acquisition of Wilson established stability to the offensive line, and as it would turn out, one of the key building blocks to the construction of the franchise's first ever Super Bowl appearance.

Entering the 1981 season, no one expected the Bengals to contend for a playoff berth much less a spot in the Super Bowl. Coming off back-to-back seasons of 4-12 and 6-10 in 1979 and 1980 respectively, the Bengals, on the surface, seemed no better than a .500 football team. But a closer look at the roster to start the 1981 season showed a team that had used the last five years since their last post-season appearance to build an offensive and defensive unit budding with talent and seasoned by NFL trial-by-fire experience. In 1981, of the 22 starters on both offense and defense, thirteen, including Wilson, were drafted or acquired between 1976-1980. Add to this mix veteran quarterback Ken Anderson and Hall of Fame offensive lineman and a member of multiple NFL championship teams, Forrest Gregg, as the head coach, and the Bengals were actually ready to make a statement to the rest of the NFL in 1981.

Cincinnati finished the 1981 regular season 12-4, tied for the most wins in a season in team history and tied for second for the highest winning percentage in a season, and their first AFC Central Division title since 1973. While both sides of the football contributed to the team's success, it was the offense which stood out as the driving force behind what many observers believed was an unexpected run to the Super Bowl. Led by the eventual 1981 NFL MVP Anderson at quarterback, and an offensive line with Wilson now starting at right tackle and featuring future Hall of Famer Anthony Muñoz at left tackle, the Bengals offense dominated not only most of the defenses it played against but the team's record book as well.

Powered by 421 points scored, 51 touchdowns, 30 touchdowns, 5,968 total net yards, 3,995 net yards passing and 361 first downs, numbers that still remain as top five regular season records in team history, the offense rolled through the regular season. It also featured a 1000-yard rusher in Pete Johnson (1,077 rushing yards), a 1000-yard receiver in rookie Cris Collinsworth (1,009 receiving yards) and a 3,000 yard passer in Anderson (3,754 yards passing). Overall, the offense finished the season ranked second in the NFL in total offense, and third in passing offense and points scored. It was, and still is by all accounts, one of the best seasons in team history. But in Wilson's mind, the regular season was just a prelude to what he, and the rest of the team, really wanted.

"To me, you get paid to play. That's what the season is for," Wilson said after retired from the NFL. "But when you get to the playoffs, it's about the ring. Not the money."[67]

Wilson's quest for the ring in 1981 began with a 28-21 home victory over the Buffalo Bills in the AFC Division Playoff round. One week later, the Bengals hosted the San Diego Chargers in their first AFC Championship game appearance and the chance for a spot in Super Bowl XVI. In a game now known more for being played in a temperature of nine degrees below zero and a wind chill factor of minus 59 degrees, Wilson and the rest of the team persevered through the frigid weather conditions and defeated the obviously overwhelmed and unprepared Chargers, 27-7. Wilson's plan of playing for the ring was to prepare to take on the San Francisco 49ers in the Super Bowl. What he didn't foresee in the two weeks prior to the game was the avalanche of requests for his time and his perceived ability to secure seats for the biggest event of the year.

"It's such a build-up with all the press calling and people trying to get tickets," Wilson recalls. "Everybody comes out of the woodwork. I had people calling that were fifth cousins removed."[68]

Once the Super Bowl started, it seemed like the rest of the Bengals were just as confounded by the pre-game hype and non-football tasks because they appeared they weren't ready for their time on the biggest football stage of them all as the 49ers jumped out to a 20-0 halftime lead. Wilson and the rest of the Bengals offense stormed back in the second half, setting post-season team records by scoring three touchdowns, completing 17 passes, amassing 17 first downs and 257 total net yards. The comeback fell short as Joe Montana and the 49ers held on for a 26-21 win and their first Super Bowl title. Despite missing out on earning the championship ring he wanted, Wilson wouldn't trade his Super Bowl experience for anything.

"It's amazing once you get there and play," Wilson has said about his only Super Bowl appearance. "That's something that nobody can take away from you. It's something you'll always have."[69]

Wilson went onto start at right tackle for the Bengals for another four years after the Super Bowl season but, unfortunately, the team did not attain the success it achieved in 1981, making the playoffs only once, a quick and early exit in the strike-shortened 1982 season. After the 1985 season, Wilson was traded to the Seattle Seahawks where he continued be reliable and durable, starting in all 60 games he played with the Seahawks. Following the 1989 season, Wilson retired from the NFL after 12 years in which, incredibly, he played in 174 out of a possible 184 games, starting an even more remarkable 172 of those games.

In 114 of those 174 games, Wilson wore a Bengals uniform and in the process became one of the best offensive lineman in team history. In his eight seasons as a starting left and right tackle, the Bengals had their most successful season in team history to that point, relying on a burgeoning offense that would become a force in the league over the next 10 years. From 1978-1985, a time when explosive offenses began to take shape throughout the league, the Bengals finished in the top half of the NFL in total offense and passing offense six times (1978, 1981-1985), points scored five times (1979, 1981, 1982, 1984, and 1985) and rushing offense four times (1979, 1980, 1984 and 1985). Wilson and the rest of the offensive line paved the way for one 1000-yard rushing season, 21 single game 100-yard rushers, two 3,000-yard passing seasons and 19 games where a quarterback threw for 300 or more yards. Without Wilson, one of the foundation pieces of the offensive line, there's no telling if the Bengals would have even made it to their first Super Bowl appearance.

To this day, whenever Wilson returns to the University of Georgia, he is still called "Moon Pie". "A lot of old time Georgia people only know me by that name," Wilson reasons.[70]

A lot of old time Bengals fans, on the other hand, only know Wilson as the working man who helped the franchise reach some of their great heights in team history. Seems only appropriate that to the fans he was nicknamed "Moon Pie" when you consider that Earl Mitchell Jr. of the Chattanooga Bakery Company always believed his now famous confection was a working man's lunch.

CHAPTER THIRTY-FOUR

ANTHONY MUÑOZ

The GOAT

It's easy now, in hindsight, to see why the Cincinnati Bengals used the third overall pick in the 1980 NFL Draft to select Michael Anthony Muñoz from the University of Southern California (USC). Inducted into the Pro Football Hall of Fame in his first year of eligibility in 1998, The Pro Football Historical Abstract described Muñoz, who played his entire 13-year NFL career with the Bengals, as someone who "played the game on a completely different level than those that came before him" and moving forward for "those that aspired to Muñoz's standard, none have reached it."[71] Looking back, you have to wonder if the Detroit Lions and the New York Jets, the two teams who selected ahead of Cincinnati in the 1980 Draft, sincerely regret passing on the impressive offensive lineman from Ontario, California.[1]

Hindsight, though, is a funny thing, a convenient way to recognize the realities of an event or a decision. Judging the Bengals' decision to draft Muñoz through this lens makes it appear obvious and smart. Truth be told, at the time of the 1980 Draft, choosing Muñoz was far from being labeled obvious or smart. In fact, most professional football executives and player

---

[1] With the number one overall pick, the Lions selected Billy Sims and the Jets followed by choosing wide receiver Johnny Lam Jones.

personnel experts believed the Bengals' selection was extremely risky and full of pitfalls. In some circles, their decision to draft the offensive tackle from USC was considered foolish.

The Bengals were not being derided because Muñoz didn't have the talent to play in the NFL. At 6'6" and 280 pounds, he was an offensive tackle with "the agility of a running back" and the skill level to become a starting offensive tackle at USC in his sophomore year in 1977. After his junior season in 1978, Muñoz was named to the All-Pac 10 conference team and was a named a pre-season All-American prior to his senior year in 1979. If that wasn't enough, he was also a member of the pitching staff on USC's 1978 National Championship baseball team.

The risk behind choosing Muñoz with such a high and valued draft pick was his questionable health and durability. Knee injuries limited him to a combined eight games played in his junior and senior seasons, placing his status as a high round draft choice in serious doubt, despite the talent and potential he obviously displayed as a four-year letterman at USC. Selecting him anywhere in the first round, much less with the third overall pick, was considered highly speculative and uncertain. Nevertheless, the Bengals remained resolute in their convictions and selected Muñoz with that fateful third overall pick in 1980, convinced they had chosen their left tackle of the foreseeable future. Thirteen NFL seasons later, it was obvious the Bengals' gamble had paid off. And then some.

The Bengals wasted no time in placing Muñoz into the starting lineup, in part because the team's offense and its offensive line were in dire need of a spark and an infusion of talent. In the previous two seasons, 1978 and 1979, the Bengals had a combined 8-24 record due mainly to an anemic offense that finished 18th in the NFL in rushing offense and 21st in points scored in 1978 while finishing 23rd in total offense and 24th in passing offense in 1979.

Another key reason why the Bengals elected to start their first round pick in 1980 in his rookie season was because the team's new head coach, Forrest Gregg, would immediately provide the teaching Muñoz needed to become a top-flight NFL offensive lineman. Gregg's credentials as an NFL offensive lineman primarily with the Vince Lombardi-led Green Bay Packers were impeccable: A five-time NFL champion, a three-time Super Bowl champion, a nine-time Pro Bowler, a seven-time member of the AP

All-Pro first team, a member of the NFL's 50th Anniversary All-Time team and a member of the Pro Football Hall of Fame since 1977. If Muñoz was going to develop into a player worthy of his high selection in the draft, having Gregg as his head coach during his formative NFL years certainly was a very good start.

Given their performance the previous two years, most NFL observers didn't question the Bengals' decision to start Muñoz in his rookie season. In their minds, what did they have to lose? What they doubted was Muñoz's durability, given the fact he had played in a very limited capacity in his junior and senior seasons and whether he had the talent or skill to establish himself as an offensive tackle worthy of the number three overall draft pick. Regardless of what their critics said, the Bengals, in essence, went all-in on Muñoz at the start of the 1980 season.

Needless to say, the gamble paid off and any questions about his durability were totally erased. By the time Muñoz ended his career, he had become the greatest Bengal of all time and arguably the greatest offensive tackle in the history of the NFL. Of the 200 games the Bengals played during career from 1980-1992, Muñoz played in 185 of them (92.5%), starting at left tackle in all but one of those 185 games.[1] His 185 games played as a Bengal is the fifth most in team history and his 13 seasons in a Cincinnati uniform places him in a tie for fourth most in club history. According to his former teammate, defensive end Alfred Williams, it was easy to see why Muñoz hardly missed a snap in his NFL career. According to Williams, his work ethic was second to none.

"When practice started, I'd see him running a mile to get warmed up," Williams said in an interview with Adam Schefter of The Denver Post. "Then he'd come back and do the conditioning afterward with everyone else. He was amazing to watch."[72]

Football observers, such as The Pro Football Historical Abstract, who ranked Muñoz as the 12th best offensive lineman in NFL history, believes it was his ability to have game come to him that led to his long and consistent career. "Rather than trying to counter their moves with his own technique, Muñoz would simply back off after the initial contact and let

---

[1] Muñoz missed the majority of those 15 games in 1992 when he was only able to start and play in eight of the team's 16 games because of knee and shoulder injuries.

the defender do his thing," The Abstract wrote. "Then he would pounce, using his quickness and agility to get right back in the guy's face and take him where he wanted him to go."[73]

The best explanation for Muñoz's longevity, however, may come not from a former teammate, coach or opponent but instead from his wife, DeDe. "I don't see any contrast between what he does and the way he is," she once observed. "Ever watch him? It's an artistic way of playing the offensive line. He makes it look easy."[74]

From the moment he took his first snap at left tackle to open the 1980 season, Muñoz not only anchored the Bengals offensive line for the next 13 seasons but he helped the franchise develop and create one of the premier NFL offenses of the 1980s. Unlike most teams of that era, the Bengals offense dominated in both the passing and running games, with Muñoz spearheading the effort.

Whether it was Ken Anderson or Boomer Esiason at quarterback, Muñoz was the centerpiece of an offensive line that allowed Anderson and Esiason to throw for 3,000 or more yards in a season seven times (1981, 1985-1990), 34 games where they passed for 300 or more yards and three seasons of 32 (1989), 31 (1985) and 30 (1981) touchdown passes, marks which rank tied for second, fourth and fifth respectively in team history. With Muñoz ensconced at left tackle, Anderson was responsible for 3,995 net yards passing in 1981, the third best in team history, while Esiason accumulated 3,957 net yards passing in 1986.

In 1982, the Bengals averaged 259.89 net yards passing per game, the best in team history. Muñoz himself contributed to the success of the passing game during this time by catching seven passes for 18 yards and four touchdown receptions. In the 13 seasons with Muñoz at the critical pass protection position of left tackle, the Bengals finished in the top half of the NFL in passing offense 10 times, finishing as high as third in 1981, 1982 and 1986.

As impressive as the passing game was from 1980-1992, the running games, the facet of the offense that linemen take the most pride in dictating and controlling, was just as, if not even more commanding. Using a mix of primary running backs such as Pete Johnson, James Brooks, Ickey Woods and Harold Green, Muñoz, who according to The Pro Football Historical Abstract, could "block straight on, he could pull and trap, he could do it all", led a running game that featured six seasons with a 1000-yard or more rusher and 47 games where a running back ran for 100 yards or more.

The sheer numbers prove that the best rushing offense in Bengals team history occurred during Muñoz's tenure on the offensive line. It was a running game that still holds the top three seasons in team history in rushing touchdowns (27 in 1988, 24 in 1983 and 24 in 1986), net yards rushing (2,710 in 1988, 2,533 in 1986 and 2,483 in 1989) and average yards per rushing attempt (4.862 in 1986, 4.813 in 1988 and 4.694 in 1989).

Not only did the rushing offense monopolize the team record book during Muñoz's 13 seasons, but it occupied the upper echelon of the yearly NFL rushing offense rankings as well. Ten times from 1980-1992, the Bengals ended the year in the top half of the NFL in rushing offense, finishing second in 1986 and leading the league in 1988 and 1989. The reason for this dominance was simple, according to The Pro Football Historical Abstract.

"From 1986-1989, the Bengals had the league's most productive running game," wrote The Abstract. "And Muñoz was the primary reason."[75]

Combine the production of both the passing and rushing offenses when Muñoz commanded the left tackle position and it should come as no surprise that the Bengals had one of the league's top total offenses and arguably the best in team history. The five best seasons in team history in first downs accrued (361 in 1981, 351 in 1988, 348 in 1986, 348 in 1989 and 344 in 1985) and total net yards gained (6,490 in 1986, 6,101 in 1989, 6,057 in 1988, 5,968 in 1981 and 5,900 in 1985) both happened during the Muñoz era. It was an offense that overpowered most of its opponents as reflected by the eleven seasons it ranked in the top half of the NFL in total offense, including finishing third over in 1985 and 1989, second overall in 1981 and 1982 and leading the league in 1986 and 1988.

All of those high powered offensive statistics compiled during the 1980s and 1990s would have been mere window dressing if the Bengals didn't turn those numbers into points on the scoreboard. Fortunately, they did, and they did it in record setting fashion. Those offenses have three of the top four seasons in points scored in team history, including the fourth most in 1981 (421) and the top two season in 1988 (448) and 1985 (441) respectively. The 61 points Muñoz and his teammates on offense scored against the Houston Oilers on December 17, 1989 is tied for the most points scored in a single game in team history. They also hold three of the top four seasons in Cincinnati history in total touchdowns, highlighted by the 59 they scored in 1988, the most in team history. Their ability to put points on the board placed them in the top half of the NFL in points scored in eight of Muñoz's thirteen seasons, leading the league in 1988 and finishing third in 1981, 1985 and 1986.

Thanks in large part to the efforts of Muñoz and the rest of the offense, the Bengals experienced their most sustained success in franchise history. In his time as the team's starting left tackle, Muñoz was a member of three AFC Central Division championship teams (1981, 1988 and 1990) and one additional post-season appearance in 1982. The 12 victories the Bengals achieved in both 1981 and 1988 are tied for the most games won in a season in team history. Coincidentally, those two seasons also marked the two times the Bengals appeared in the Super Bowl, allowing Muñoz to be only one of six individuals to play in both of Cincinnati's Super Bowl appearances. Even though the Bengals lost both of those Super Bowl games to the San Francisco 49ers, Muñoz was part of multiple offenses that set several post-season team records.

In a 1982 wild card playoff loss to the New York Jets on January 9, 1983, the Ken Anderson led offense set the team post-season record for net yards passing in a game with 333 yards. Led by this punishing run blocking technique, Muñoz helped the running back trio of Woods, Brooks and Stanley Wilson gain a team post-season record of 254 net yards rushing against the Seattle Seahawks in a 21-13 victory in a 1988 AFC divisional playoff game on December 31, 1988. The Bengals offense really exploded in the 1990 post-season when they scored five touchdowns and 41 points, both post-season team records, in a 41-14 dismantling of the Houston Oilers in an AFC wild card matchup on January 6, 1991.

1990 also marked the last time Muñoz played in the post-season with the Bengals as the team went a combined 8-24 the next two seasons. After the 1992 season in which he only played eight games due to injuries, the Bengals released Muñoz in 1993. He attempted to reunite with his former head coach in Cincinnati, Sam Wyche, who had just been hired by the Tampa Bay Buccaneers as their head coach in 1992 by signing with the

Bucs in 1993. Unfortunately, the Buccaneers released Muñoz prior to the start of the 1993 season, and instead of pursuing options with another NFL team, he chose to retire and end his professional football career. By that point, he had nothing left to prove. After 13 years of play in the NFL, he had cemented his legacy as a Cincinnati Bengal and made the case for being the greatest left tackle in the history of the National Football League.

Muñoz's resume and list of achievements is unparalleled. His 11 Pro Bowl selections are the most by any Cincinnati Bengal and is tied for fourth most by any player in NFL history. He was elected first team AP All-Pro nine times and on two other occasions second team AP All-Pro. He was selected the NFL Alumni Lineman of the Year and the National Football League Players Association Lineman of the Year four times and in 1981, 1987 and 1989 he was tabbed the NFL's Offensive Lineman of the Year. He was chosen as an offensive lineman on both the NFL's 1980s All-Decade Team and the league's 75ht Anniversary All-Time Team.

In 1989, he received Athletes in Action's Bart Starr Man of the Year Award, given to the NFL player who best exemplifies outstanding character and leadership in the home, on the field and in the community. In 1991, the NFL named him the Walter Payton Man of the Year for his excellence on the field and his volunteer and charity work off the field. In their lists of the 100 Greatest Players in NFL History, The Sporting News ranked Muñoz 17th and the NFL Network placed him 12th on theirs. In both instances, he was the highest ranked offensive lineman. Any doubts about Muñoz's place in NFL history were erased when he was inducted into the Pro Football Hall of Fame in his first year of eligibility in 1998.

Even more important than the accolades he received was the respect and admiration Muñoz earned from his coaches, his peers and his opponents. "Anthony always makes the right adjustments," his offensive line coach in Cincinnati, Jim McNally told Sports Illustrated. "[His] only negative is that he has no negatives." His head coach from 1984-1991, Sam Wyche believed "if pro sports could point to one guy who would be the ideal to look up to, Anthony would be it. All of us try to set examples until something goes wrong, and then we reveal our true selves. Anthony's real self is the one the rest us try to be."[76]

The quarterback he protected for eight seasons, including his MVP season in 1988, Boomer Esiason, saw first-hand the greatness of his left tackle. "If I were as good at my position as Anthony is at his," Esiason once said, "then I'd be 10 times better than Joe Montana."[77]

Those who played against him marveled at his athleticism. "He has the best feet of any tackle I've gone against," said Houston Oiler defensive end William Fuller. "Because he has such great hand-foot coordination you never catch him out of position."[78] Fellow Hall of Famer, defensive end Bruce Smith, was more succinct.

"There are no comparisons between him and other tackles," Smith said during his own time as a dominant defender. "He's proven it year after year that he's the best."[79]

Trying to encapsulate Muñoz's impact on the football field in a short sentence or two is in many respects a fruitless exercise. It simply won't do justice to his 13-year NFL career. Nevertheless, the NFL Alumni Association came about as close as anyone could after one of the four times Muñoz was named their Lineman of the Year.

"The NFL has three levels of offensive linemen," the Alumni Association said in a statement. "The bottom rung is for players aspiring to make the Pro Bowl. The next step is for those who have earned all-star status. Then there's Anthony Muñoz. He's alone at the top."[80]

To the city of Cincinnati and Bengals fans everywhere, there's an even more apt description—Michael Anthony Muñoz: The Cincinnati Bengals Greatest of All Time.

CHAPTER THIRTY-FIVE

ROSS BROWNER

The Swimmer Gone Astray

Looking back, it's hard to believe that when he was a youngster growing up in Warren, Ohio in the late 1960s, Ross Browner was more interested in swimming and diving than any other sport. At the time it seemed logical since, according to Browner, he loved it. "I practically grew up at the Warren YMCA," Browning remembers. "I competed as a swimmer and a diver. I put a lot of time into the sport."[81]

But as Browner grew into his early teenage years, his focus began to change. It was a transformation that would become very fortuitous to the Cincinnati Bengals organization nearly 10 years later. It was a change made out of necessity and to a certain degree, desire.

"It was like this," Browner once described. "All my brothers and friends were playing football in our side yard. I didn't want to get left behind. Plus, I was noticing that the girls were going for the football players."[82]

It was at this point in his life when Browner decided to trade his swimsuit and goggles for shoulder pads and a helmet. Foregoing his chance to make his mark in a swimming pool or the diving well, Browner recalls football as just a routine, but says, "...then all of a sudden it became a passion."[83]

And so began the football life of Browner, one of the most dominant defensive players of his time and an integral part in the history of the Cincinnati Bengals.

Browner's talents on the football field first became evident during his time at Warren Western Reserve High School. In his senior year in 1972, he was named to the first team Ohio AAA All-State squad at defensive end. His play at Western Reserve caught the eye of legendary college head coach Ara Parseghian and his current employer, the iconic football program at the University of Notre Dame. Parseghian knew as soon as he saw Browner that he wanted him in a Fighting Irish uniform.

"It was very apparent that this guy was going to be something special," Parseghian once said about his recruitment of Browner.[84]

Parseghian's assessment of Browner's ability proved prescient. More importantly for Irish fans, they got to witness first hand early on what their head coach had seen. Initially recruited to play tight end, Browner was moved to the other side of the line of scrimmage and the Irish's starting defensive end his freshman year in 1973, helping Notre Dame to their first National Championship since 1966. Even though he was just playing his first year of college football, Notre Dame offensive coordinator, Tom Pagna, knew Browner was the real deal.

"Ross had all the tools—size, agility, speed and toughness," Pagna recalled. "He was a prototype defensive end."[85] Browner wasted no time showing his athleticism and skill when in the first game of the 1973 season against Northwestern, he blocked a punt and in the process broke the punter's leg. By the end of the season, he had made 68 tackles, third best on the team.

After being suspended by the university for one year following the 1973 season,[1] Browner returned to the team and the starting lineup in 1975. Over the next three seasons, not only did Browner lead the Irish defense from his end position but by the time his collegiate career was finished, he had established himself as one of the best players in the history

---

[1] Along with five other players, including two of his roommates and teammates, Browner was accused of raping a female student on campus. Even though the student refused to press charges, the university took disciplinary action. If not for the lobbying by Parseghian to the school's president, Father Theodore Hesburgh, Browner and his teammates could have easily been expelled instead of serving a one-year suspension.

of college football. In his junior season in 1976, Browner was a unanimous All-American defensive end, named the UPI Lineman of the Year and was the winner of the annual Outland Trophy, the award presented by the Football Writers Association of America to the best college football interior lineman in the country.

His performance in that year's Gator Bowl in which Notre Dame defeated Penn State 20-9, eventually earned him a spot in the Gator Bowl Hall of Fame in 1999. Browner and the rest of the Irish entered his 1977 senior season with high expectations and neither he nor the rest of the rest the team disappointed.

Browner dominated the college football landscape in his senior season, and to many college football historians was the best player in the country in 1977. He was once again a unanimous All-American and named the UPI Lineman of the Year. He received the Rotary Lombardi Award as the best college football lineman or linebacker and the Maxwell Award as the best college football player in the nation, the first lineman ever to win the award. He also placed fifth in the Heisman Trophy voting, a rare occurrence for a defensive lineman, and was selected to play in two college all-star games, the 1978 Japan Bowl and the 1978 Hula Bowl. Meanwhile, the Irish won their second National Championship during Browner's tenure when they defeated Earl Campbell and the Texas Longhorns, 38-10, in the 1978 Cotton Bowl.

Five years after arriving in South Bend, Indiana, Browner left Notre Dame as one of the school's greatest players and one of college football best defensive ends ever. In his four years as a starter, the Irish went 39-7 and won two National Championships. He still holds the school records for tackles for minus yardage in a season (28 for 230 yards) and the career marks for tackles by a front four lineman (340), tackles for minus yardage (77 for 515 yards) and fumbles recovered (12). His career stat line includes 10 passes deflected, two blocked kicks, two safeties and one touchdown. Browner was selected as one of Notre Dame's 55 Greatest Players Since 1953 by USA Today's 2010-11 College Football Encyclopedia, named one of three defensive ends on Sports Illustrated's College All-Century Team[1],

---

[1]   The other two defensive ends were Florida's Jack Youngblood and Pittsburgh's Hugh Green.

and ranked number 84 on collegefootball.com's Top 100 players of all-time. In 1999, he was inducted into the College Football Hall of Fame.

Needless to say, Browner's performance at Notre Dame made him a prime candidate to play at the next level in the NFL. As the 1978 NFL Draft drew near, it wasn't a question of if he would be selected in the first round but a matter of how long he would have to wait before his name was announced.

One team with an early first round pick in 1978 who hoped Browner was still available when it came time for them to make their selection, were the Cincinnati Bengals. They had the eighth overall pick in the draft and if owner/general manager Paul Brown had his way, Browner would become a Bengal. In fact, to hear Browner tell it, Brown had decided six years earlier he was drafting the kid from Warren, Ohio as soon as he saw him play in a high school all-star game.

After Browner was selected by the Bengals with their first round pick in 1978, Paul Brown had something to say. Browner recalls, "He told me, 'Son, I kept my eye on you all these years. I drafted you because I didn't want to play against you.'"[86] Nine seasons later, it became clear why Brown wanted the Bengals offense to avoid playing against Browner at any cost.

Browner wasted no time in making an impact, becoming the Bengals' starting defensive right end in his rookie season in 1978 and leading the team in sacks (6.5), forced fumbles (2) and fumble recoveries (3). It was a performance trend he would continue over the next eight seasons in Cincinnati as he led the team in sacks three more times (1979, 1985 and 1986) and forced fumbles four more times (1981, 1982, 1984 and 1986). He also led all of the Bengals defensive linemen in solo and total tackles three times (1980-1982), passes defended four times (1980, 1981, 1983 and 1984) and forced fumbles twice (1983 and 1986).

Unfortunately, Browner's consistent performance failed to translate into any sustained success for the Bengals themselves. Cincinnati went 65-72 in his nine years with the franchise, including six seasons where the team finished at or below .500. Despite the lack of winning seasons, Browner and the rest of the defense did their best to keep the Bengals competitive. From 1978-1986, the nine seasons Browner started at right defensive end, the Bengals finished in the top half of the NFL in total defense (1978, 1980, 1981, 1983 and 1984) and rushing defense (1980-1984) five times and points allowed four times (1978, 1980, 1981 and 1983).

Statistically, the 1982 and 1983 seasons stand out in particular. The 1982 defense holds the team record for fewest points allowed in a season (177), fewest total net yards allowed in a season (2,893)[1] and ended the year with the third best rushing defense in the NFL. In 1983, the Bengals had the NFL's number one ranked total defense and finished tied for second as the league's best rushing defense. They also allowed only 270.44 net yards per game in 1983, the fourth lowest in team history.

But by far the best season for Browner and the rest of the Bengals was 1981, a year that culminated in the franchise's first ever Super Bowl appearance. After finishing the regular season with a 12-4 record and an AFC Central Division Championship, the Bengals defeated the Buffalo Bills 28-21, in the AFC divisional Round and the San Diego Chargers, 27-7, in the AFC Championship to earn a berth in the Super Bowl against the San Francisco 49ers. The Bengals lost to Joe Montana and the 49ers, 26-21, in Super Bowl XVI but not because of Browner's play. Playing in what he later considered, "the most magnificent game I've ever played in my life",[87] Browner had one sack and, at the time, set the record for most tackles by a defensive lineman in a Super Bowl, with nine. He would play in one more playoff game in 1982, finishing his NFL post-season career with 26 solo tackles for an average of 6.5 per game and 32 total tackles for an average of 8.0 per game.

At the end of the 1984 season, like many NFL players during that time, Browner was lured by the big money contracts being offered by the upstart United States Football League (USFL). He signed with the Houston Gamblers for the 1985 season which began on February 9, a little more than a month after the end of the Bengals 1984 season. Once the Gamblers season ended, the organization determined they could no longer sustain operations. In fact, during the 1985 season, they had trouble making payroll, needing an advance from the league to simply go to the playoffs. Ownership sold the team's assets to Donald Trump's New

---

[1]   It is worth noting that due to an NFL player strike, only nine regular season games were played in 1982.

Jersey Generals, essentially merging both teams. In the end, the Gamblers/ Generals never played another down as the league folded before the start of the 1986 season.

Apparently seeing the writing on the wall, Browner decided to return to the NFL for the 1985 season. The Bengals welcomed him back with open arms and he returned to his starting right defensive end position. He would go on to play two more seasons in Cincinnati before joining the Green Bay Packers in 1987. After playing 11 games with the Packers in 1987, Browner retired from the NFL.

In his retirement, Browner was asked how he approached playing in the trenches in a game he chose as a teenager over the daily grind of competing lap-after-lap in the YMCA swimming pool. His response harkened back to the violent battles of the Roman Empire and the days of mortal hand-to-hand combat.

"That's what I always thought of it as," Browner said. "Just being a destroyer and go in there as a gladiator, just really approaching the game where I have to be the conqueror, or I have to be the victor in this whole fight against offensive and defensive lineman and this battle against our opponent.

"I went in with a total mentality of going in and being a destroyer of offenses."[88]

In his nine seasons as a Bengal, Brower was just that. A destroyer of offenses. He finished his career in Cincinnati with 381 solo tackles and 516 total tackles, an average of 42.3 solo tackles and 57.3 total tackles per season. He also had 17 passes defended, 13 forced fumbles, 11 fumble recoveries and one interception. In 127 games played (he started in 121 of them), Browner's 59 career sacks as a Bengals is the third most in team history. It was a period of dominant play from the defensive end position that earned Browner a spot on the franchise's 40th Anniversary Team in 2007.

And to think Browner's football career almost never happened. For if you would have asked him about his career aspirations back in his younger days in Warren, Ohio, he probably would have talked about his dreams of becoming an Olympic swimmer or diver. Thankfully for the Bengals and their fans, Browner's brothers and perhaps more importantly, the girls in his Warren, Ohio neighborhood, did not hang out at the Warren YMCA but at the football field instead.

CHAPTER THIRTY-SIX

CRIS COLLINSWORTH

The Second Choice

As the Cincinnati Bengals prepared for the 1981 NFL Draft, the primary decision makers for the team, owner/general manager Paul Brown, and head coach Forrest Gregg, knew they faced a critical juncture in the relatively short history of the franchise. After making the playoffs in three of their first eight years of existence, the Bengals had not qualified for the post-season since 1975. In the previous three seasons, they had gone a combined 14-34 under three different head coaches, including Gregg, who had just finished his first season the year before with a record of 6-10.

Despite the sub-par record in 1980, both Brown and Gregg believed they were close to turning things around in Cincinnati. The Bengals had won three of their last four games in 1980 and their first round draft choice from 1980, offensive tackle Anthony Muñoz, was beginning to emerge as one of the premier offensive linemen in the NFL. Both men agreed that the Bengals needed a game-breaking wide receiver to help them get back to the playoffs and contend for a championship, a player who could stretch the field in Gregg's sophisticated passing game. After completing their scouting and due diligence of the draft eligible wide receivers, it seemed Brown and Gregg had settled on using the 10th overall pick in the 1981 Draft on University of Kansas senior wide receiver, David Verser.

Verser landed on the Bengals' radar thanks in large part to his final collegiate season in 1980 when he had 30 receptions for 576 yards and five touchdowns. He finished his career at Kansas with 77 receptions for 1,476 yards, 11 touchdowns and a total of 1,607 yards from scrimmage. As draft day drew closer, most experts were projecting the Bengals to use their first round draft choice to select the Kansas wide receiver.

The decision to select Verser with their first pick was not, however, unanimous amongst the rest of the coaching staff inside the Bengals war room. Wide receivers coach and former University of Florida halfback, Lindy Infante, agreed the team needed a receiver. But instead of choosing Verser, he lobbied hard for the team to select a fellow Gator, senior wide out Cris Collinsworth.

Alumni favoritism aside, Infante had good reason to believe Collinsworth was worthy of the Bengals' first round selection. Born in Dayton, Ohio, Collinsworth had the athletic pedigree and personal resume similar to many NFL first round draft choices. His father, Abraham Lincoln Collinsworth[1], was a legendary basketball player in the state of Kentucky, first as one of the top scorers in Kentucky High School Athletic Association history and then as a member of the University of Kentucky's infamous "Fiddling Five" 1958 National Championship team.

Abe's son Cris began making his own mark at Astronaut High School in Titusville, Florida, where he was a four-sport star in baseball, football, basketball and track. As a senior, he was named a high school All-American quarterback and was the Florida High School Athletic Association's Class 3A 100-yard dash state champion in 1976.

He parlayed his football talents into a scholarship at the University of Florida where head football coach Doug Dickey recruited him to play quarterback. In his first game as a Florida quarterback in the fall of 1977 against the Rice Owls, Collinsworth threw a 99-yard touchdown pass to Derrick Gaffney, tying the mark for the longest touchdown pass in NCAA history. Unfortunately, the long TD pass was not enough for Dickey to keep Collinsworth as one of this quarterbacks because he decided to switch to an I-formation offense the following season. According to Collinsworth, losing his spot as one of the team's signal callers was necessitated by being

---

[1]   Collinsworth's father was given his name because he was born on the same day, February 12, as President Lincoln.

personally inflicted with "a disease called 'lack of spiral'".[89] Dickey moved his former quarterback to wide receiver for the 1978 season, a transition Collinsworth remembers being more than a little rough.

"When I first switched over, about the only thing I could catch was my breath," Collinsworth said in a 1981 interview. "I swear it was two weeks before I could catch the routine pass. They called me 'Old Stone Hands'."[90]

Fortunately for the Gators, Collinsworth quickly went from "Old Stone Hands" to "Old Sure Hands". In his first season as a wide receiver in 1978, he was the team's leading receiver (39 receptions, 745 yards receiving, 19.1 yards per reception and nine touchdowns), selected first team AP and UPI All-SEC and named a second team AP All-American. He even returned 15 kickoffs at an average of 26.3 yards per return that included a 97-yard return for a touchdown against LSU on October 7, 1978. He followed up his sophomore season with an equally impressive junior year in 1979. He once again led the team in receiving (41 receptions, 593 yards, 14.5 yards per reception and two touchdowns), named first team AP and UPI All-SEC and an honorable mention selection on the AP All-American team.

Sadly, the Gators were unable to match Collinsworth's performance in 1979 as they went 0-10-1 under first year head coach, Charley Pell, who had replaced Dickey after the 1978 season. Worse yet, the Gators were combined 4-17-1 in the two years Collinsworth was a wide receiver. Hardly anyone expected Florida to improve in 1980, much less make noise in the uber-competitive Southeastern Conference. Much to everyone's surprise, the Gators vastly improved from the year before, finishing the season 8-4 and earning a berth in the Tangerine Bowl, the school's first bowl appearance since 1976. It also marked, at the time, the biggest one-year turnaround in NCAA Division I football history. It was an unprecedented reversal of fortune, and to hear Pell tell it, it never would have happened without his team captain Collinsworth and his "unique ability to give 100 percent all the time." In Pell's eyes, Collinsworth displayed "the best leadership I've ever been associated with."[91]

For the third straight year, Collinsworth led the Gators in receiving (40 receptions, 599 yards, 15.0 yards per reception and three touchdowns)[1]

---

[1] Collinsworth also led the SEC in receiving in 1980.

and was an AP and UPI first team All-SEC wide receiver. He was voted first team All-American by the Newspaper Enterprise Association (NEA) and second team All-American by the AP and UPI. In the school's first bowl game in four years, Collinsworth's 166 receiving yards in Florida's 35-20 victory over Maryland in the Tangerine Bowl is the third most by a Gator in a bowl game. As if that wasn't enough, he also earned first team Academic All-American honors in 1980.

Collinsworth finished his four-year letterman career at Florida with 120 receptions for 1,937 yards, five 100-yard receiving games and 14 touchdowns. He also had two rushing touchdowns and 30 kickoff returns for 728 yards (24.2 yards per return) and one touchdown. His 34 consecutive games with a reception from September 16, 1978 to December 20, 1980 ranks second in school history. After his football career was completed, Collinsworth was inducted into the University of Florida Hall of Fame as a Gator Great in 1991, ranked as the 12th best Gator football player of all-time by The Gainesville Sun in 2008 and named by the USA Today's 2010-11 College Football Encyclopedia as one of five wide receivers on Florida's 55 Greatest Players Since 1953. More importantly, his play at Florida put him in a position to have an NFL assistant head coach and former Gator to push hard for his employer to draft Collinsworth in the first round of the 1981 NFL Draft.

Based upon his performance at Florida, Infante had no problem making the case inside Bengals headquarters as to why they should take Collinsworth with their 10th overall pick in the 1981 Draft. It is safe to assume, however, that Infante was met with double-barrel resistance regarding Collinsworth's draft stock, one spoken and the other unspoken. The obvious negative attribute was Collinsworth's size. At a height of 6'5" and a weight of 192 pounds, many members of the coaching staff, particularly Gregg, believed Collinsworth was too small and lean to take the kind of punishment he would receive from NFL defenders while still providing the kind of production they expected from a number one wide receiver.

The other objection to selecting Collinsworth with a high draft choice was not so easily discussed. Simply put, Collinsworth was a white man trying to play what had been labeled a black man's position. It was a stereotype Collinsworth brushed aside.

"I see myself as someone who has to grit his teeth and scratch for everything he does," Collinsworth told Sports Illustrated in 1981. "But I don't believe you're fast or slow because you're black or white and you don't have to pattern yourself after somebody your own color."[92]

Infante made a strong argument for Collinsworth's selection in the first round and as draft day approached he hoped he had convinced both Brown and Gregg to choose the Gator wide receiver over Verser. By the time Day 1 of the draft was over the verdict was in and Infante had received some good news and some bad news. The bad news was that Infante had been outvoted. With the 10th overall pick, the Bengals chose Verser. The good news was that the wide receivers coach would have a chance to work with the player he wanted the Bengals to draft in the first round, when they selected Collinsworth in the second round with the 37th overall pick. The Bengals believed they had hit the jackpot by drafting two of the best wide receivers in the draft. Meanwhile, Collinsworth was simply hoping to secure a steady paycheck.

"I was more scared about making the team than anything else," Collinsworth said during the 1981 season. "They (Bengals) picked Verser and they already had Isaac Curtis, Pat McInally and Steve Kreider. There weren't many openings left. I think the fear of being rejected helped me a lot."[93]

In spite of his own self-doubts entering training camp, it was clear early on that Collinsworth would not have to worry about making the Bengals roster. In fact, after watching him play and practice, Collinsworth's new teammates knew he was something special. Among those who took notice were fellow wide receiver McInally, who called Collinsworth, "a natural" and quarterback Jack Thompson who stated, "He'll sell out his body to get the ball." Even his head coach, Gregg, had to retract his previous misgivings about Collinsworth's size and durability.

"I was wrong," Gregg said during the 1981 season. "After the first pre-season game, I knew he was tough enough. He gets laid out, but he bounces back up."[94]

By the time the Bengals opened their regular season in 1981, Collinsworth had turned those early positive impressions into a spot in the starting lineup at wide receiver against the Seattle Seahawks in Week 1 of the season. It marked the beginning of an incredible rookie season for Collinsworth and an equally remarkable season for the Bengals. Collinsworth finished his first season with what would be a career-high 67 receptions for a team best 1,009 yards and eight touchdowns. Those eight receiving touchdowns not only led all Bengals wide receivers but it was also the eighth most in the NFL. It was a breakout season that garnered Collinsworth nationwide attention. He was named second team UPI All-AFC, second team AP All-NFL, selected to the Pro Bowl and graced the cover of Sports Illustrated, the first Bengal ever to do so.[1]

Collinsworth's surprisingly exceptional rookie season coincided with a landmark season for the Bengals. They finished the regular season 12-4, winning their first division title since 1973. They qualified for the playoffs for the first time since 1975 and appeared in the franchise's first ever Super Bowl. The Bengals' milestone 1981 season was due in large part to an offensive explosion led by NFL MVP, quarterback Ken Anderson, and his rookie wide receiver from the University of Florida.

The 1981 offense established the standard by which all future Bengals offenses are measured and still maintains several spots in the team's record book. They own top-five team season records for first downs (1st with 361), total net yards passing (3rd with 3,995 yards), points scored (4th with 421), total net yards (4th with 5,968 yards), net yards passing per game (4th with 249.69 yards per game) and total touchdowns (tied for 5th with 51). They finished second in the NFL in total offense and third in passing offense and points scored.

The only thing missing was a Super Bowl championship. Collinsworth did his part to bring a title to Cincinnati, catching five passes for 107 yards against the San Francisco 49ers in Super Bowl XVI. Unfortunately, one of those receptions, a 19-yard pass from Anderson to the 49ers five yard line, ended in a lost fumble after being tackled by defensive back Eric Wright. The 49ers recovered the fumble at the eight yard line and proceeded to march 92 yards for a touchdown and a 14-0 lead. It was a deficit from

---

[1]   Collinsworth's more highly touted rookie teammate, Verser, failed to make a similar impact. Verser did not start a single game and had only six receptions in 1981. In the end, he became one of the team's biggest draft busts, playing only four seasons in Cincinnati and retiring from the NFL in 1987 with a total of 23 receptions and three touchdowns.

which Collinsworth and the Bengals never recovered, losing 26-21 in their inaugural Super Bowl appearance.

Over the next six seasons, Collinsworth remained one of the Bengals' usual starting wide receivers while becoming the primary target for Anderson and his successor at quarterback, Boomer Esiason.[1] From 1982-1987, Collinsworth led the Bengals in receptions and receiving yards five times (1982-1986) and receiving touchdowns three times (1983, 1984 and 1986). He finished in the top ten in the NFL in 1982 in receptions (4th with 49), receiving yards (4th with 700 yards) and receiving yards per game (4th with 77.8 yards per game); in 1983 in yards per reception (10th with 17.1 yards per catch) and receiving yards per game (5th with 80.7 yards per game); in 1985 in receiving yards (8th with 1,125 yards); and in 1986 in receiving touchdowns (5th with 10 touchdowns). During this six-year stretch, he averaged 56.2 receptions, 910.3 receiving yards and 4.5 touchdowns per season.

Even though the Bengals only made the playoffs once in those six years, Collinsworth was recognized nationally as one of the game's top receivers. In 1982, he was named second team All-NFL by the Associated Press. In 1983, Pro Football Weekly and the UPI selected him first team All-AFC and the AP and NEA named him second team All-NFL. In 1985, he earned UPI second team All-AFC honors. He also was selected to two Pro Bowls in 1982 and 1983.

By the beginning of the 1988 season, Collinsworth lost his starting spot at wide receiver but he still contributed to a record setting offense and the franchise's second trip to the Super Bowl. Despite playing a part-time role, Collinsworth was part of an innovative offense that still holds the team records for points scored (448) and touchdowns (59) in a season and the third best season in total net yards gained (6,057). The Bengals used this offensive explosion to steamroll their way to Super Bowl XXIII against their previous Super Bowl opponent, the San Francisco 49ers.

But similar to what happened in their only other Super Bowl

---

[1]   Collinsworth's career in Cincinnati almost came to an abrupt end after just four years. Following the 1984 season, he signed a multi-year contract with the Tampa Bay Bandits of the USFL for the 1985 season. But when he failed a Bandits team physical because of a bad ankle, the contract was voided and Collinsworth returned to the Bengals for the 1985 season.

appearance, the Bengals fell just short to the 49ers, this time by the score of 20-16 when Joe Montana found wide receiver John Taylor open in the end zone for the game winning score with only 34 seconds left in the game. Collinsworth, who became one of six players to appear in both of the Bengals Super Bowl games, had three receptions for 40 yards but it wasn't enough. For the second time, he failed to leave a Super Bowl champion. Worst of all, the two losses had been by a combined nine points, creating an empty feeling that nearly thirty years later, Collinsworth still has a hard time forgetting.

"Honestly, there used to be there wasn't an hour that went by that I didn't think about it," Collinsworth said in a 2015 interview about the two Super Bowl losses. "Then there was probably not a day that went by I didn't think losing those two. Now, it's probably not a week that goes by that I didn't think about it. You always think about it."[95]

As it turned out, Super Bowl XXIII was Collinsworth's last NFL game, creating a unique set of career bookends that began with a Super Bowl season in his rookie year and finished with a second Super Bowl appearance in his final NFL game. In his 107-game regular season NFL career, all with the Bengals, and 90 of which he started, Collinsworth had 417 receptions for 6,698 yards and an average of 16.06 yards per reception, all of which rank fourth on the team's all-time receiving list. He finished with four 1000-yard receiving seasons and had 18 100-yard receiving games, the fifth most in team history. His 216 points scored, the result of his 36 touchdown receptions, is tied for 17th in team history and is tied for seventh amongst all Bengals wide receivers. He ended his career with a 67-53 regular season record, two AFC championships and three Pro Bowl selections.

As a starting wide receiver for the Bengals from 1981-1987, Collinsworth was part of several offenses that dominated the NFL and in some cases revolutionized the way the game was played. In each of those seven seasons, the Bengals finished in the top half of the NFL in total offense and passing offense, including having the number ranked offense in the league in 1986. The offense also ended up in the top half of the league in points scored five times, finishing as high as third on three different occasions (1981, 1985 and 1986).

Collinsworth's legacy with the Bengals does not end with just his regular season performance. Cincinnati made the playoffs three times in his eight seasons with the team and Collinsworth played a significant role in the team's post-season success during the 1980s. He is the Bengals' post-season leader in career receiving yards (354) and average yards per reception (16.86) and is second in career receptions (21). He holds the team's top two single playoff game performances in average yards per reception (21.40 vs San Francisco 49es in Super XVI and 17.14 on January 9, 1983 vs New York Jets) and his 120 receiving yards against the Jets on January 9, 1983 in a first-round playoff game is the second most in franchise post-season history.

But beyond his accomplishments on the football field, Collinsworth added to his iconic status with Bengals fans by his actions off the field. From the moment he arrived in Cincinnati in 1981, it became apparent Collinsworth had found a home and a city of football fans and non-football fans alike who embraced him as one of their own, even though he was, for the most part, a product of Florida. He resonated with football devotees with his fearlessness and his willingness to sacrifice his body to make a play. No single play personified this workman-like attitude more than when Collinsworth faced the Bengals arch rivals, the Pittsburgh Steelers, for the very first time. It was a play he vividly recalled in an interview later that season.

"My first catch against the Steelers was a crossing route—the kind where they see what kind of man you are, "Collinsworth said. "It's the kind of route all us honkies run. I just went out and put a little move on [Mel] Blount, and Kenny Anderson drilled the ball right in for about 22 yards. From then on, I was O.K. I had done stepped into the lion's den and came out alive."[96] The football fans of Cincinnati, known for their blue collar work ethic, immediately became forever enchanted.

Collinsworth also cast his blithe and intoxicating personality on those in town who had no interest in the city's NFL team. He was a breath of fresh air, a professional athlete who did not act like one, someone everyone could identify with or could easily hang out with at the neighborhood bar. Even though he spent his formative years in Florida, most people around Cincinnati considered Collinsworth one of their native sons, a reverence usually reserved for people who in fact were raised in the city, like Pete Rose, Roger Staubach or Barry Larkin.

The feeling of being at home in Cincinnati was something Collinsworth found mutual. After he retired from the NFL, he continued to live in the Greater Cincinnati area, earning a Juris Doctor from the University Of Cincinnati School Of Law and raising a family with his wife, Holly. He began a broadcasting career as a sports radio talk show host on Cincinnati's WLW, replacing former Bengals tight end, Bob Trumpy. Like he had done with his football skills at the University of Florida, he turned his talents behind the microphone into a career on the national stage. Fifteen Sports Emmys later, Collinsworth is the lead analyst for NBC's Sunday Night Football and one of the most recognized and respected sports television personalities in the country.

To the city of Cincinnati, and Bengals fans in particular, Collinsworth is simply known as one of, if not the best, wide receivers in team history. He is, to this day, one of the most popular and revered players ever to wear a Bengals uniform and is considered one of the main reasons why the team flourished in the 1980s.

And chances are, if you would have asked Forrest Gregg and Paul Brown back in 1981 which of their first two draft choices that year would reach these kind of heights, they probably would have said David Verser. Chances are, the thought that Cris Collinsworth would be that player, never crossed their mind.

Chances are, however, Lindy Infante knew it could have happened and thankfully he was on the Bengals staff in 1981, determined, like any other sound running back and wide receivers coach, not to let a talent like Collinsworth to slip through the team's hands.

Even if it was the team's second choice.

CHAPTER THIRTY–SEVEN

CARL PICKENS

The Forgotten Star

Any professional sports team with a history of 40 years or more has a period of time in their existence they wish they could completely erase. When George Steinbrenner purchased the New York Yankees in 1973, he inherited a team that had not won a World Series title since 1962 or an American League pennant since 1964, the longest gap between American League titles for the Yankees since 1920. From 1965-1972, the franchise had an un-Yankee like 636-649 record and even though Steinbrenner eventually restored the team's championship legacy, it took another three seasons after he bought the team for the Yankees to win an American League pennant. It took four seasons to capture a World Series crown, representing a 16-year drought between championships that most Yankee fans call "The Blackout in the Bronx".

Most people equate continued success in the NBA with the Boston Celtics, their 17 NBA titles accounting for nearly 25 percent of all of the league's championships and 21 conference titles justifying their label as the most successful franchise to date in the four traditional North American professional sports leagues. Celtic fans, however, lament the times between championship numbers 16 and 17, a period of 23 seasons in which Boston made the NBA Finals only twice and finished the season below .500 11 times, including a span of eight consecutive losing seasons from 1994-2001.

Prior to that championship dry spell, the longest the Celtics went without a winning a title was 13 seasons when they first entered the league in 1946.

Even the vaunted New England Patriots, the NFL franchise many consider the most successful team of the 21st Century, have not been immune to a stretch of seasons they and their fans would soon like to forget. After making their first ever Super Bowl appearance in 1985, the Patriots endured a 10-year stretch in which they finished with a combined 63-96 record (.396) that included a 1-15 season in 1990 before reaching their second Super Bowl in 1996.

So, it should come as no surprise that the Cincinnati Bengals, a professional football team with over 40 years of history, have experienced their own period they wished was only a bad dream but in reality was a nightmare. For the Bengals, their version of the Dark Ages began in 1991 and did not end until the 2003 season when they finished a cathartic 8-8. In the 12 seasons prior to that 2003 sense of relief season, the Bengals went a combined 55-137, a purgatorial-like .286 winning percentage, and a won/loss record that set several dubious team records for consecutive games lost, and lowest winning percentage in a season.[1] Cincinnati had only one season where they finished with a .500 record or better (8-8 in 1996), a span of bad football that cost three head coaches (David Shula, Bruce Coslet and Dick LeBeau) their jobs and caused a serious case of fan empathy.

But from under this shadow in the team's history, there emerged a bright spot wearing the Bengals' infamous orange and black. For eight seasons from 1992-1999, Carl Pickens was a fixture on the short lists of the best wide receivers in the game. Yet, unless you were one of the dwindling fans who followed the Bengals, or a fantasy football owner during this time, Pickens' accomplishments went relatively unnoticed. In fact, he is probably best remembered by most for the stir he created off the field at the end of his Bengals career, not by his performance on the field. And that is unfortunate because Pickens certainly put up the kind of numbers

---

[1]   Some of those records include most games lost in a season (14 in 2002), lowest winning percentage in a season (.125 in 2002), consecutive games lost (11 from 1992-1993), consecutive home games lost (11 from 1998-1999), consecutive road games lost (15 from 1992-1994) and consecutive games lost in one season (10, Games 1-10 in 1993)

which, had he played on a more successful team, would have placed him unquestionably as one of the best players in team history. As it is, he is a forgotten wide receiver who, at times, dominated his opponents and still remains statistically one of the best who played his position in team history.

Pickens first garnered national attention at Murphy High School, a small school in the Smoky Mountains of North Carolina. In addition to his wide receiver duties, Pickens played free safety at Murphy High, recording 15 interceptions in three seasons. But it was his play at wide receiver that had every major college football program knocking on his door. In his senior season in 1987, Pickens had 71 receptions and 24 touchdowns, earned Parade High School All-American honors and was named Mr. Football USA by ESPN Rise as the national player of the year. Needless to say, he was a highly prized recruit.

"You're talking about a guy who never came off the field in high school," the then- University of Tennessee wide receivers coach Kippy Brown said when talking about Pickens. "He punted. He returned punts. He returned kickoffs. He played free safety. He played wide receiver."[97]

Playing for Brown and the Volunteers seemed a logical choice for Pickens. He attended high school and lived just 100 miles from the University of Tennessee's campus in Knoxville, thereby giving his family the opportunity to see him play in college with little travel. More importantly, the Volunteers at the time was known as "Receivers U" because of the high grade wide outs such as Anthony Hancock, Willie Gault, Tim McGee and the five first-round picks in the previous eight NFL drafts they had recently produced. For Pickens, the choice was easy.

"Being a receiver," Pickens said when he signed with Tennessee, "why not go where the receivers are and be one of the best."[98]

After being red-shirted in 1988, Pickens began his freshman year in 1989 playing mostly on the defensive side as a free safety. He had four interceptions and was named the Defensive Most Valuable Player in Tennessee's 31-27 victory over Arkansas in the 1990 Cotton Bowl. Even though he was named as one of the defensive backs on the 1989 All-SEC Freshman Team, Pickens was not happy about the fact that he played sparingly at wide receiver, catching only seven passes for 81 yards and two touchdowns. Pickens openly expressed his displeasure of averaging only five snaps a game at wide receiver his freshman year, causing Brown to advise his young wide out that he needed to "learn to handle adversity better."[99]

Whether or not Pickens took his coach's word to heart is anybody's guess. But by his sophomore year in 1990, he had become the Volunteers number one receiver. Pickens led the SEC with 917 receiving yards, the 12th best in school history on 53 receptions and six touchdowns. He was named SEC Offensive Player of the Week thanks to his 201 receiving yards against Kentucky, and his 13 receptions against the then number one ranked team in the country, Notre Dame, remains a school record for most catches in a game. At the end of the season, Pickens had earned first-team AP, UPI and American Football Coaches Association (AFCA) All-SEC honors.

Pickens continued his stellar play in his junior season in 1991, once again leading the SEC with 877 receiving yards on 49 receptions and five touchdowns. He was named the SEC Offensive Player of the Week after catching four passes for 172 yards and two touchdowns in Tennessee's 30-21 victory over Auburn. He finished the season on the AP and AFCA's All-SEC first team squad and was selected first team All-American by the AFCA, The Football News, The Scripps-Howard Newspapers and The Gannett News Service. He also received second team All-American honors from the AP and the UPI.

Despite having another year of college eligibility, Pickens elected to forego his senior season and declared for the 1992 NFL Draft, closing out a college career that still ranks ninth in career receiving yardage (1,875), tenth in career kickoff return yards (777) and 12th in career all-purpose yards gained (2,848) in school history. A three-year letterman from 1989-1991, Pickens, who spent only two seasons as a full-time wide receiver, was named by the USA Today's 2010-11 College Football Encyclopedia as one of five wide receivers on the University of Tennessee's Greatest Players Since 1953. A brief college career notwithstanding, his head coach at Tennessee, college football Hall of Famer Johnny Majors, called Pickens "probably the most outstanding football talent I've had as far as all-round ability."[100]

As a testament to his enormous talent and potential, Pickens was slotted by most NFL organizations as an early round selection in the 1992 NFL Draft in spite of his short college career at wide receiver and his sometimes disruptive behavior off the field. One of those teams was the Cincinnati Bengals who were in the market for a wide out after the departure of seven-year veteran Eddie Brown following the 1991 season. When it came time for the Bengals to make their second round pick, Pickens was still available, so without hesitation, they selected him with the 34th overall pick.

With a dearth of high quality wide receivers on their roster to open the 1992 season, the Bengals inserted the rookie Pickens into the starting lineup. Better yet, he immediately made an impact. Starting 10 of the team's 16 games at wide receiver, Pickens had 26 receptions for 326 yards and one touchdown[1]. He also led the team with 18 punt returns for 229 yards and one touchdown for 95 yards against the Green Bay Packers on September 20.[2] His 12.7 punt return average for the season was the NFL's second highest in 1992. It was a performance so impressive that Pickens was named the Associated Press 1992 NFL Offensive Rookie of the Year.

Pickens followed up his strong rookie year with a solid second season in 1993. He finished with 43 receptions for 565 receiving yards and his six touchdown catches led all Bengals wide receivers. As the 1994 season approached, both the Bengals and Pickens himself expected him to have a breakthrough year.

But as the 1994 season reached the halfway point, Pickens and the Bengals had experienced anything but a breakthrough season. The Bengals lost their first seven games while Pickens struggled to produce, recording only 15 receptions for 216 yards and two touchdowns during the 0-7 start. Things didn't look to get any better in game eight of the season as the Bengals prepared to face the two-time defending Super Bowl champions, the Dallas Cowboys. As it would turn out, the game against the Cowboys

---

[1] His lone touchdown in 1992 was a dramatic one. His fourth quarter, game-tying, 23-yard touchdown reception with 59 seconds left against the Chicago Bears on ESPN's Sunday Night Football on November 8 enabled the Bengals to steal a 31-28 victory on the road at Soldier Field in Chicago.

[2] This game is known most notably for the debut of Brett Favre as the Packers starting quarterback of the future. After the starter, Don Majkowski injured his ankle in the third quarter, Favre led Green Bay on a 92-yard touchdown drive with 1:07 left in the game to lead the Packers to a 24-23 victory. The rest, as they say, is history.

would debut a new era for the Bengals and would mark the beginning of Pickens's run as a top flight NFL wide receiver.

After failing to achieve any kind of success with David Klingler or Erik Wilhelm starting at quarterback through the first seven games of the season, head coach David Shula named third-string quarterback, Jeff Blake, the starter against the Cowboys. Instead of the disaster many had predicted, Blake almost engineered a huge upset, completing 14 of 32 passes for 247 yards and two touchdowns in a close fought 23-20 loss. More importantly, the game against Dallas unveiled what would become a special relationship between Blake and Pickens.

"When I first got to Cincinnati, Carl and I hit it off right away," Blake recalled in 2015. "We had a lot in common, we hung out together, we ate together, we practiced together and we played together. That's why we were able to produce the way we did. If we didn't have that chemistry off the field, there is no way we would've had it on the field. You read each other's minds before the play, during the play and after the play. It made the game fun and exciting."[101]

For the remainder of the 1994 season, Pickens and Blake had fun at their opponents' expense and for the first time since 1990 made Bengals football exciting. Pickens finished the season leading the team in receptions (71), receiving yards (1,127) and touchdown catches (11) as the Bengals won three of their last eight games. His 11 touchdown receptions is tied for fourth most receiving touchdowns in a season in team history and was the third most in the NFL in 1994. He had five 100-yard receiving games in 1994, that included four consecutive games with 100 or more receiving yards, the second most in team history. Even with the slow start to the season, Pickens was named second team All-AFC by the UPI.

With Blake beginning his first full season as the Bengals starting quarterback in 1995, Pickens' statistical output continued to skyrocket. Once again Pickens had five 100 yard receiving games and led the team in receptions (99), receiving yards (1,234) and touchdown catches (17) as the team improved to 7-9. His 99 receptions rank third all-time in team history and was the 10th most in the NFL in 1995. His 17 touchdown receptions not only is the most in one season in team history and led the NFL in 1995, but is the fifth most touchdown receptions by a player in one season in NFL history. Pickens earned his first Pro Bowl selection in 1995 and was named first-team All-AFC by the UPI and Pro Football Weekly as well as second team All-NFL by the Associated Press.

Even though he had received national recognition, and as a consequence the full attention of his opponents because of his performance in 1994 and 1995, Pickens continued his dominant play in 1996. Just as he had done the previous two seasons, he led the team in receptions, receiving yards and touchdown catches in 1996 as the Bengals finished the year 8-8, their best season since 1990. His 100 receptions were the third most in the NFL in 1996 and it marked the first time a Bengals wide receiver had 100 or more catches in a single season. His 1,180 receiving yards was the eighth most in the NFL and his 12 touchdown receptions was the third most in the NFL--and is tied for the second most in a season in team history. Pickens' ability to dominate a game was on full display in Week 13 of the season against the Atlanta Falcons. He torched the Falcons secondary for 11 receptions, 176 receiving yards and three touchdowns in a 41-31 Bengals victory, a performance that earned him the AFC Offensive Player of the Week. At the end of the season, Pickens was named to his second Pro Bowl and was selected first team All-AFC by Pro Football Weekly and the UPI. He also received first team All-NFL honors from the Pro Football Writers and second team All-NFL from the Associated Press.

Over the following three seasons, Pickens maintained his successful and productive play, solidifying his partnership with Blake and his sidekick at the other wide receiver position, Darnay Scott. From 1997-1999, Pickens strong-armed his opponents with an average of nearly 64 (63.6) receptions and over 818 (818.3) receiving yards and five (5.3) touchdowns per season, headlined by the 1998 season when he led the team with 82 receptions and 1,023 receiving yards. One group of opponents he particularly harassed were the Pittsburgh Steelers. In the 18 games he played against the Steelers as a Bengal, Pickens had 91 receptions, 1,289 receiving yards, a 14.16 yards per reception and six touchdown catches. His dominance against Pittsburgh was showcased in the Bengals' 25-20 win in Week 6 of the 1998 season. Pickens shredded the Steelers that day for 13 receptions, 204 receiving yards and one touchdown, setting the team record for most receptions in a game and earning him the AFC Offensive Player of the Week honors.

Unfortunately, the Bengals couldn't match the accomplishments achieved by Pickens in his eight seasons with the team from 1992-1999. During his time with the team, the Bengals were a far from auspicious 40-88 (.312). And even though it appeared the franchise had turned things around when Blake was installed at quarterback in 1995, creating the exciting "Shake and Blake" connections with Pickens and Scott, the Bengals fell to a combined 7-25 in 1998 and 1999. It seemed those last two years had killed any momentum or goodwill the previous three seasons had generated inside the Bengals' locker room.

Ironically, the one player on the 1999 Bengals roster least likely to be disgruntled was the one labeled by many observers of the team as temperamental, cantankerous, prickly and cancerous—Carl Pickens. In spite of the team's 4-11 record with one game left in the 1999 season, Pickens, who many felt was about to go ballistic over the team's dreadful play, had, instead, every reason to be delighted. He was about to complete the final year of a five-year, $23.25 million contract, which included a $3.5 million signing bonus, and it appeared he was about to receive a boatload of cash when the 2000 season began. It seemed the enigmatic wide receiver had found his happy spot.

The situation changed dramatically, though, on the Monday before the regular season finale against the Jacksonville Jaguars when owner/general manager, Mike Brown, announced he was renewing head coach Bruce Coslet's contract for the 2000 season. It was a decision that surprised many around the league considering Coslet's 21-36 record as the Bengals head coach. In Pickens' mind, it was a decision he found insulting and undermined any chance for the Bengals to contend for a championship.

"I don't understand it. We're trying to win, we're trying to turn this thing around here. And they bring Coslet back," Pickens angrily told the media two days after the announcement. "What can you do? Obviously, the players don't call the shots around here."[102]

To no one's surprise, Coslet was upset by Pickens' comments. "It's embarrassing for Carl Pickens to say something like that," Coslet said in response to his wide receiver's opinion. "I've been more supportive of him than anybody in this organization. Anybody. I took him from a 30-catch-a-year to a 100-catch-a-year Pro Bowler in the offense that I ran."[1103]

Meanwhile, Mike Brown was incensed over what Pickens had said and was bound and determined to prevent any future disparaging comments made by any player under contract with the Bengals. From that point forward, Brown instituted what became known as the "Carl Pickens Clause" into a player's contract, a provision that would cause a player to forfeit all or some of his signing bonus if he insulted the organization in public. Roundly and harshly criticized by the National Football League Players Association, Brown made it clear he would only enact the clause under extreme circumstances. Regardless of if and when the Bengals elected to enforce it, the mere mention of the "Pickens Clause" sealed the wide receiver's fate with the franchise. Prior to the start of the 2000 season, Pickens was released.[2]

The fallout of his comments at the end of the 1999 season and the subsequent loyalty clause that bears his name has also marred Pickens' legacy with the Bengals as well. It has, to a large degree, made him more notorious for being a malcontent than for what he achieved on the football field during some very difficult years. And while he won't be confused as one of the organization's all-time model teammates, to dismiss his accomplishments simply because he ruffled the feathers of some of his teammates, coaches and management by his actions and opinions is unfair and an injustice.

From a pure performance perspective, Pickens is one of the top five wide receivers in team history. After eight years with the Bengals that encompassed 120 games played and 111 games started, the name Pickens

---

[1] As a matter of full disclosure, Pickens apologized for his comments later that same day. "I want to say to Bruce Coslet, my teammates, the Bengals organization and Bengals fans that I regret the comments I made today in our locker room," Pickens said in a statement. "They were ill-advised and were the product of my frustration from a long and tough season."
As for whether his initial comments had any merit, it is worth noting that Coslet quit three games into the 2000 season.

[2] Pickens signed with the Tennessee Titans for the 2000 season, playing in only nine games before he was released. He signed as a free agent with the Dallas Cowboys in April 2001 but announced his retirement one month later.

is found throughout the team's receiving and scoring record books. His 530 receptions, an average of 66.25 per season, is the second most in team history. His 6,887 receiving yards, an average of 860.87 yards per season and 12.99 yards per catch, ranks third in team history and includes four 1000-yard receiving seasons as well as 19 100-yard receiving games, the fourth most in franchise history. His 63 touchdown catches are second best in team history and his 64 total touchdowns places him fourth on that list. Pickens had 10 consecutive games from November 27, 1994 to October 1, 1995 in which he scored a touchdown, a feat unequaled by any other Bengals player. In eight seasons, Pickens scored 388 points, the eighth most in team history and the second most by a Bengals wide receiver.

The individual offensive numbers produced by Pickens from 1992-1999 are even more impressive when you take into account the teams he played with. The best performance the Bengals could muster during Pickens' eight seasons was in 1996 when they finished fifth in the NFL in points scored, 10th in total offense and 12th in passing offense. Even then, Pickens played a large part in the team's success, personally accounting for 19.35 percent of the Bengals points scored, 22.62 percent of the total offense and 34.38 percent of the team's passing yards for the entire 1996 season. In his eight-year tenure in Cincinnati, Pickens was responsible for 16.41 percent of the team's points scored, 17.86 percent of the total offense and 27.96 percent of the Bengals net passing yards.

It's true that even with Pickens piling up the receptions, receiving yards and touchdowns, the Bengals were in the midst of a very dark period that lasted through the majority of the 1990s and half of the 2000's, a drought of success Pickens couldn't eradicate. But without Pickens, the 1990s would have been a total eclipse. His play was a bright chapter in an otherwise bleak volume of Bengals football.

In due time, maybe, just maybe, his performance in a Bengals uniform during a very exacting time will do go down in team history as the true "Carl Pickens Clause".

CHAPTER THIRTY-EIGHT

RODNEY HOLMAN

The Reluctant All-Pro

When looking back on his 14-year professional career, you have to believe Rodney Holman always dreamed of playing in the NFL. Named to multiple Pro Bowls, All-Conference and All-NFL teams while finishing as the Cincinnati Bengals all-time leader in receptions by a tight end, it seems obvious that Holman had a singular goal in mind while growing up in Ypsilanti, Michigan—to make it big in the NFL. And by the looks of it, Holman achieved all of his NFL ambitions and then some. In other words, Holman's career had the appearance of a feel-good NFL Films type of story.

Sometimes, though, the truth gets in the way when attempting to write the perfect biographical script. Such was the case when articulating the career path Holman took to become a highly successful NFL tight end. The fact is, Holman never had a burning desire to play in the NFL, let alone become one of the league's best tight ends of the late 1980s and early 1990s.

"I didn't watch much football. I played to the best of my ability," Holman recalled after his playing days were over, apparently eliminating any presumption he had fulfilled his boyhood dreams. "I never brought it home."[104]

Even though he never had any NFL aspirations, Holman was a star football player at Ypsilanti High School and an even bigger wrestling standout, going 144-0 as a 191 pound all-state wrestler. His skills on both the wrestling mat and the football field drew the attention of several college football heavyweights, including Ohio State's Woody Hayes, Alabama's Bear Bryant and Michigan's Bo Schembechler, all hoping to sign Holman to a football scholarship. After completing his own due diligence on all the schools that were trying to secure his services, Holman ultimately decided bigger wasn't necessarily better.

"There were 500 or more per class at Michigan," said Holman, who was using his football skills to further his education, not to improve his NFL chances. "At Tulane, the classroom had 50, maybe 75. I could have more of a one-on-one relationship between the professor and the student."[105] So with academics at the forefront, Holman accepted a football scholarship from Tulane University in New Orleans, Louisiana, starting in the fall of 1978.

Holman wasted little time making his presence felt at Tulane, becoming the starting tight end his freshman year in 1978 and remaining a starter until he graduated four years later. In his sophomore year in 1979, he tied for the team lead in receptions (47) and set the single season record for most receptions by a tight end in school history. It was also the year that Holman was introduced to Lindy Infante, a man who would play a large part in Holman becoming an NFL tight end.

In 1979, Infante was the offensive coordinator at Tulane and introduced a scheme that according to Holman, was ideal for his position since "a majority of the routes were intermediate for the tight ends and running backs, with the wide receivers stretching the defense."[106] It was an offense that was efficient and lethal, and as Holman aptly put it, "just piled up the first downs."[107] Infante left Tulane after the 1979 season to become the quarterbacks' coach for the Cincinnati Bengals, a move that would become significant for Holman two years later.

In the meantime, Holman finished his last two seasons at Tulane, completing a career many consider as the best for a tight end in school history. A four-year letterman from 1978-1981, Holman was either a second team, third team or honorable mention All-American in each of his last three seasons. In 1981, he was named to the All-South Independent team and was selected to play in the Blue-Gray All Star Classic. He finished his career as the school's all-time leader in receptions (135) and receiving yards (1,512) by a tight end[1] and helped lead Tulane to consecutive bowl games for the first and only time in school history. His accomplishments would eventually gain him induction into the Tulane Hall of Fame in 1990 and the Allstate Sugar Bowl Hall of Fame in 2013.

By the time his college career ended in 1981, Holman was already on the radar of many NFL scouts and executives. The problem was, Holman seemed disinterested and indifferent about continuing his football career. "The Bengals had sent me a questionnaire during my junior year," Holman recalled. "I just filled it out and sent it back."[108]

Looking back, it's obvious why the Bengals sent him the pre-draft questionnaire in 1980 since his former offensive coordinator at Tulane, Infante, had completed his first year as Cincinnati's quarterback coach. What is surprising is that Holman's responses apparently did not alarm the Bengals' because when he became eligible for the NFL Draft in 1982, Infante, who by now was the team's offensive coordinator, was convinced Holman was ready for the NFL. The team trusted Infante's instincts, drafting the tight end from Tulane in the third round with the 82nd overall pick.

As for Holman, being selected by the Bengals was totally unexpected. "I was caught off guard," Holman later recalled.[109] Many NFL observers seemed to agree with Holman's assessment of his selection as well. The Bengals were coming off a 1981 season that was capped off by their first Super Bowl appearance and engineered in large part to Infante's high octane offense which featured All-Pro tight end Dan Ross. Ross finished the 1981 regular season with a then team record 71 receptions, 910 receiving yards and five touchdown catches. He almost single-handedly won Super Bowl XVI for the Bengals with his 11 reception, 104 receiving yards and two touchdown performance in the team's 26-21 to the San Francisco 49ers.[2] With Ross and third-year veteran, M.L. Harris (both

---

[1]   His 135 receptions places him 11th among all players in Tulane history.

[2]   Ross' 11 receptions remained a Super Bowl record until tied by Jerry Rice (Super Bowl XXIII), Wes Walker (XLIII) and Deion Branch (XXXIX). It was eventually broken by Demaryius Thomas in Super Bowl XLVIII when he caught 13 passes. Ross' record of 104 receiving yards by a tight end in a Super Bowl was tied by Vernon Davis in Super Bowl XLVII.

of whom combined for 84 receptions, 1,092 receiving yards and seven touchdowns) returning for the 1982 season, it appeared on the surface that Holman was drafted simply as a favor from Infante, his former college coach. Based upon his indifference to the prospect of playing professionally and the stacked talent the Bengals already had at the tight end position, there was a sense that Holman's NFL career would probably amount to a very small cup of coffee.

At first, it looked like the skeptics would be proven right, even after Holman made the team in his rookie season in 1982. In his first three seasons with the Bengals, Holman started in only two games, catching a total of 26 passes for 272 yards and two touchdowns. His lack of time in the starting lineup and his relatively low production did not, however, accurately reflect his development as an NFL tight end. Holman played in every game in those first three seasons, quickly gaining a reputation as a sure-handed receiver and an effective and devastating blocker in the team's running game. His performance was so impressive that when Ross left for the USFL in 1984 and Harris' role began to diminish, Holman was inserted into the starting lineup at the beginning of the 1985 season. It also marked the genesis of an eight-year span in which Holman became an elite NFL tight end and arguably the best tight end in Bengals team history.

Over each of the next eight seasons as the Bengals starting tight end, Holman led all tight ends on the team in receptions and receiving yards, averaging 36.5 catches and 507.12 receiving yards per season. He averaged 13.89 yards per catch and four touchdown receptions per year during this eight year stretch, highlighted by his 1989 season in which his nine touchdown catches led the team and was the sixth most in the entire NFL.

Holman's first year as a starter, 1985, also signaled the emergence of head coach Sam Wyche's "No Huddle" offense, a scheme under which all of the players in the team's offense, including Holman, thrived. In a period from 1985-1992, the Bengals set the team records in a season for points scored (448 points in 1988), touchdowns (59 in 1989), rushing touchdowns (27 in 1988), total net yards (6.490 in 1986), net yards rushing (2,710 in 1988) and average yards per rushing attempt (4.862 yards per attempt in 1986). In those eight years, the offense finished in the top half of the NFL in rushing offense all eight seasons, including leading the league in 1988 and 1989, in total offense seven times (1985-1991), highlighted by having the league's top offense in 1988. They also finished in the top half of the league in passing offense six times (1985-1989 and 1991) and points scored five times (1985, 1986, 1988-1990) with a league leading 448 points scored in 1988.

Those offenses also set several single game team records as well with Holman making a substantial contribution to several of those milestones. In their 52-21 victory over the New York Jets on December 21, 1986, Holman's six receptions for 129 yards and one touchdown was part of a 621 net yard performance by the offense, setting the team record for net yards gained in a single game.[1] His two touchdown receptions in the Bengals' 56-23 win over the Tampa Bay Buccaneers on October 29, 1989 accounted for one-quarter of the team's eight touchdowns and one-third of their six passing touchdowns, both team records for total and passing touchdowns in a game.

When the Bengals tied the team record for points scored in a game in a 61-7 blowout of the Houston Oilers on December 17, 1989, he supplied five receptions for 44 yards and one touchdown. Holman's most impressive individual performance occurred when he led the team with 10 receptions for 161 yards as the offense set the team record for net yards passing in a game with 443 in their 34-31 victory on the road against the Los Angeles Rams on October 7, 1990.[2]

Holman was recognized by the national media for this contributions to the offense that went beyond his individual achievements in several of the team's record setting performances. In 1988, Holman was named to his first Pro Bowl and earned second-team All-AFC by the UPI. In 1989, Holman was selected to his second Pro Bowl while being named first All-AFC tight end by The Pro Football Weekly and the UPI, first team All-NFL tight end by the Newspapers Enterprise Association (NEA) and Pro Football Weekly and second team All-NFL by the Associated Press. He earned his third consecutive Pro Bowl selection in 1990 in addition to being named first All-AFC by Pro Football Weekly and the UPI and second team All-NFL by the Associated Press and the NEA.

---

[1] The 416 net yards passing the Bengals offense gained in the same game ranks fifth in team history.

[2] The Bengals offense accounted for 582 total net yards that day against the Rams, the fourth best in team history.

Thanks in large part to the explosive offenses they employed from 1985-1992, the Bengals qualified for the playoffs twice, in 1990 and, most notably in 1988 when they reached the Super Bowl for the second time in their history. In both of those post-seasons, Holman played a significant part in the team's success, leading the team each post-season in receptions (7 in 1988 and 4 in 1990) and receiving yards (82 yards in 1988 and 102 yards in 1990). His two receptions for 51 yards helped the Bengals set the team's post-season records for points scored and touchdowns (5) in a game in their 41-14 1990 wild card Playoff game against the Houston Oilers on January 6, 1991.

The post-season was also the scene of Holman's greatest professional disappointment. Heading into Super Bowl XXIII, he led the team in receptions during the playoffs and was hoping to add to that total while bringing home the Bengals' first-ever NFL championship. Holman struck out on both counts, failing to record any receptions and then watching Joe Montana engineer the winning touchdown drive in the waning seconds of the fourth quarter in the San Francisco 49ers 20-16 victory over the Bengals. "It was a great game," Holman would later recall.[110] As for being held without a catch in the game, Holman offered no excuses.

"I had a rookie linebacker on me," Holman remembers.[111] That rookie linebacker was Bill Romanowski, a future 16-year NFL veteran who would go on to win three more Super Bowl rings and earn two Pro Bowl selections in 1996 and 1998.

But it may have more than just Romanowski's play that kept Holman off the stat sheet. Super Bowl XXIII was played at Joe Robbie Stadium in Miami, and according to Holman, the field and the weather played a big part in why the Bengals came up just short.

"The turf (grass) was brand new [at Joe Robbie Stadium]," Holman remembers. "There was a torrential rain storm the night before, then the sprinklers came on to compound the problem. I sunk my hand into the turf. If was soft. The field was slow.

"We had two 1000-yard rushers (James Brooks and Ickey Woods). Eddie Brown had the best hands that I had ever seen. Tim McGee couldn't get traction. We couldn't use our speed. (The Niners) ran intermediate routes with Jerry Rice and John Taylor."[112]

After experiencing the agony of defeat in the Super Bowl and two disappointing seasons in 1991 and 1992, the Bengals decided to move the franchise in a new direction prior to the start of the 1993 season. Perennial All-Pro offensive tackle Anthony Muñoz was released and the 1988 NFL MVP quarterback Boomer Esiason was traded to the New York Jets to allow their first round draft choice in 1992, David Klingler, the opportunity to start behind center. Another casualty of the team's roster overhaul was Holman, who was released after the 1992 season. He immediately became a free agent and was signed by the Detroit Lions in 1993. Holman played three seasons in Detroit, retiring from the NFL following the 1995 campaign. Reluctant though he might have been to take part in the NFL, Holman finished his career by playing in 212 games, the second most by a tight end in NFL history.

Nearly 78 percent of those 212 games Holman played, or 165 to be exact, were in a Cincinnati uniform. Holman finished his 11-year career as a Bengal with 318 receptions, the ninth most by all receivers and the most by a tight end in team history. His 204 points scored ranks him 22nd on the team's all-time scoring list and is the second most by a Bengals tight end.

Even though the franchise sported a mediocre 80-88 regular season record (.476) in his 11 seasons with the team, Holman played in six playoff games as a Bengal, arguably saving his best performances for the post-season. His 16.73 yards per reception during the playoffs is the second best in team history while his 184 career post-season receiving yards ranks third. In the record setting wild card Playoff win over the Houston Oilers on January 6, 1991, Holman caught a 46-yard pass from Esiason which still stands as the fifth longest reception in Bengals' playoff history.

In the minds of many, the most remarkable aspect of Holman's illustrious career in Cincinnati was that he achieved such success even though he never expressed a strong desire to play in the NFL. Holman still remembers how stunned his college coaches were about his passive attitude towards a career in the NFL.

"They asked me, 'Do you want to play pro football?'", Holman remembers. "'I can't believe with your talent that you would say that.'"[113]

But if those college coaches had looked a little closer, football had never seemed a priority to Holman. In high school in Ypsilanti, while his play on the football field had college coaches clamoring for his signature on their scholarship offers, he appeared more passionate about wrestling, as evidenced by his undefeated high school record. When it did come time for him to decide what college to attend, Holman eschewed the football powerhouses like Alabama, Ohio State, Michigan State and Michigan and instead chose a lesser known school, Tulane University, because "it was a nice change of scenery, and a real good education."[114] Is it any wonder then, that Holman was not about to follow the script everyone else believed contained the storybook ending of a successful career in the NFL?

Interestingly, the choices Holman made early in his life demonstrate why he became one of the best NFL tight ends of his time, despite his unwillingness to embrace a life in professional football. He never let football define him, even when he had college football Hall of Fame coaches and NFL scouts telling him he was crazy not to make the game a career. He valued an education over the spoils and accolades accorded to someone with his athletic skills, thereby ignoring an easier path to potential fame and riches. More importantly, when it came time to do his job on the football field, even when it wasn't his preferred occupation, Holman exhibited the discipline, intelligence, self-confidence and skills he developed as a high school and college student athlete to excel at a top-flight level and become the consummate pro.

So you can label Rodney Holman "The Reluctant NFL Tight End" if you so desire.

Just make sure you add, "Cincinnati Bengals All-Time Great" in the same sentence.

CHAPTER THIRTY-NINE

TONY McGEE

Touchdown Tony

L*ike most teenagers growing up* in the state of Indiana, Tony McGee dreamed of having a high profile basketball career. Growing up in the projects and the government housing of Terre Haute, Indiana, McGee envisioned playing basketball at a Division I college and then eventually, the NBA. He was well on his way to fulfilling his aspirations while attending South Vigo High School in Terre Haute, showing enough promise to have both the University of Pittsburgh and Indiana University offer him a scholarship to join their basketball program.

Meanwhile, in addition to being a stand-out on the basketball court at South Vigo, McGee excelled on the football field. In his senior year in 1988, he played both offense and defense for a South Vigo football team that won their sectional and regional championships before losing to the eventual state champion, Indianapolis' Ben Davis, in the semi-finals. As a tight end, McGee had 29 receptions for 620 yards and four touchdowns in 1988 and as a member of the defensive line, he accounted for 60 total tackles and nine tackles for a loss. Just like those schools who recruited him to play basketball, several Division I college football programs offered McGee a scholarship. Evidently, the South Vigo senior had a decision to make when it came to his choice of colleges—"Do I play football or basketball?"

It was by no means an easy call for McGee to make, particularly for someone born and raised in the hoops-crazed state of Indiana. In the end, though, McGee ultimately concluded his size wasn't suitable for a post player like himself in the college game. So he forewent his dreams of basketball stardom in favor of playing Division I college football. After sifting through all of the football scholarships he was offered, McGee signed with the University of Michigan and began his career in the fall of 1989.

At the time McGee became a member of the Michigan football roster, the Wolverines were about to finish a decade in which they achieved an 80-27-2 record, four Big Ten titles and four Rose Bowl appearances. Michigan continued their winning ways upon McGee's arrival, even after legendary head coach, Bo Schembechler, retired after McGee's freshman year in 1989, and was replaced by long-time assistant coach, Gary Moeller. The Wolverines went 29-7 in McGee's first three years with the team, ending each season no lower than eighth in the final AP rankings and finishing either champion or co-champion of the Big 10 Conference.

Unfortunately for McGee, he made little or no impact on his team's success. In his first three seasons from 1989-1991, McGee had a grand total of four receptions, and as he entered his senior season in 1992, he figured he was playing his final season of organized football. Needless to say, the chances he would continue his career in the NFL never crossed McGee's mind.

"When you have four catches going into your senior year, you're not trying to sign an agent," McGee later recalled.[115] By the time his senior season was over, though, McGee's phone was probably ringing off the hook with incoming calls from agents anxious to sign him.

In short, McGee had a breakthrough senior season in 1992, as the Wolverines went 9-0-3, winning another Big 10 title and appearing in the Rose Bowl for the third time in four years. He ended the year with 38 receptions, tied for ninth most by a tight end in school history, for 467 yards, the 11th most by a Michigan tight end in a single season. His six touchdown catches in 1992 tied for second for most touchdown receptions by a tight end in school history. Named an All-Big 10 tight end and an All-Academic Big 10 in 1992, McGee saved his best performance as a Wolverine in his final game. His six receptions for 117 yards and touchdowns in Michigan's 38-31 victory over Washington in the 1993 Rose Bowl vaulted the Wolverines to fifth in the final AP college football poll.

Based on his senior season, McGee's chances of playing in the NFL changed overnight. In August 1992, no one had considered him an NFL prospect. Fast forward to February 1993 and there were several teams interested in selecting him in the upcoming NFL Draft in April. One of those teams was the Cincinnati Bengals, a franchise in the midst of a roster overhaul and who had just released their starting tight end from the previous eight seasons, Rodney Holman. Looking to replace Holman's 318 career receptions and 34 touchdown catches, the Bengals believed McGee's performance in his senior year at Michigan was indicative of what he could do in the NFL and that he could fill the void created by Holman's departure. Granted, drafting a player with only one statistically impressive college season was a bit of a gamble, but the Bengals brass were not discouraged. They selected McGee in the second round of the 1993 NFL Draft with the 37th overall pick.

McGee wasted no time in making the Bengals' decision look shrewd. In his rookie year in 1993, McGee admirably picked up where Holman left off, finishing the season with 44 receptions for 525 yards in 15 games, all of which he started. It was also the beginning of an impressive streak for McGee of 117 consecutive games played from 1993-2000,[1] the fifth longest streak in team history. Besides the one game in 1993, McGee missed only seven more games in his nine years with the Bengals, playing a total of 136 games, starting in all but two of them.

McGee made the most of his time in those 136 games he played, leading all tight ends on the team in receptions and receiving yards in each of those nine seasons, averaging 33.2 receptions and 421.7 receiving yards per season and leading all Bengals receivers in touchdowns catches (6) in 1997. His best year was 1995 when he recorded a personal best 55 receptions and 754 yards receiving. He also registered two 100-yard receiving games in 1995, a six reception, 118-yard effort in a 24-21 victory

---

[1] During this stretch, McGee started in every game from 1994-1999.

over the Indianapolis Colts on September 3 and an eight reception 109 yard performance against the Houston Oilers on September 24.[1]

From a performance standpoint, McGee's transition from the college game to the NFL went as smooth as could be expected. Not only did he start every game from the time he entered the league but his production compared favorably to all of the other tight ends in the league. It appeared that McGee had adjusted well to life in the NFL.

Where life differed for McGee from his time at college, was the performance of the team he was playing for. After spending four seasons with a Michigan program that went 38-7-3, McGee found himself playing for an NFL team struggling to achieve respectability, attempting to return to their winning ways of the 1980s. In his nine seasons in Cincinnati, the Bengals finished with a 45-99 record (.312), ending only one season with a record of .500 or better (8-8 in 1996) and never coming close to reaching the post-season. McGee endured several extended losing streaks including 10 consecutive losses in 1993, nine consecutive games lost in 1998 and during 1998 and 1999, a string of 11 consecutive games lost at home.

Even with McGee's solid production, the Bengals offense struggled. Using nine different starting quarterbacks from 1993-2001, the offense finished in the top half of the NFL in total offense (1996, 1997 and 1999) and points scored (1995-1997) only three times and in passing offense a scant twice (1996 and 1997). The lone bright spot during his nine year stretch was the team's running game in 2000. It finished second in the league in total rushing offense and included two of the top three net yards rushing in a game in team history—292 yards against the Arizona Cardinals on December 3 and a franchise best 407 yards against the Denver Broncos on October 22.[2]

Unaccustomed to playing on a losing football team, McGee was forced to evaluate success on the field from a completely different perspective. "There are so many things surrounding the team that you can't control," McGee recalled. "You had to say, as an individual, 'How am I playing?'"[116]

Another aspect of the game McGee couldn't control was his health. In

---

[1]   McGee had one other 100-yard receiving game as a Bengal when he caught seven passes for 102 yards against the Seattle Seahawks on September 26, 1993.

[2]   This game also featured Corey Dillon rushing for 278 yards, the team record for rushing yards in a game.

his first eight years in the NFL, he was relatively healthy and injury-free as evidenced by the fact that he only missed three games from 1993-2000. In 2001, however, his run of good fortune in the health department ended, and as it would turn out, so would his tenure with the team.

In the game against the Tampa Bay Buccaneers on December 2, 2001, McGee sprained the medial collateral ligament in his left knee, an injury doctors determined severe enough to place him on season-ending injured reserve with five games left in the season. What no one knew at the time was that the six-yard reception he made against the Buccaneers when the injury occurred would be his last catch as a Cincinnati Bengal. On April 25, 2002, the Bengals granted McGee his unconditional release.

McGee wasn't unemployed for long. Two days later, he signed with the Dallas Cowboys where he played in all 16 games in 2002. After short stints with Tampa Bay and then the Cowboys again, he finished the 2003 season by playing in three games with the New York Giants. When the Giants did not re-sign him after the season, McGee retired from the NFL. By then, he had played in 156 NFL games, starting in all but six of them and, according to The Pro Football Historical Abstract, establishing himself as one of the best tight ends in league history. Based upon their analytical score, McGee is the 50th best tight end of all-time with a career Q score of 117.0 and 2,029 career adjusted yards gained.[117]

The overwhelming majority of those milestones occurred when McGee wore a Bengals uniform. In his nine seasons in Cincinnati, McGee amassed 299 receptions, 10th on the team's all-time reception list and the second most by a tight end in team history. His 3,795 receiving yards are the 12th most in team history and the third most by a Bengals' tight end. He accounted for 122 points on 20 touchdowns and one two-point conversion, making him the fourth highest scoring tight end in franchise history. By any measure, it was a solid career but, according to McGee, one with a tinge of regret. He readily admits he wasn't a student of the game or someone who ate, drank, and slept football 24 hours a day. Years after his playing days were over, he wondered aloud what might have been had he put in the extra effort.

"If I had known the things that I know now when I was playing," McGee said in 2014, "the mental strength, the work ethic approach, the understanding of the processes, I'd be a beast."[118]

Ironically, McGee could have used those same words to describe whether choosing football over basketball was the right move for him back in 1989. No one, not even McGee, will ever know if he would have become an NBA beast. You can imagine that the thought, all these years later, has crossed McGee's mind. But as McGee once said about failing to make the playoffs while playing in Cincinnati, "You can't miss what you never had."[119]

Hopefully, McGee takes solace and satisfaction in what he did have—a nine-year career in Cincinnati as one of the Bengals' best tight ends of all time.

CHAPTER FORTY

REGGIE KELLY

The Reverend

A*ll too often, especially in* today's statistical driven analysis of the game, a player's value to their team, regardless of the sport, is almost entirely based upon the numbers he or she compiles on game day. In baseball, a player's value is measured by his batting average, home runs, and runs batted in or by games won and his earned run average. In basketball, the standard assessment of a player has increasingly become more about how often you reach double digits in three of the five statistical categories in a game, points scored, rebounds, assists, steals or blocked shots, more commonly known as the triple double, than any other aptitude.

Football is no different. Players at the skill positions, such as quarterback, running back, wide receiver or tight end, earn All-American honors in college and are named to All-Pro and Pro Bowl teams once they reach the NFL primarily on statistics like yards gained and touchdowns scored that they produce. Simply put, in the minds of most football fans and observers, the bigger the number you manufacture on Saturday or Sunday, the higher your value to the underlying success of the team.

In recent years, such organizations like Baseball Prospectus, 82.Games and Football Outsiders have gone beyond the use of traditional statistics to determine a player's worth by creating a set of data meant to unearth, what Football Outsiders calls an "analytics revolution [that] is about learning

223

more about the intricacies of the game instead of just accepting the boilerplate storylines produced by color commentators, lazy beat reporters and crotchety old players from the past." To that end, statistics like Wins Above Replacement (WAR), Defense adjusted Value Over Replacement (DVOA) and Simple Ratings have become just as common, or in some cases, replaced slugging percentage, yards per carry and points per game as a measuring stick for a player's relevance and significance to a team.

But even with the advent of advanced metrics and innovative statistics widely accepted by the NFL since the beginning of the 21st Century, sometimes the value a player adds to his team goes deeper than just the traditional statistics he produces or the DVOA he yields. Sometimes just a player's presence on the field and in the locker room, attributes not determinable by a traditional or advanced data point, is worth more than any one touchdown scored in the last minute of a tie game. Such was the impact Reggie Kelly made as a member of the Cincinnati Bengals.

In his eight seasons as a Bengal from 2003-2010, seven as the team's starting tight end, Kelly wasn't a celebrated receiver, averaging only 17.9 receptions and 107.7 yards receiving per year. Other than the fact that he led all tight ends on the team in receptions and receiving yards in 2006, 2007 and 2008, you will be hard pressed to find Kelly's name in the Bengals' record book. Yet when you asked his teammates during his time in Cincinnati who the unheralded MVP of those teams was, Kelly's was the name universally spoken.

"We just got better on a number of levels," quarterback Carson Palmer said when he learned the Bengals signed Kelly for the 2010 season after he missed the 2009 season due to a ruptured left achilles tendon. "He brings maturity, leadership and he's a great role model for younger players. Aside from his ability to put his hand on the ground in a three point stance and block anybody."[120]

"When you come into the league, you aspire to be a guy like Reggie Kelly," remarked All-Pro tackle and future locker room leader, Andrew Whitworth. "He adds so much to the running game because he's big and tough. And he's like a father figure in the locker room. Or a big brother. Guys know they can go to him for anything. And he's so calm."[121]

Kelly first began thinking about a career in the NFL as a youngster in the small town of Aberdeen, Mississippi, on Sunday afternoons, immediately following a full day of watching football on television. "After the game, all the neighborhood boys would gather in someone's backyard where we played football and that's where I first dreamed of playing in the pros."[122] Kelly said in 2012. He went on to letter in football, as well as basketball and power-lifting at Aberdeen High School, earning a football scholarship to attend Mississippi State University and head coach Jackie Sherrill in the fall of 1995.

Kelly was a four-year letterman and a three-time member of the Southeastern Conference Honor Roll at Mississippi State from 1995-1998, starting in half of the 44 games he played. He finished his career with 29 receptions, 474 receiving yards, 16.3 yards per reception and two touchdown catches. In his senior season in 1998, he was a part of the Bulldogs team that won the SEC West and a berth against Texas in the 1999 Cotton Bowl. More importantly, Kelly's play in the 1998 season earned him a spot in the 1999 Senior Bowl and the opportunity to show his skills in front of a wide array of NFL coaches, scouts and executives.

Kelly made the most of this Senior Bowl invitation, particularly impressing the Atlanta Falcons who chose him in the second round of the 1999 NFL Draft with the 44th overall selection. Kelly was a solid contributor for the Falcons, averaging 17.25 receptions and 197.5 receiving yards per season in his four years in Atlanta. He had two touchdown catches as a Falcon, including his first NFL score, a 37-yard reception from quarterback Chris Chandler against the St. Louis Rams on September 24, 2000. Even though Kelly put up decent numbers in his 62 games as a Falcon, Atlanta elected not to re-sign him when his contract expired after the 2002 season. Anxious to find a replacement for tight end Tony McGee who left following the 2001 season, the Bengals signed Kelly as an unrestricted free agent to a four-year contract prior to the 2003 season.

As it would turn out, joining the Bengals was a win-win for both Kelly and the franchise. His arrival in Cincinnati coincided with the beginning of the Marvin Lewis era as the team's head coach as well as the drafting of who the Bengals believed was their franchise quarterback of the future, Carson Palmer. Thanks to these new additions, along with a roster that already included Willie Anderson, Rich Braham, T.J. Houshmandzadeh, Chad Johnson, Rudi Johnson and Brian Simmons, it seemed Kelly was coming to a team on the cusp of ending; this was at the time, a 13-year post-season drought.

As for the Bengals, they added not only an NFL proven receiver at the tight end position but because of Kelly's league wide reputation as an excellent run blocker, they in essence were able to field three tackles on the offensive line. Off the field, Kelly earned the nickname, "The Reverend" and brought a calming, mentoring influence to a locker room full of young, talented, and frankly highly egotistical individuals on the brink of becoming breakthrough NFL stars. Kelly's presence on the roster wasn't lost on the new coaching staff. "He gives us flexibility and options as well as being the ultimate professional," offensive coordinator Bob Bratkowski would later say.[123]

It didn't take long for Kelly and the new look and new-minded Bengals to meet the high expectations many had forecast. Over the next seasons from 2003-2008, the Bengals returned to NFL respectability due in large part to a resurgence in the team's offense. Finishing in the top half of the NFL in point scored five times (2003-2007) and total offense and passing offense four times (2003, 2005-2007), the offense led the team to four seasons with a record of .500 or better, their best stretch of football since the middle of the 1980s.

For his part, Kelly played a significant role in the offense's and the team's restoration. New York Jets head coach, Rex Ryan called him "the Bengals 'secret weapon'",[124] Kelly proved to be a reliable receiving option (115 receptions for 928 receiving yards and three touchdowns from 2003-2008), finishing with the fifth best DVOA by a tight end in 2006 according to Football Outsiders. As a run blocker, Kelly was moved all over the field because of his ability to block anyone, an attribute Bratkowski was eager to use to the team's advantage.

"Reggie was used in situations when we brought him into the backfield as a back to protect on third down when we knew people were going to use matchups," said Bratkowski, the offensive coordinator in all of Kelly's eight seasons with the Bengals.[125]

Inside the locker room, Kelly had an even bigger impact, earning the respect and admiration of all of his teammates. In 2007, the players named him the winner of the team's Ed Block Courage Award, an annual honor given to a player who symbolizes courage in the face of difficulty. By then, his true value to the team's success as team leader and mentor was firmly in place.

Without question, the best season for the Bengals during Kelly's time in Cincinnati was 2005. After back-to-back 8-8 seasons in 2003 and 2004, the Bengals qualified for the post-season for the first time in 15 years in 2005, going 11-5 in the regular season and winning their first-ever AFC North Division championship. Kelly (and the rest of the offense) was a big contributor to their having made the playoffs in 2005, ending the season with the sixth best total offense, the fifth best passing offense and scoring the fourth most points in the NFL. Their 32 passing touchdowns and 421 points scored in 2005 ranks tied for second and tied for fourth respectively in team history.

As an unofficial member of the offensive line, Kelly contributed to one of the best pass blocking seasons in Bengals history. The 21 sacks and 1.31 sacks per game Kelly and the line allowed are both the second fewest in team history. Even though the season ended with a bitter loss to the Pittsburgh Steelers in the AFC wild card Playoff round, the performance of the 2005 team marked the first step in the team's turnaround from a league laughing stock to a perennial playoff contender.

The Bengals' next trip to the post-season was in 2009 when they won their second AFC North title with a 10-6 regular season record. Unfortunately for Kelly, the Achilles injury he'd suffered in pre-season training camp prevented him from participating in the franchise's second playoff appearance in five years. The Bengals brought him back in 2010 primarily to mentor and teach their newest tight ends, Jermaine Gresham and Chase Coffman, but released him following the end of the season. Kelly returned to Atlanta in 2011 but after recording only one reception for seven yards the entire year, he retired from the NFL.

Kelly's statistical resume certainly won't gain any Pro Football Hall of Fame consideration. In his 184 NFL game career, Kelly had 195 receptions for 1,767 receiving yards and five touchdowns, numbers that are, admittedly, pedestrian at best. Even his 125 career receptions for 970 yards as a Bengal are only the sixth and ninth best respectively for a tight end in team history.

But when it comes to being a polished professional, an unquestioned locker room leader, and a mentor to his teammates. Kelly is understandably a first ballot Hall of Famer. Kelly's value is such that his qualities espouse a culture of success throughout the team, which parallels any number of receptions or touchdowns a player can produce. Kelly, the founder and CEO of KYVAN Foods, a line of soul food and tailgating fare, recently provided the secret to his NFL success despite the lack of any gaudy statistics.

"If you do the little things right," Kelly said, 'the big things will follow and that's what carried me through my NFL career."[126]

Or as "The Reverend" would say, "Here endeth the lesson."

CHAPTER FORTY-ONE

BOB TRUMPY

Calling a Legend

Even though it happened over 30 years ago, I still remember the first time I was a caller on Cincinnati's long running radio show, "Sports Talk". It was the fall of 1980 and I was, by most standards, a precocious 16-year old who stood firm in his opinions and convictions, especially when they had anything to do with sports. So, when I called into "Sports Talk" I believed I was on the right side of the fence when it came to the issue being discussed.

In this instance, I was ready to express my thoughts on whether the city of Cincinnati should pursue an NHL or NBA expansion franchise. I steadfastly believed the NHL was the best option, citing the recent relative success of the Cincinnati Stingers in the World Hockey Association (WHA) and the fact that the city had already had their NBA opportunity but lost it when the Cincinnati Royals left due to poor attendance in 1972 and became the Kansas City-Omaha Kings. It was an argument I had successfully made numerous times to classmates and adults so voicing it over the phone was, it seemed, just a different setting in which to do what I had always done before—convince everyone listening that Cincinnati was better off attempting to secure a NHL franchise.

And yet, as I waited on hold, I was scared to death.

I didn't doubt my ability to make my point but I was overconfident.

Curiously, waiting on hold for what would be a significant period of time, did not cause any anxiety since the callers ahead of me were taking the opposite side of the argument so there wasn't any chance for my opinion to be stale and redundant. And surprisingly, appearing on a radio show broadcast for the very first time on the 50,000-watt behemoth, 700 WLW with a very large audience listening in didn't cause me any nervous apprehension.

No, the reason I was shaking with intimidating fear while my time on the air crept closer was entirely based on the person hosting the show, the person who ultimately would determine if my opinion was conclusive and strong or flimsy and assailable. I was about to speak to Bob Trumpy, and the thought of it terrified me to no end. Unlike some callers who would later admit they were intimidated by his intelligence, his seemingly vast knowledge of all sports and even to a certain degree, his deep, distinctive voice, the source of my panic was all about getting the chance to talk to a former NFL star who, in my mind, was the best tight end of his era and an all-time great for my favorite team, the Cincinnati Bengals. In essence, I feared the worst—I would lose my nerve when attempting to speak to a Bengals legend.

Unless you were a Bengals fan from 1968-1977, football fans are probably only familiar with Trumpy from his work at NBC Sports beginning in 1978. Over the next 20 years, Trumpy was an analyst on the network's NFL broadcasts, including serving as the number one analyst for NBC from 1992-1994, working alongside legendary play-by-play announcer Dick Enberg in which they worked two Super Bowls together. And while it was a stellar broadcasting career, his time as an NFL tight end was just as outstanding.

Born in Springfield, Illinois, Trumpy attended Springfield High School after his family moved back to the area from Trenton, Illinois in his sophomore season. He became an all-state performer in football and basketball while at Springfield, an athletic career that eventually earned him a spot as a charter member of the Springfield Illinois Sports Hall of Fame in 1991 and the Springfield High School Hall of Fame in 1996. It also helped him procure a football scholarship to the University of Illinois beginning in 1963. The following year, Trumpy played in nine games for the Illini, finishing the 1964 season eighth in the Big 10 in receptions (28), seventh in receiving yards (428) and fifth in yards per reception (15.3) to go along with his two touchdown catches.[1]

Trumpy played only one season at Illinois before transferring to the University of Utah. Like he had done at Illinois, Trumpy played only one year at Utah, contributing nine receptions, 159 receiving yards, a 17.7 yards per reception average and two touchdowns in nine games for the Utes in the 1966 season. Even though Trumpy was eligible for the 1968 AFL/NFL Common Draft, very few football observers believed any AFL or NFL team would select him.

Fortunately for Trumpy, the Cincinnati Bengals were about to embark on their inaugural season in the AFL in 1968 and, quite frankly, they needed all the able bodies they could get their hands on. Consequently, the Bengals chose Trumpy in the 12th round of the 1968 Draft with 301st overall selection. Not much was expected from Trumpy as he entered his and the Bengals first ever training camp. In fact, the chances he would even make the team in 1968 seemed slim at best. Fortune, however, was on Trumpy's side when he arrived in Cincinnati prior to the 1968 season.

The Bengals were led in their first season by their owner, general manager and head coach, the legendary Paul Brown. One of the many decisions Brown made when putting together his first team was to hire an up-and-coming assistant from California, Bill Walsh, as his wide receivers and tight end coach. Walsh saw in Trumpy the prototypical tight end in what would become his infamous West Coast Offense, a player who at 6'6" was "remarkably tall compared to other tight ends of his era," remarked The Pro Football Historical Abstract.[2127]

Under Walsh's and Brown's tutelage, Trumpy went from relative obscurity at the University of Utah to starting in the Bengals' first AFL game at tight end, and more impressively, making a significant impact in the franchise's debut season. Trumpy led the team in 1968 in receptions (37), receiving yards (639) and touchdown catches (3) as the Bengals

---

[1] One of Trumpy's teammates at Illinois was a center and linebacker who would become one of the greatest players in NFL history, a man by the name of Dick Butkus.

[2] In an interesting piece of irony, Trumpy replaced Walsh as the number one NFL analyst at NBC in 1992.

finished their inaugural season with a 3-11 record. For his efforts, Trumpy was named to the 1968 AFL Pro Bowl team.

Trumpy picked up where he left off in his rookie season the following year and in doing so, over the next four years became the number one target for quarterbacks Greg Cook and Virgil Carter. In 1969, he led all Bengals tight ends with 37 receptions and an AFL sixth best 835 yards receiving for an average of 22.57 yards per reception, the third highest yards per catch in the AFL and the second highest in franchise history. His nine touchdown receptions led all Bengals receivers in 1969 and was the fourth most receiving touchdowns and the fifth most total touchdowns in the entire AFL. A third of those touchdowns came against the Houston Oilers on November 6 when Trumpy scored on three passes of 40, 70 and 14 yards from Cook to become the first Bengals tight end to score three touchdowns in one game. Trumpy's performance in his second professional season earned him first team All-AFL honors from the AP, the Hall of Fame, the Newspapers Enterprise Association (NEA), The New York Daily News, Pro Football Weekly and the UPI, second team All-AFL honors from The Pro Football Writers and The Sporting News and his second straight selection to the AFL Pro Bowl.

In 1970, the AFL merged with the NFL, giving Trumpy and his teammates the opportunity to display his talent on a wider, national stage. He didn't disappoint and neither did the Bengals. Trumpy ended the year with 29 receptions for 480 yards and two touchdowns, and a spot on the newly minted 1970 AFC Pro Bowl team. He also garnered first team All-AFC selections from the AP and The Sporting News and second team All-NFL honors from The Pro Football Writers and the NEA.

More importantly, Trumpy's play helped the Bengals to an incredible run of seven consecutive wins to end the season that resulted in an improbable AFC Central Division title and a trip to the NFL playoffs in their first year in the league and their third professional football season overall. Even though they lost to the Baltimore Colts 17-0, in the first round of the playoffs, the performance of Trumpy and the rest of the Bengals went beyond the expectations for a player and a team in only their third year of professional play.

Trumpy followed up his 1970 season with another solid year in 1971. He led all Bengals receivers in receptions (40) and receiving yards (531) in addition to catching two touchdown passes. The 1972 season was no different for Trumpy as he led all tight ends on the team with 44 receptions, 500 receiving yards and two touchdown catches. Unfortunately, the Bengals failed to match Trumpy's success in those two seasons, missing the playoffs in both years while going a combined 12-16 in 1971 and 1972.

As the 1973 seasons unfolded, the Bengals' offense began to change. Ken Anderson settled in as the team's starting quarterback and he had two new weapons at his disposal, rookie running back, Boobie Clark and rookie wide receiver, Isaac Curtis. Clark and Curtis became the primary receiving targets for Anderson, combining for 90 receptions, 1,190 receiving yards and nine touchdown catches, with Clark being named the 1973 AFC Rookie of the Year.

Meanwhile, the offense's new focus reduced the number of opportunities and receptions Trumpy received. In his first five years from 1968-1972, he averaged 37.4 receptions and 597 receiving yards per season. Over the next five years from 1973-1977, he averaged 22.2 receptions and 323 receiving yards per season. The upside to the decrease in Trumpy's production was that the Bengals started to win more often. From 1973-1977, they finished a combined 40-30 during the regular season, qualifying for the playoffs twice, once as the AFC Central Division champion in 1973 and as a wild card team in 1975. It was a trade-off Trumpy gladly accepted.

"When I was getting the ball all the time, we were 4-10," Trumpy remarked in October 1974. "With Isaac in there, we're 10-4. I'd much rather win than be famous."[128]

Trumpy, who despite playing a lesser role in the offense, earned his fourth Pro Bowl appearance in 1973 and led the team in touchdown receptions with seven in 1976,[1] is probably best remembered by Bengals fans during this time for his part in a memorable play against the Miami Dolphins on November 22, 1977. Trailing the Dolphins 17-16 in a driving rainstorm at Riverfront Stadium with 2:35 left in the fourth quarter and the ball at the Miami 29-yard line, the Bengals coaches called for the "Triple Pass". The play started with Anderson handing the ball off to running back Archie Griffin who then handed it to wide receiver John

---

[1]   Trumpy's seven touchdown catches was the seventh most in the NFL in 1976.

McDaniel on a reverse. McDaniel then returned the ball to Anderson who hoped to find Trumpy open in the end zone. As Trumpy recalled after the game, the pressure was squarely on his shoulders.

"We've been running that play for 10 years," Trumpy said in a post-game interview. "I drop it and I'm looking for a job sweeping floors somewhere."[129] Trumpy didn't drop it and his 29-yard touchdown reception, the only touchdown catch he would have in 1977, gave the Bengals an exhilarating 23-22 victory. It also essentially eliminated Miami's chances of making the playoffs. This was a fact that then Dolphins head coach, Don Shula, reminded Trumpy about every time he saw him.

"Shula called it the reverse pass," Trumpy has said. "He'll see me and say, 'That damn reverse pass. I remember that.'"[130]

The only negative aspect of Trumpy's career was his play in the post-season. In his first two playoff appearances in 1970 and 1973 against Baltimore and Miami respectively, Trumpy did not have a single reception. In his final playoff game in 1975 against the Oakland Raiders, Trumpy caught one pass for a negative seven yards. To make matters worse, the Bengals lost all three playoff games by a combined score of 82-44.

Trumpy's scant production in the post season should not and does not take away from what he accomplished in his 10-years in a Bengals uniform. His 298 career receptions is the third most by a Bengals tight end, and ranks 11th on the team's all-time receptions list. He amassed 4,600 receiving yards, the most by a Bengals tight end and the ninth most by any player in team history. He also leads all tight ends in Cincinnati history in yards per reception (15.4) and points scored (210) while placing sixth and 20th on those lists respectively amongst all players in Bengals team history.

Trumpy's achievements also place him as one of the best tight ends in NFL history as well. The Pro Football Historical Abstract ranks him as the 18th best tight end of all-time with a career Q score of 160.48 and 2,194.0 adjusted yards gained. The Abstract lists three of his seasons as some of the best ever, including 1969 when he received a perfect 10.0 Q score and gained 382.5 adjusted receiving yards.[1131]

---

[1] The other two seasons The Abstract recognized were 1971 and 1972. In 1971, Trumpy received an 8.2 Q score and gained 280.5 adjusted receiving yards. In 1972, his Q score was 7.4 and he finished with 260.0 adjusted receiving yards.

Trumpy's statistical production was, at the time, uncommon for someone who played the tight end position. Unlike the roles today's tight ends play, such as Rob Gronkowski, Antonio Gates, Jason Witten and Jimmy Graham, the football played during Trumpy's era did not utilize the tight end as a primary offensive weapon, making his numbers even more impressive. The offensive philosophy championed by Walsh and Brown to use the tight end more extensively and aggressively, enabled the Bengals to enjoy success which, at the time, was unusual for an expansion franchise.

In their first 10 seasons from 1968-1977, Cincinnati had a surprising 73-66-1 regular season record, won two division titles and qualified for the playoffs a total of three times. Trumpy, who played in 128 games, 97 as a starter, during those 10 years, and the rest of the offense, served as a primary catalyst for the Bengals' unprecedented start in the NFL. They finished in the top half of the NFL in points scored eight times (1970-1977) and in passing offense (1972-1977) and total offense (1971-1975 and 1977) six times while possessing the number one ranked passing offense and the number two total offense in 1975.

Trumpy's playing career ended after the 1977 season[1] but his association with the NFL continued for another 30 years. In addition to his work at NBC Sports, Trumpy worked as the analyst for Westwood One Radio on their NFL Sunday Night Football broadcasts from 2000-2007. It was a body of work that earned him the Pro Football Hall of Fame's Pete Rozelle Radio-Television Award in 2014 for lifetime achievement in NFL broadcasting and long-time exceptional contributions to radio and television in pro football.

Looking back on my phone call to Bob Trumpy in 1980, it is a good thing I didn't know I was talking to a future member of the Pro Football Hall of Fame. If I had, I'm certain my nerves would have gotten the better of me and I would have suffered from a case of the relatively unknown disease known as "sports talk radio stage fright".

Besides, I was already intimidated before I was taken off hold and heard Trumpy's boom, "Mark, from Anderson Township, you're on Sports

---

[1] Years later, when asked to reflect on his legacy in Cincinnati, Trumpy joked, "They retired my size, not my number."

Talk." Because I knew then, like I know now, that I was about to talk to an all-time Cincinnati Bengals great and a future member of the team's Hall of Fame.

And that's something I'm sure both Trumpy and I could have agreed upon.

CHAPTER FORTY-TWO

T.J. HOUSHMANDZADEH

The Underrated Wide Receiver

G rowing up as a teenager in Barstow, California, T.J. Houshmandzadeh had a premonition, something he believed was a harbinger of bad things to come.

"I'd be out on the streets at night and I'd just get this bad feeling that something was going to happen," Houshmandzadeh remembers. "I'd say, 'O.K., I'll see you all tomorrow.' I'd read in the paper the next day that somebody in the group I was with got shot. I just had the sixth sense to avoid something really bad."[132]

Thankfully for the Cincinnati Bengals, Houshmandzadeh's intuitive convictions were just as strong as the physical skills he possessed over an eight-year span from 2001-2008 in becoming one of the team's all-time best wide receivers in franchise history.

Houshmandzadeh's journey to NFL stardom was by no means a conventional one. He dropped out of Barstow High School in 1995 because, as he admits, "I just didn't go to school. I would be out all night. It's hard to get up and go to school when you're out all night."[133] Over the next two years, he would earn his GED and receive a fortuitous phone call from his Barstow High football coach, Junior Monarrez.

At the time of the call, Monarrez was a member of the football staff at Cerritos College, a small community college 17 miles southeast of downtown

Los Angeles. Monarrez offered his former player Houshmandzadeh an opportunity to join the football team at Cerritos for the 1997 season because "somewhere along the line, he got himself focused."[134]

Houshmandzadeh took full advantage of his high school coach's overture by making an immediate impact. In his first year at Cerritos in 1997, he finished the season with 622 receiving yards in addition to an 87-yard punt return for a touchdown and a 100-yard kickoff return for a score. It was a performance that earned Houshmandzadeh the team's Special Team's Award and Freshman of the Year honors as well as being selected first-team Mission Conference at the wide receiver position. He continued his impressive play in his second season at Cerritos in 1998, earning first-team Mission Conference honors for the second consecutive season as well as being named the team's Most Valuable Player. Houshmandzadeh ended his Cerritos career as a two-time letterman with 65 receptions for 1,152 receiving yards and 13 touchdowns. He also earned high praise from his head coach at Cerritos, Frank Mazzota.

"He's just such a tough guy," Mazzota said when asked about his former star wide receiver and kick returner. "He's not the fastest guy in the world, but that sucker will catch the ball and he doesn't care who's around him."[135]

Another coach Houshmandzadeh impressed was Dennis Erickson who in 1999 was the head football coach at Oregon State University. Erickson offered him a scholarship for the 1999 season and he accepted. In his first season at Oregon State, Houshmandzadeh contributed 24 receptions for 378 yards, a 15.8 yards per reception average and two touchdowns as the Beavers ended the season 7-5 and earning a berth in the Oahu Bowl against Hawaii.

The following season, his 48 catches led the team in receptions and seventh best in the Pac-10 Conference in 2000. Houshmandzadeh also finished in the top in the conference in receiving touchdowns (4th with seven), receiving yards (9th with 730) and yards per catch (10th with 15.2 yards per reception). And like he had done at Cerritos, he returned punts as well at Oregon State, ending the year with 28 punt returns for 278 yards, good enough for second best in the Pac-10 conference.

Houshmandzadeh's play as both a wide receiver and a punt returner helped the Beavers in 2000 to an 11-1 record, the most successful season in school history. The 11 wins set the school record for wins in a single season and earned them a berth in the Bowl Championship Series against Notre Dame in the 2001 Fiesta Bowl. The Beavers crushed the Irish, 41-9, with Houshmandzadeh contributing six receptions for 74 yards and one touchdown catch of 23 yards in a victory that propelled Oregon State to a final ranking of third in the Associated Press poll and fourth in the coaches' poll. Houshmandzadeh personally capped off an exceptional season by being selected to play in the 2000 East-West Shrine college all-star game.

Two years after Erickson took a chance on a high school dropout from Cerritos Community College, Houshmandzadeh made his head coach look like a recruiting genius. In his two years at Oregon State, he caught 72 passes for 1,108 yards, an average of 15.4 yards per catch, and nine touchdowns. He also returned 49 punts for 459 yards, an average of 9.4 yards per return. More importantly, once his collegiate career was over, he earned the highest praise from the man who had given him the opportunity to excel in Corvallis, Oregon.

"He's one of the most accountable players I've ever been around," Erickson said following Houshmandzadeh's final college season. "He's a warrior, probably is the best way to put it."[136]

But despite an impressive statistical output in his two seasons at Oregon State and his exposure to NFL scouts and executives at the East-West Shrine Game, Houshmandzadeh's stock in the 2001 NFL Draft wasn't very high. In fact, as draft day neared, those teams looking to add a wide receiver were more interested in his Oregon State teammate, Chad Johnson. One of those teams was the Bengals, who in the second round of the draft, selected Johnson as a compliment to their first round choice from the previous year, wide receiver Peter Warrick.

After they selected Johnson and the rest of the draft unfolded, the Bengals continued to look for another wide receiver. When it came time for them to make their fifth round selections, Houshmandzadeh's college coach, Erickson, lobbied Bengals offensive coordinator, Bob Bratkowski, to take his former player with their next draft pick. The Bengals passed on Houshmandzadeh in the fifth round[1] but when he was still available

---

[1] Instead, the Bengals selected Victor Leyva, a guard from Arizona State, in the fifth round. Leyva played in a total of 10 games for the Bengals in three seasons before being released.

with their seventh round pick and the 204th overall selection in the 2001 Draft, they, like Frank Mazzota and Dennis Erickson had done before them, took a gamble on the wide receiver who survived a tumultuous early life in Barstow, California. It was a draft choice Houshmandzadeh's wide receiver coach at Oregon State, Eric Yarber, believed was the equivalent of a high end bank heist.

"I told Bratkowski you need to go to jail for stealing T.J. in the seventh round," Yarber later recalled. Houshmandzadeh, meanwhile, was even more frank in his assessment of the 2001 Draft.[137]

"There's no way you can explain why I got drafted where I got drafted," Houshmandzadeh said. "There's no way."[138]

In his first three seasons in Cincinnati, however, it looked like the Bengals and the rest of the NFL were right about Houshmandzadeh. He started only six games from 2001-2003, missing all but two games in 2003 because of a severe hamstring injury. When he did play, Houshmandzadeh caught a combined 62 passes for 720 yards and only one touchdown. His lone highlights in his first three years were as a special teams player where he led the team in punt returns in 2001 and 2002 that included an 86-yard punt return at Cleveland on November 25, 2001, the third longest in the NFL in 2001 and which remains tied for the third longest punt return in team history. His 126 total punt return yards in that game against the Browns is the team record for punt return yards in a game.

His fortunes changed in 2004 when Warrick sustained a knee injury during the season. Houshmandzadeh was inserted into the starting lineup at the second wide receiver position to replace Warrick and he wouldn't relinquish the spot until after the 2008 season.[1] Over the next five years, Houshmandzadeh would become one of the top receivers in the NFL, averaging 89 receptions, 1,013 receiving yards and 7.2 touchdown catches per season from 2004-2008. He played a key role in the renaissance of the Bengals offense and in leading a turnaround for the franchise, who in 2005 made their first playoff appearance since 1990. Led by quarterback Carson Palmer, the Bengals finished in the top half of the NFL in points scored four times (2004-2007) and in total offense and passing offense

---

[1] Thanks in large part to Houshmandzadeh's performance, the Bengals released Warrick prior to the start of the 2005 season.

three times (2005-2007) while setting franchise marks for points scored (421 points, tied for fourth in team history) and passing touchdowns (32 tied for second) in 2005 and net yards passing (2nd with 4,012) and net yards passing per game (3rd most at 250.75 yards per game) in 2007.

Personally, Houshmandzadeh played his best during a three-year stretch from 2006-2008 when he led the Bengals in receptions each season. In 2006, his 90 receptions were the seventh most in the NFL while his 77.2 receiving yards per game ranked eighth. In 2007, his first and only season when he was named to the Pro Bowl, Houshmandzadeh led the NFL and set the team record for receptions in a season with 112, becoming only of two Bengals receivers in team history with at least 100 receptions in a single season. His 12 receiving touchdowns that year, which included eight consecutive games where he scored a touchdown, the third longest such streak in team history, was seventh best in the NFL and ranks tied for third for most receiving touchdowns in a season in team history. He ended the 2008 season with 92 receptions, good enough to finish sixth in the NFL. By then, Houshmandzadeh had proven his value to his teammates and coaches, even if the rest of the football world didn't seem to notice.

"T.J.'s very physical. I've never seen anybody with such great balance," said Palmer, who compared Houshmandzadeh to Pittsburgh Steelers' wide receiver, Hines Ward. "He gets hit so hard, he's standing on one foot and he keeps his balance and winds up breaking a tackle and still getting up field."[139]

"T.J's an intellectual player. He really knows why things are done, why defenses do things," said Bratkowski, the Bengals offensive coordinator from 2001-2010. "That allows him to go use his ability and put himself in the right spot. He has great hands. He catches a lot of contested balls. He's great with run after the catch and very precise in his route running."[140]

Unfortunately for Houshmandzadeh, he went relatively unknown to the rest of the NFL outside of the Bengals' locker room, despite having the seventh best DVOA among wide receivers in the NFL in 2005 and the fifth best DYAR in 2006 according to Pro Football Outsiders. Once again, he was overshadowed by his Oregon State and now--Bengals teammate, Chad Johnson. With his choreographed touchdown celebrations and his overall bravado, Johnson got far more publicity nationally than Houshmandzadeh and, fairly or unfairly, far more credit for the Bengals success, especially at the wide receiver position. As usual, Houshmandzadeh addressed this slight with his trademark frankness and brevity. "I think I'm the most under-rated receiver in the game," he said in 2006.[141]

At the conclusion of the 2008 season, Houshmandzadeh decided he no longer wanted to live in the shadows of Johnson so he aggressively pursued his options as an unrestricted free agent. "For the last three years in Cincinnati, they knew I was underpaid," Houshmandzadeh concluded. "But that's how they get down. I can't fault them for that, but that's just how it is."[142]

The Bengals wanted to re-sign Houshmandzadeh but in the end, they fell short in their pursuit to the Seattle Seahawks, who signed him before the start of the 2009 season to a five-year, $40 million contract, with $15 million guaranteed. "Cincinnati's offer wasn't enough for me to continue to play there," Houshmandzadeh told the Seattle media after signing his contract. "I think I should be able to start fresh."[1143]

Houshmandzadeh lasted only one season in Seattle, and after playing with Baltimore in 2010 and Oakland the following season, his 11-year NFL career ended after the 2011 season. And even though he may not have received the notoriety he wanted while he was there, Houshmandzadeh's best years came when wearing a Bengals uniform. He finished his career in Cincinnati with 507 receptions, the third most in franchise history and 5,782 receiving yards which ranks ninth in team history and includes two 1,000-yard receiving seasons (2006 and 2007) and 13 100-yard receiving games.[2] His 38 touchdowns for 228 points scored ranks 17th on the team's all-time scoring list and is ninth best among all wide receivers. He also added 55 punt returns for 447 yards (8.1 yards per return average), 33 kickoffs for 700 yards (21.2 yards per kick return) and in his lone playoff appearance with the Bengals in 2005, he caught four passes for 25 yards and one touchdown.

It was, without question, a career no one saw coming. For a high

---

[1] Houshmandzadeh also added, "I want to win some games for once." As it turned out, the Bengals won the AFC North Division and made the playoffs in 2009 while the Seahawks finished 5-11.

[2] Three of those 13 100-yard receiving games occurred in three consecutive games in 2007, tied for the third longest streak of consecutive 100-yard games in team history.

school dropout who barely made it out of his hometown alive, only to find a lifeline from his former high school coach at a small community college that earned him a scholarship to a Division I school. To being the last player selected by an NFL team in their college draft and turning that presumed slight into an eight-year career that established him as one of the best receivers in franchise history. It is a story even the seemingly clairvoyant Houshmandzadeh could not have predicted while roaming the streets of Barstow, California.

Back then, Houshmandzadeh only saw danger in his future. Good thing for him and the Bengals, he also had the foresight to avoid it.

CHAPTER FORTY–THREE

ISAAC CURTIS

The Game Changer

One of the surest ways for a professional athlete to secure their legacy is to have a rule in their sport or league adopted and named in their honor. Lew Alcindor, who later changed his name to Kareem Abdul-Jabbar, was so dominant near the basket in his first year as the center for the UCLA basketball team in 1967, the NCAA banned the dunk shot after the season and called it the "Lew Alcindor Rule".[1]

Wayne Gretzky and his Edmonton Oiler teammates created so much havoc and scored seemingly at will when skating four-on-four against their opponents during an offsetting minor penalty that the NHL introduced the "Wayne Gretzky Rule" for the 1985-86 season which required both teams to play at full strength when offsetting penalties were called.[2]

NFL Hall of Famer defensive end, Deacon Jones, terrorized quarterbacks during the 1960s and early 1970s, thanks in large part to the devastating head slap he inflicted on an offensive lineman on his way to the backfield. Even though he retired after the 1973 season, the NFL

---

[1] The NCAA rescinded the rule and allowed dunking at the start of the 1976-77 season.

[2] Like the "Lew Alcindor Rule", the NHL reversed course at the start of the 1992-93 season and returned to four-on four matchups when offsetting minor penalties occurred.

paid homage to the player credited with creating the statistic known as the quarterback sack in 1977 when the league enacted the "Deacon Jones Rule," which prohibited the use of Jones' signature head-slap-to-the-helmet maneuver. In each of these cases, the play of these three legends forced their respective leagues to change the dynamic and the way their games were played.

In the case of the legendary Cincinnati Bengals' wide receiver Isaac Curtis, the NFL only needed to see him play for one season before acknowledging that they had to modify the rules that pertained to contact between receivers and defensive backs down field. When Curtis began his NFL career in 1973, the rules allowed defensive backs to make full contact with a receiver anywhere on the field as long as it did not interfere with the receiver's ability to catch the ball.

As the 1973 regular season unfolded, it appeared those rules had no effect on Curtis, who caught 45 passes for 843 yards, nine touchdowns and an average of 18.7 yards per catch in helping the Bengals win the 1973 AFC Central Division title. The permissible contact down field didn't faze Curtis because the defensive backs he faced did not have the speed to cover or catch up with him past the line of scrimmage.

While preparing to play the Bengals in the first round of the 1973 playoffs, Miami Dolphins head coach, Don Shula, realized he had no one in his defensive secondary who could cover Curtis, a matchup he feared his mentor, Bengals' head coach Paul Brown, would attempt to exploit as often as possible. Shula, therefore, instructed his defensive backs to bump, push, hold, and maul and harass Curtis at every opportunity anywhere on the field. Shula's game plan worked as the Dolphins held Curtis to one reception for nine yards in Miami's 34-16 victory over Cincinnati in the AFC divisional playoffs.

Shula's strategy also succeeded in infuriating his former head coach Paul Brown. After watching Shula and the rest of the league batter Curtis and stifle his passing game, Brown, an influential member of the league's competition committee in charge of adding and modifying the rules of the game, lobbied in the off-season for an overhaul of how defensive backs defended receivers down field. His efforts to convince the majority of the remaining NFL owners to eliminate the contact beyond the line of scrimmage proved successful, culminating in what became known as the "Isaac Curtis Rule" for the start of the 1974 season.

Beginning in 1974, the "Isaac Curtis Rule" eliminated the cutting and roll blocking of receivers downfield eligible to catch a pass. More significantly, the rule prohibited any contact by a defender with a receiver five yards beyond the line of scrimmage. Any non-incidental contact by the defender after those five yards would be flagged for holding, a five-yard penalty resulting in an automatic first down. Arguably, the adoption of the "Isaac Curtis Rule" forever changed the face of the NFL, transitioning the game from the ground and pound, three yards and a cloud of dust offenses of the 1960s and 1970s, to the wide-open pass happy scoring fest it has become today. To many former players, the league can thank Curtis and his incredible speed and skill for making the league as popular as it is today.

"He changed the game," former teammate and current NFL analyst Cris Collinsworth has said about Curtis. "There's no question, because no one could keep up with him." Because of Curtis, Collinsworth argues, the NFL "put in the five-yard bump rules and all that crazy stuff that it all eventually became."[144]

Before his talents as a wide receiver were immortalized by the NFL rule book, Curtis grew up in Santa Ana, California as a stand-out running back and track star at Santa Ana High School. In fact, in the eyes of some, he was more than just a high school senior who had the skill set to play at the Division I college level.

"Isaac Curtis is the best running back to ever play in Orange County," long-time local high school football coach, Tom Baldwin, once said. "He never got the recognition because he played on such a great team his senior season."[145]

Curtis decided to continue his athletic exploits at the University of California-Berkeley where he was a member of both the football and track teams. Even though he was a two-sport star at Cal, Curtis always believed one of those two took precedent.

"I was a football player that ran track," Curtis noted. "Although I guess you could also say I was a track guy that played football. But I always considered myself a football player first."[146] After looking at his performance on the Cal track team, however, one can only imagine how dominant Curtis could have been had he considered himself a track guy first.

Curtis helped lead California to the 1970 NCAA Track and Field championship in his freshman year, finishing first as a member of the 440-yard relay team, second in the 100-yard dash and fourth in the 220-yard dash. His 100-yard dash time in 1970 of 9.3 seconds is the second fastest in school history while his 21.04 seconds time in the 200-meter dash is the 10ᵗʰ fastest. A three-time track All-American at Cal, Curtis had the seventh fastest time in the United States in the 100-meter dash in 1970 and the ninth fastest in 1972.

Meanwhile, Curtis was no slouch on the football team for the Golden Bears either. A two-year letterman and starting running back for head coach Ray Willsey, Curtis rushed for 427 yards for three touchdowns on 103 attempts and accounted for 644 yards of total offense and four total touchdowns in 1970. The following season he gained 475 rushing yards for five touchdowns on 110 attempts and added 175 receiving yards on 15 receptions.

Unfortunately, Curtis' time at California came to a sudden end after his junior year in 1971. An investigation into his academic records indicated he had failed to take the test to predict a 1.6 grade point average prior to his admission to the school, an oversight which was an NCAA infraction. As part of their penalty for the violation, California forfeited the 1970 NCAA Track and Field championship and declared Curtis athletically ineligible. The NCAA additionally placed the school on indefinite probation, making them ineligible for post-season play in football and track.

Despite being declared ineligible at California, the NCAA did allow Curtis the opportunity to transfer to another Division I school to continue his collegiate career. After weighing several offers, Curtis settled on a school that had only been playing at the Division I level since 1969 but whose head coach was turning heads with his innovative and successful pass-oriented offense and his unique recruiting perspective.

Don Coryell had built a program at San Diego State University prior to 1969 which in his words, "won games by throwing the ball without the best personnel"[147] and by recruiting primarily junior college transfers. It was a recipe good enough for the Aztecs to win three Division II California Collegiate Athletic Association conference titles in his first seven seasons and two small college undefeated seasons in 1966 and 1968. The success continued for Coryell and San Diego State once they began playing at the Division I level. In their first three seasons at the top tier of college football, the Aztecs went 26-7 from 1969-1971, capturing two Pacific Coast Athletic Association (PCAA) titles in 1969 and 1970 in the process.

With the 1972 season approaching, Coryell was intrigued by the prospect of having the speedy former California running back on his team. He offered Curtis the opportunity to complete his final year of college eligibility but under the condition that he switch positions from running back to wide receiver. It was a move Curtis warmly embraced.

"I always felt it was a natural position for me," Curtis said of his move to wide receiver. "I could always catch."[148] By the time he completed his lone season at San Diego State, both Curtis and Coryell were proven right—he was a natural at wide receiver and he could catch.

Curtis finished the 1972 season as the team leader in receptions with 44 and receiving yards with 832 as the Aztecs ended the year 10-1 and winners of the PCAA for the third time in four years. In addition to his seven touchdown catches, Curtis had three 100-yard receiving games, including a personal high 166 yards receiving against Long Beach State on November 25. Not only did he earn first team PCAA honors for his performance but Curtis also won the 1972 John Simcox Memorial trophy as the team's Most Valuable Player and played in the post-season College All-Star and the East-West Shrine games.

At the end of the 1972 season, both Coryell and Curtis used their experiences at San Diego State as a stepping stone for bigger and better things. Coryell parlayed his enormous success in his 11 seasons as the Aztecs head coach into an equally transformative NFL head coaching career beginning in 1973. In 14 seasons as head coach of the St. Louis Cardinals and most notably the San Diego Chargers, Coryell finished with a career 111-83-1 (.572) coaching record and introduced one of the greatest passing offenses in NFL history known simply as Air Coryell.

At the same time his college head coach was beginning his eventual memorable NFL career, Curtis, who was inducted into San Diego State's athletic Hall of Fame in 2008, and his ability to spread the field with his incredible speed, piqued the interest of the legendary NFL head coach, Paul Brown and his wide receivers coach in Cincinnati, Bill Walsh. In Curtis, both Brown and Walsh saw a unique offensive weapon that was a perfect complement to their young starting quarterback, Ken Anderson and a building block in their efforts to make the young franchise competitive in the NFL.

Both Brown and Walsh were also impressed with Curtis' determination to become a world class football player and everything that entailed, and not just someone with world class speed who happened to play football. "I always considered myself a football player first," said Curtis, who credits Walsh with helping him become a top-flight receiver. "Some of these sprinters come into the pros, they're afraid of contact. They only know how to run straight ahead."[149]

It's also worth presuming that Brown and Walsh valued Curtis so highly because they believed the young wide receiver was the prototypical player of the NFL future. Walsh in particular must have been salivating at the chance to use Curtis's speed, agility, physicality and hands in his innovative offense that would evolve into the legendary West Coast offense. Whatever the reason, the Bengals wasted no time in choosing Curtis in the 1973 NFL Draft, selecting him in the first round with the 15th overall pick.

As evidenced by the strategy Shula employed in the playoffs later in the year, Curtis made an immediate impact in his rookie season in 1973. A starter in all of the team's 14 games, Curtis led the team in receptions (45), receiving yards (843) and touchdown catches (9) and finished fourth in the NFL in yards per reception (18.7 yards per catch) and receiving touchdowns, fifth in receiving yards, sixth in receiving yards per game (60.2 yards per game) and tenth in total touchdowns. It was a debut season worthy enough to earn Curtis a Pro Bowl selection and a spot on the UPI's second team All-AFC roster.

The following season, with the rule bearing his name in place, Curtis led the Bengals in receiving yards (633) and touchdown receptions (10) while his 21.1 yards per reception was the second highest in the NFL in 1974 and is the fifth best in team history. His 10 touchdown receptions was also the second highest in the league that season and was the seventh most total touchdowns in the NFL in 1974. Once again, the post-season accolades rolled in for Curtis. He received his second Pro Bowl selection and was named first team All-AFC by the AP, The Sporting News and the UPI and second team All-NFL honors from the AP, The Pro Football Writers and The Newspaper Enterprise Association (NEA).

The 1975 season was an excellent one for both the Bengals and Curtis. Cincinnati finished the season 11-3, a .786 winning percentage that is the best in team history, and qualified for the post-season as the AFC wild card entrant. Curtis played a large role in the Bengals' success in 1975, leading the team in receptions (44), receiving yards (an eventual career high, 934) and touchdown catches (7). His 21.2 yards per reception not only led the NFL in 1975 but remains the fourth best season in franchise history. He finished second in the league in receiving yards and receiving yards per game (66.7 yards per game) and ninth in receiving touchdowns. Curtis was also responsible for 139 of the 441 passing yards the Bengals gained against Buffalo on November 17, the third most net yards passing in a game in club history.

Even though the Bengals lost their first round playoff game against the Oakland Raiders on December 28, 1975, unlike his first playoff game, Curtis was not held completely in check, catching three passes for 20 and one touchdown in the 31-28 defeat. Once the 1975 season was complete, Curtis had earned his third consecutive Pro Bowl invitation along with such honors as first team All-AFC from Pro Football Weekly and The Sporting News, first team All-NFL from the NEA and Pro Football Weekly, second team All-AFC from the UPI and second team All-NFL from the AP and the Pro Football Writers.

Curtis continued a four year run of excellence in 1976 when he led the team in receptions (41) and receiving yards (766) while leading all Bengals wide receivers in touchdowns with six. He finished 10th in the league in yards per reception (18.7 yards per catch) and his 85 yard touchdown reception against the New York Jets on December 12 is the fifth longest reception in team history. Despite the fact the Bengals missed out on making the playoffs in the last week of the 1976 season, Curtis made his fourth consecutive trip to the Pro Bowl and was named first team All-AFC by The Sporting News and the UPI, first All-NFL by the NEA and second All-NFL by the AP and the Pro Football Writers.

Over the next four seasons Curtis continued his workman-like production even though Cincinnati dropped from perennial playoff contention by going a combined 22-40. From 1977-1980, he averaged

38.5 receptions, 572.5 receiving yards and four touchdowns per season, leading the team in receptions (47) and receiving yards (737) in 1978 and receiving touchdowns (8) in 1979. Despite the team's poor performance during this time, Curtis still managed to have the sixth highest yards per reception (18.9 yards per catch) and the eighth most receiving touchdowns in the NFL in 1979. He also led all Cincinnati wide receivers in receptions (32 and 43) and receiving yards (605 and 610) in 1979 and 1980 and touchdown catches (3) in 1978 and 1980.

At the start of the 1981 season, the Bengals began the process of finding Curtis' heir apparent as the team's number one wide receiver when they selected wide outs David Verser and Cris Collinsworth with their first two picks in the 1981 NFL Draft. In his typically-quiet and professional style, Curtis did not publicly balk about the team's new direction, but he mentored the two new receivers as well, a role former teammate Dave Lapham believed benefited not just Verser and Collinsworth but everyone on the team.

"He was like E.F. Hutton," Lapham said of Curtis. "When he talked, people listened. And he didn't throw a lot out there."[150]

Collinsworth immediately jumped at the chance to learn from one of the league's best wide receivers. Problem was, when he tried to copy the moves Curtis made on the field, Collinsworth was at a loss. "I would watch it on tape and I would try to do it and I could not physically make the moves that he would," Collinsworth lamented.[151]

The first-year student apparently learned enough since by the end of the 1981 season, Collinsworth replaced Curtis as Ken Anderson's primary passing target. But before he ceded his number one wide receiver position, Curtis continued to contribute to the Bengals offense in his last four years with the team. From 1981-1984, Curtis, in a largely secondary role, averaged 29.5 receptions, 408.7 receiving yards and 1.25 touchdown catches per season. More importantly, his production helped the Bengals return to NFL prominence, culminating in back-to-back playoff seasons in 1981 and 1982 and the franchise's first ever Super Bowl appearance against the San Francisco 49ers. Even with the emergence of Collinsworth as the Bengals' featured wide receiver, Curtis enjoyed the most productive post-season games of his career, combining for nine receptions, 155 receiving yards and one touchdown in four playoff games played in 1981 and 1982.

After recording only 12 receptions in 1984, Curtis retired from the NFL. But by then he had established himself as the first great wide receiver in Cincinnati Bengals history. In his 12 seasons, Curtis was a hallmark of longevity, stability, consistency and proficiency, traits that enabled the Bengals to achieve unexpected success in their early years as an NFL franchise and for Curtis to make an indelible mark on the team's record book. He played in 167 games or 95.4% of the 175 games the Bengals played from 1973-1984, starting in 159 of those games or 90.8% of the time. In his 12 years as a Bengal, Curtis averaged 34.7 receptions, 592 receiving yards and 4.4 touchdown catches per season, a remarkable feat of consistency considering, with the exception of the 1984 season and the 1977 when he missed half the year due to an injury, he had no more than 47 and no fewer than 23 receptions and no more than 934 and no fewer than 320 receiving yards in a single season.[1]

Before Curtis arrived in Cincinnati in 1973, the franchise was only five years old and even though they made the playoffs in 1970, the Bengals still struggled to win on a regular basis, compiling a 27-42-1 (.387) record in those first five seasons. In the 12 years that followed, they went 94-81, qualified for the playoffs four times, won two AFC Central Division titles, one AFC Championship and made their first ever Super Bowl appearance. A major reason for the turnaround was the presence of Curtis and the performance of his teammates on offense. With Curtis manning the wide receiver position, the Bengals finished in the top half of the NFL in passing offense 10 times (1973-1978, 1981-1984), including the number one ranked passing offense in 1975 and in total offense (1973-1975, 1977-1978, 1981-1984) and points scored (1973-1977, 1979, 1981, 1982 and 1984) nine times.

Although it has been over 30 years since he last played, Curtis' name remains prevalent in the franchise's career receiving record book, an accomplishment made even more impressive by the fact that he amassed his statistics during a time when the NFL was not the pass-heavy league that it is today. Heading into the 2016 season, Curtis is still the team's all-time leader in yards per reception with a career 17.07 average and his

---

[1]   His single season low of 23 receptions and 320 receiving yards both occurred in the strike-shortened 1982 season.

14.15 yards per reception in the playoffs is the third highest in Cincinnati post-season history. His 7,101 career receiving yards ranks second in team history and 20 100-yard receiving games are the third most by a Bengals receiver.

The first player to catch 400 passes in a Bengals uniform, Curtis finished with 416 career receptions, the fifth most in team history, with 53 of those catches resulting in a touchdown, the third most receiving touchdowns and the fifth most total touchdowns in Bengals history. Curtis' 318 total points scored in his 12 seasons places him 10th on the team's all-time scoring list and is third amongst wide receivers. Given this track record of achievements, it is not surprising for Lapham, who witnessed Curtis's performance first hand, to state, "There's no question he was good as anyone in his era."[152]

It's fairly common for football fans to attempt to compare a player from the past to someone currently playing. Lapham was asked to do such a thing regarding his former teammate Curtis. "He's Larry Fitzgerald with speed," Lapham initially summarized.[153] But upon reflection, the former offensive guard and current analyst for the Bengals radio broadcasts felt it necessary to provide more details about Curtis's ability than just a simple one-on-one comparison.

"He might have the best hands of anyone I've ever seen," Lapham added. "He was always catching the bottom third of the ball at the last minute."[154]

Lapham then summed up his appreciation of the former track star who made the over-the-shoulder touchdown spike cool, with the most apt description of the impact Curtis made on both the Bengals and the National Football League.

"Anybody they change a rule for, that says it all."[155]

CHAPTER FORTY–FOUR

TIM McGEE

A Hard Loss to Swallow

To this day, *Tim McGee* has never seen a replay of Super Bowl XXIII, the game best known for Joe Montana's fourth quarter drive and his last minute touchdown pass to John Taylor that sealed the San Francisco 49ers 20-16 victory over the Cincinnati Bengals. And if he can help it, McGee, a starting wide receiver on the 1988 Bengals team that lost to Montana and the 49ers, never will.

"I'll never watch it," says McGee, who caught two passes for 23 yards for the Bengals in Super Bowl XXIII. "It's not like you have to go into a team meeting and one of the requirements is to watch the game. I can't help but watch the John Taylor catch. They always show it. We can't help but (relive it). It happens every year because they show it."[156]

McGee's refusal to watch his gut-wrenching loss in the Super Bowl is understandable. Thankfully, due to his play in a nine-year NFL career, eight of which he spent in a Bengals uniform, McGee has plenty of his own positive highlights he can check out in his retirement without having to dwell upon the bitter loss to the 49ers in football's biggest game.

Born and raised in Cleveland, Ohio, McGee was a stand-out split end at his hometown John Hopkins High School where future NBA all-star Charles Oakley was a teammate on the football team. He capped his high school career with an outstanding season in which he recorded

58 receptions, 1,240 yards and eight touchdowns catches and a spot on the Northeast Lakes All-District team in his senior season. Upon his graduation in 1982, McGee accepted a football scholarship to the University of Tennessee.

The decision for a split end to attend and play for head coach Johnny Majors and the Volunteers in 1982 was an easy one. By the time he arrived in Knoxville, the Tennessee football program had become known as "Wide Receiver U" because of their recent reputation of producing such top flight receivers as Willie Gault, Mike Miller, Clyde Duncan, Lenny Taylor and Joey Clinkscales. Due to the depth at wide receiver, McGee played sparingly in his first two seasons at Tennessee, catching a total of 19 passes for 286 yards and two touchdowns. When play began in 1984, however, his status with the Volunteers changed in a big way.

McGee became the team's starting wing back in 1984 and he immediately lived up to the school's "Wide Receivers U" distinction. In his first year as a starter for the Volunteers, McGee led the team in receptions in 54 and 809 receiving yards for six touchdowns. On two separate occasions, he caught 10 passes in one game, first against Florida on October 13 and then against Vanderbilt on December 1, the latter earning McGee SEC Player of the Week honors for his 10 reception, 190 receiving yards and two touchdown catches performance against the Commodores. It was a season-long effort that earned him second team All-SEC wide receiver honors from the Associated Press.

In his senior season in 1985, McGee again started at wing back and was named captain of the team that became known as the "Sugar Vols" thanks to their SEC Championship and a subsequent invitation to the 1986 Sugar Bowl. For the second consecutive season, McGee led Tennessee in receiving, finishing the year with 50 receptions for 947 yards and seven touchdown catches and earning him first team All-SEC wide receiver honors from the AP, the UPI and the American Football Coaches Association. More importantly, he helped the Volunteers to their first conference title since 1969 and a date against head coach Jimmy Johnson and the University of Miami (FL) in the Sugar Bowl. Tennessee steamrolled the Hurricanes 35-7, with McGee leading all receivers with seven receptions for 94 yards and recovering a fumble in the end zone for a touchdown. The impressive victory vaulted Tennessee to number five in the final AP poll and number four in the UPI and USA Today's coaches' poll.

Meanwhile, McGee was earning his fair share of post-season honors as well. He was named first team NCAA Consensus All-American wide receiver after being selected for similar honors by the Associated Press, the American Football Coaches Association, the Newspapers Enterprise Association, the Gannett News Service and the Scripps Howard Newspapers. He also received an invitation and played in the 1986 Hula Bowl college all-star game.

McGee ended his distinguished collegiate career with 123 receptions, 2,042 receiving yards, a 16.6 average yard per reception and 15 touchdown catches. When he graduated from Tennessee in 1985, he held the school records in a season for receptions (54 in 1984) and receiving yards (947 in 1985) as well as being the career leader in receptions, receiving yards and touchdown catches. Needless to say with those kind of achievements, he graduated Magna Cum Laude from "Wide Receiver U".[1] Because they were experiencing an offensive makeover under head coach Sam Wyche and quarterback Boomer Esiason at the time, the Bengals gladly and enthusiastically selected McGee in the first round of the 1986 NFL Draft with the 21st overall pick.

When he arrived at training camp in Cincinnati for his rookie NFL season in 1986, McGee faced a situation similar to the one he encountered as a freshman at Tennessee. He was joining a Bengals team with two established wide receivers, Steve Kreider and Mike Martin, one Pro Bowl wide receiver, Cris Collinsworth and Eddie Brown, the reigning NFL Offensive Rookie of the Year, already on their roster. Even with his college credentials, McGee found himself at the bottom of the wide receiver depth chart, just like he had at Tennessee in the fall of 1982.

The ensuing logjam at wide receiver limited McGee's playing time on offense in 1986 as evidenced by the 16 receptions for 276 yards and one

---

[1] Even though it has been over 30 years since he last played at Tennessee, most of McGee's receiving records remain in the top 10 in school history. His career receiving yards still ranks sixth while his career receptions is ninth best and his receiving yards in a season and his career touchdown catches are both 10th on the school's all-time list. He also has the sixth most 100-yard receiving games in a season (5 in 1985) and the eighth most in a career (8).

touchdown catch he registered in his rookie season. But instead of existing as just another wide receiver making a minimal contribution, McGee added to his own value by becoming the Bengals' leading return man on kickoffs and doing it at a near All-Pro level. He returned 43 kickoffs, third most in the NFL, for a league leading 1,007 yards, including a 94-yard kickoff return against the Minnesota Vikings on October 23 that was the fifth longest in the NFL in 1986. McGee's solid 23.4 average yards per kick return, the league's fourth highest in 1986, impressed the voters at Pro Football Weekly enough to name him a first team All-AFC kick returner for 1986.

Another group apparently also impressed by McGee's performance on special teams in 1986, was the Bengals' offensive coaching staff. Beginning with the 1987 season, McGee moved up the depth chart and eventually into the starting lineup. He ended up starting six games in the strike shortened 1987 season, finishing with 23 receptions, 408 receiving yards, one touchdown and an impressive 17.7 yards per reception. Those contributions did not go unnoticed by Wyche and the rest of the coaching staff because when the 1988 season opened, McGee had made his way into the starting lineup on a full-time basis. It was a position he would maintain for the next five seasons.

In those five seasons from 1988-1992 when he was a regular starting wide receiver for the Bengals, McGee averaged 46 receptions, 768.8 receiving yards, 4.4 touchdown catches and a 16.1 yards per reception per season. He led the team in receiving yards three times (1989, 1990 and 1992) and receptions (1989) and touchdowns (1991) once while leading all Bengals wide receivers in receptions in 1992 and touchdowns in 1989. He ended up in the top 10 in the NFL in yards per reception twice during this time, finishing sixth in 1990 (17.1 yards per catch) and eighth in 1988 (19.1 yards per reception).

McGee's most notable season with the Bengals was 1989, the year he became Esiason's primary target due to Collinsworth's retirement. Inheriting the number one wide receiver position did not overwhelm McGee at all, a fact both Esiason and McGee acknowledged prior to their Week 13 game at Cleveland, a homecoming of sorts for the John Jay High School graduate.

"Timmy has finally come into his own," Esiason said in the days leading up to the game against the Browns. "He's really having a great year. He doesn't have that Cris Collinsworth shadow to worry about anymore and he's settled into his role."[157]

"I've been happy with my progress, given the circumstances, but it has made a big difference this year to know that the split end job was all mine," said McGee, who ended up with seven receptions for 94 yards and a 38-yard touchdown catch in his return to his hometown in a 21-0 victory on December 3. "I won't have people asking any more, 'When is Boomer going to start looking your way more often?'"[158]

McGee completed his breakthrough season in 1989 with 65 receptions for 1,211 yards, the ninth highest receiving yards in the NFL and the sixth Bengals player to register 1,000 or more receiving yards in a season in team history. His 18.6 yards per reception was the sixth best average in the NFL and his 75.7 receiving yards per game was the 10th highest in the league in 1989. McGee finished the year with five 100-yard receiving games, tied for the second most in team history, and his eight touchdowns for 48 points placed him fourth on the team's scoring list for the season.

McGee contributed to two record-setting performances by the Bengals offense in 1989 as well. In their October 17 game against the Tampa Bay Buccaneers, the Bengals scored 56 points, the fourth most in team history, on the strength of eight total touchdowns and six passing touchdowns, both team records. McGee was the player responsible for two of those scores, a 14-yards touchdown pass from Esiason and a 46-yard toss from Erik Wilhelm. Then, on December 17 against their division rival, the Houston Oilers, the Bengals tied the club record by scoring 61 points, equaled the team record of eight total touchdowns in a game and matched the second highest mark in Bengals history for passing touchdowns in a game with five. Once again, McGee played a role in the scoring, catching a 74-yard touchdown from Esiason in the third quarter.

Those two offensive outbursts were just small examples of the potency the Bengals offense exhibited during McGee's time as a regular starter from 1988-1992. In those five seasons, the offense finished in the top half of the NFL in total offense four times (1988-1991) and in passing offense (1988, 1989 and 1991) and points scored (1988-1990) three times. The Super Bowl season of 1988 stands out in particular with the offense finishing first in the league in total offense and points scored and setting the franchise record for points scored (448) and total touchdowns (59) in a season. They also recorded 351 first downs and gained 6,057 total net yards in 1988, the second and third most productive marks respectively in team history.

Following the 1992 season, McGee exercised his right as a free agent and signed with the Washington Redskins for the 1993 season. Used primarily as a third wide receiver in a three wide receiver package, McGee started in 12 of the 13 games he played for the Redskins in 1993, ending the season with 39 receptions, 500 receiving yards and three touchdown catches. He returned to Cincinnati in 1994, playing a part-time role in which he caught 13 passes for 175 yards and one touchdown in 14 games played. It would mark McGee's final season with the Bengals and the NFL as he retired prior to the start of the 1995 season.

McGee's eight year career with Cincinnati may not have the flash or the notoriety of his fellow Bengal contemporaries like Collinsworth and Carl Pickens, but it still ranks as one of the best by a wide receiver in team history. His 282 career receptions as a Bengal is 13th on the team's all-time reception list and ninth amongst all wide receivers, while his 4,703 receiving yards is the ninth best in team history. The 1,211 receiving yards he gained in 1989 is the 11th best season in club history, and he finished with 11 100-yard receiving games. McGee accounted for 25 touchdowns and 150 points, ninth best amongst all the wide receivers in team history and his 16.68 career average yards per reception is the third best in franchise history. He also added seven receptions for 60 yards in five post-season games.

Unfortunately, the stinging loss to the 49ers in Super Bowl XXIII still haunts McGee. Even after nearly 30 years, that last-minute loss seemingly dominates McGee's recollections of this entire NFL career.

"I think it gets worse with time," said McGee, who was inducted into the Greater Cleveland Sports Hall of Fame in 2008. "When you're retired you don't get another opportunity. The celebrations are really hard to watch. You take it kind of personal. We never got to experience that. I never got to experience that."[159]

Admittedly, a loss of that nature is hard to swallow and difficult to eradicate from your memory. Nevertheless, McGee has no reason to let Super Bowl XXIII define his career. Because even though he failed to experience a championship, he did enjoy a solid NFL career and a celebrated tenure with the Cincinnati Bengals.

And that's something a lot of his peers never got to experience.

CHAPTER FORTY-FIVE

CHAD JOHNSON

Ochocinco

One day, in the middle of his first training camp in the summer of 2003 as the head coach of the Cincinnati Bengals, Marvin Lewis was approached by his third-year wide receiver, Chad Johnson. Johnson was coming off a 2002 season, his first as a starting NFL wide receiver and his second in the league, in which he led the Bengals in receptions and receiving yards and finished fourth in the NFL in yards per reception with an average of 16.9 yards per catch. In the minds of both the team's front office and their fan base, the 2003 season would determine if the young receiver had the talent to produce consistently or if he was just another flash in the pan. With an ESPN crew filming the practice nearby, Johnson wanted a word with his new head coach.

"I want to be the best of all-time," the ESPN cameras picked up Johnson saying to Lewis. "I want to be better than (Jerry) Rice."[1160]

It's now been over a decade since Johnson expressed his intentions to Lewis. And with his NFL career coming to an end after the 2012 season, there has been sufficient time to judge how close Johnson came to fulfilling his own lofty expectations. Regrettably, despite finishing with 766 career receptions, 35th on the NFL's all-time list, for 11,059 receiving yards, 33rd

---

[1] Lewis responded to Johnson by telling him, "I know, and we're going to help you."

most in league history, and 67 receiving touchdowns, Johnson failed to eclipse the marks set by Rice in his remarkable professional career.

That said, Johnson can arguably claim he is the greatest wide receiver in Bengals history. Like any player of this stature, Johnson not only made an obvious impact on the field, but how his play energized the organization and its fan base was just as meaningful and consequential.

"In all my years growing up in Cincinnati, I've never experienced a personality like Chad Johnson," said WLW radio station account executive Brian Horton in 2005. "People absolutely love him. He's changed the Bengals' personality. We had Corey Dillon and Carl Pickens, and that was a bad vibe. Chad's positive and entertaining. Everybody wants to see what he's going to do next."[161]

Born in Miami, and raised by his grandparents, Betsy and James Flowers, Johnson almost didn't get the chance to charm and excite the city of Cincinnati. "I lost friends to drugs and jail," Johnson says of his time growing up in Miami. "Everyone has a route when you're young. Once you veer off that path it's tough to come back. I veered off a couple of times. But when it counted, I was able to get myself right. I wanted to play this game so bad, it's what got me to where I am. I wasn't good in school. All I wanted to do was play ball."[162]

Johnson stayed on the right path by playing football at Miami Beach Senior High School and in the process learned the "Miami Football Doctrine", a philosophy he would practice throughout his career. "It's Miami. Everything is competition. Everything," is how Johnson initially explained the attitude he faced on the football field. "Everything is a trash talking competition of every age group.

"The trash talking starts early down there. It's just the way we were brought up. It's why so many starts that dominate the NFL are from down that way."[163]

Johnson had the skills to play at the collegiate level but because of his self-confessed aversion to school and the work that went with it, he was forced after high school to continue his passion for football by enrolling at Santa Monica Community College in California.[1] He played two seasons

---

[1] After graduating from Miami Beach Senior High School, Johnson attended Langston University in Oklahoma but transferred to Santa Monica Community College in 1997.

for Santa Monica in 1997 and 1999[1], finishing with 120 receptions for 2,100 receiving yards, 23 touchdown and a splendid 17.5 average yards per reception. His performance at Santa Monica impressed Oregon State University head coach Dennis Erickson enough to offer Johnson a scholarship for the 2000 season.

Johnson made the most of his only year of eligibility at Oregon State by playing in all 12 games, catching 37 passes for 806 yards. His eight touchdown catches that included a school record 97-yard reception against Stanford on October 14, led the Pac-10 conference in 2000 and is tied for eighth most in school history. He also finished fifth in the conference in receiving yards and second in yards per reception, a 21.8 yards per catch that was also the third highest in the NCAA in 2000.

Johnson and the rest of his Oregon State teammates enjoyed one of the best seasons in school history, ending the regular season with a 10-1 record and a berth in the Fiesta Bowl against Notre Dame on New Year's Day 2001. Johnson contributed four receptions for a game high 93 receiving yards and two touchdown catches of 74 and 4 yards in the Beavers 41-7 demolition of the Irish, a victory that gave Oregon State a school record 11 wins in a single season.

With only one season of Division I football under his belt, being invited to participate in the college all-star Senior Bowl classic in Mobile, Alabama, gave Johnson the chance to showcase his NFL potential. By the time all of the draft gurus, coaches and scouts had left Mobile, one thing was certain—Johnson had more than capitalized on his opportunity.

ESPN draft expert, Mel Kiper Jr., described Johnson as the "most impressive player at Senior Bowl practices"[164] and raved about his "tremendous physical ability."[165] In the game itself, Johnson shone, catching a 29-yard pass from Rutgers quarterback Mike McMahon and according to Kiper, was "one of the best players on the field."[166] More importantly, his performance in Mobile impressed Bob Bratkowski, who at the time was an assistant for the Pittsburgh Steelers and a member of the coaching staff assigned to the Senior Bowl team Johnson played on.

"Nobody came close to covering him," said Bratkowski who, one week after the Senior Bowl, became the Bengals' offensive coordinator. "He was

---

[1]   Johnson sat out the 1998 season so he could concentrate on his academics.

heads and tails better than anyone else." Nevertheless, Bratkowski and his new employer remained reluctant about selecting Johnson in the upcoming NFL Draft. "The big question about him," Bratkowski said, "was why did he bounce around so much?"[167]

Fortunately for Johnson and the Bengals, Bratkowski had previously worked for Erickson and he was confident the report he would receive from Johnson's head coach at Oregon State would be unfettered and totally truthful. Appeased by what Erickson said about his work habits and attitude, the Bengals selected Johnson in the second round of the 2001 NFL Draft with the 36th overall pick.[1]

Johnson was joining a franchise desperate for his competitive attitude and his passion to succeed. Heading into the 2001 season, the Bengals were still looking for their first winning season since 1990 and had gone a combined 11-37 in their last three seasons. Undeterred by the team's run of losing seasons at the time of his arrival, Johnson was always determined not only to make the Bengals a winning franchise but to also make his mark on the NFL.

"I want to help turn this organization around—do it being exciting, being entertaining and being a good guy," Johnson said in 2005. "When I've taken my team to the playoffs, and, hopefully, this year, help take us to the Super Bowl—when I've done those things, then I'll consider myself one of the best."[168]

Johnson's quest to re-energize the franchise and become one of the game's all-time greats, began in a somewhat part-time role in his rookie season in 2001, playing 12 games and starting three. He ended the year with 28 receptions for 329 receiving yards and one touchdown but because of the team's depth at wide receiver, which included former first round draft choice, Peter Warrick and veteran Darnay Scott, Johnson's moments to shine were limited. That scene changed, however, prior to the start of the 2002 season when Scott was released, opening the door for Johnson to become a bigger contributor to the Bengals offense. Like

---

[1] The Bengals and Bratkowski would use this relationship with Erickson to vet Johnson's teammate at Oregon State, T.J. Houshmandzadeh. Because of Erickson's feedback and prodding, they would draft Houshmandzadeh in the seventh round of the 2001 NFL Draft.

he had done at the Senior Bowl, Johnson took full advantage of the opportunity.

Playing in all 16 games in 2002 and starting in all but two of them, Johnson led the team in receptions with 69 and receiving yards with 1,166, the first of six consecutive years where he gained 1,000 or more receiving yards in a season. The 2002 season marked a turning point in Johnson's NFL career, the beginning of a five-year run as arguably the best wide receiver in the game and in the process, the beginning of a rebirth for the Bengals franchise as well.

Not only was 2003 the debut season for Marvin Lewis as the Bengals' head coach and a new direction for the franchise, but it also signaled the emergence of Johnson as a dominant--and the most flamboyant--wide receiver in the league. Over the next five seasons from 2003-2007, Johnson averaged 92.4 receptions, 1,374 receiving yards and 8.6 touchdown catches per season, while leading the team in receiving yards all five years and receptions and touchdown catches three times (2003-2005). During this five year span, he finished in the top 10 in the NFL in receiving yards[1] and receiving yards per game[2] five times, receptions three times[3] and receiving touchdowns twice.[4] He also had the league's sixth highest yards per touchdown catch in 2006 (14.4 yards per touchdown) and the ninth most yards from scrimmage in 2007 (1,487 yards).

Johnson's performance from 2003-2007 earned him numerous awards and honors, certifying him as one of the most decorated wide receivers of the decade. Selected to the Pro Bowl in each of these five seasons, Johnson was named first team All-NFL by the AP, The Pro Football Writers and The Sporting News in 2005 and 2006, first team All-AFC by Pro Football Weekly in 2003, 2004 and 2005 and second team All-NFL by the AP in 2003. He also earned the AFC Offensive Player of the Week award when he caught 12 passes for 103 yards and three touchdowns in the Bengals 35-7 victory over the Tennessee Titans on November 25, 2007. Heading

---

[1] 2003: 4th, 1,355 yards; 2004: 6th, 1,274 yards; 2005: 3rd, 1,432 yards; 2006: 1st, 1,369 yards; 2007: 3rd, 1,440 yards.

[2] 2003: 5th, 84.7 yards per game; 2004: 7th, 79.6 yards per game; 2005: 5th, 89.5 yards per game; 2006: 1st, 85.6 yards per game; 2007: 6th, 90.0 yards per game.

[3] 2003: 5th, 90 receptions; 2004: 3rd, 95 receptions; 2005: 5th, 97 receptions

[4] 2003: 4th, 10 touchdowns; 2005: 4th, 9 touchdowns.

into the 2008 season, the Pro Football Historical Abstract already had Johnson ranked as the 35th best wide receiver in NFL history. Clearly, Johnson had become a player to watch.

"I love watching him play," former Bengals wide receiver Cris Collinsworth said. "He's a real star-quality NFL player."[169]

By then, Johnson had also become a star-quality celebrator of touchdowns and a full-blown outspoken entertainer. His inventory of post-touchdown high jinks included giving CPR to the football, sporting a future Pro Football Hall of Game gold jacket, performing the Riverdance, using the goal line pylon to putt the football and during the Christmas holidays, displaying a sign after he scored that read, "Dear NFL, please don't fine me again! Merry Christmas!" Publicly, the league was unamused by Johnson's escapades. Privately, Johnson believed, the NFL thought otherwise.

"Even though it's something they don't like, I guarantee they think what I'm doing is entertaining," Johnson said in 2005. "I know they have to like it because nothing I do is mischievous."[170]

While the NFL may have disliked Johnson's antics, the Bengals and their fans were delighted because all those touchdown celebrations meant the team was winning. The Bengals went from laughing stock to playoff contender, compiling a 42-38 regular season record from 2003-2007 which included their first playoff appearance and first winning season in 16 years when they won the AFC North Division in 2005. Johnson and the rest of the offense played a key role during this stretch, finishing in the top half of the NFL in points scored in each of those five years and in total offense and passing offense four times (2003, 2005-2007). Their 32 passing touchdowns in 2005 and their 4,012 net yards passing in 2007 each place second in team history and their 421 points scored in 2005 is tied for fourth best in club history.

Yet despite the outburst on offense and the modicum of success the team experienced from 2003-2007, all was not happy inside the Bengals' locker room and the front office. After coming off a disappointing 7-9 season in 2007, many blamed Johnson and his emotional and perceived narcissistic behavior for the team's lack of consistency. "I was labeled selfish and a cancer and it hurt," Johnson said on ESPN's Mike and Mike radio show once the 2007 season was concluded. "Fingers were pointed at me this year."[171] It was a stigma attached to Johnson that both his teammates and former players believed was unfair but an understandable assessment.

"He wears his emotions on his sleeves sometimes," his quarterback since 2004, Carson Palmer once remarked. "He's an emotional player. He's very competitive, and he wants the ball."[172]

"There's a really fine line that's hard to distinguish between, 'I want the ball because it's going to make me rich and famous' and 'I want the ball because I help our team win,'" Collinsworth empathized. "I really believe Chad Johnson is on the team side. In Chad's mind, when he's complaining, it's because he thinks it's in the team's best interest."[173]

As for Johnson, he believed he was misunderstood, even speaking in the third person to justify his case.

"The outside world doesn't know Chad," Johnson said in 2005. "The outside world only sees a cocky, arrogant, trash-talking receiver that's very, very good.

"But I want people to understand the hard work I put in each week, the hours of watching film, the hours of going over the game plan and sitting in the meeting with coaches. No other player sits up there and goes over the game plan with their coaches in their off days. I wish people would understand. I'm not just talk. My foundation is right. The thing that's made me successful is all the hard work."[174]

With critics breathing down his neck, Johnson spent most of the months following the 2007 season demanding a trade out of Cincinnati, going so far as to miss the Bengals off-season workout programs and practices and to verbally ask Washington Redskins owner, Dan Snyder, to call him. The Bengals, meanwhile, let it be known they had no intentions of trading their number one wide receiver, so when training camp opened for the 2008 season, Johnson returned for his eighth season in Cincinnati. Unfortunately, Johnson experienced his worst season since his rookie season, catching only 53 passes for 540 yards and four touchdowns. Likewise, the Bengals stumbled badly themselves, starting the season 0-8, losing Palmer to a season-ending injury early on and finishing with a disappointing 4-11-1 record.

The Bengals rebounded the following year, winning the AFC North Division for the second time in five years with a 10-6 record. Johnson returned to his previous form in 2009 as well, leading the team in receptions (72), receiving yards (1,047) and touchdown catches (9). Those nine receiving touchdowns were the ninth most in the NFL and helped Johnson earn his sixth Pro Bowl appearance. The only disappointing aspect of the season was the team's abrupt exit in the playoffs, a 24-14 loss at home to the New York Jets in the AFC wild card Playoff round. As was the case in his 2005 playoff appearance, Johnson wasn't a factor against the Jets, catching only two passes for 28 yards.[1]

The 2010 season looked promising for the Bengals, especially after acquiring All-Pro wide receiver, Terrell Owens, to team with Johnson. The expected offensive fireworks never materialized in 2010 as Owens played most of the season with a broken hand, while Johnson dealt with a nagging ankle injury that limited his production to 67 receptions, 831 receiving yards and four touchdown catches. What looked like a possible Super Bowl season in August resulted in a disastrous 4-12 season in January. The 2010 season would also mark the end of the Chad Johnson era in Cincinnati.

On July 28, 2011, Johnson, then known as Chad Ochocinco after he changed his last name in October 2006 in an homage to his uniform number 85 and to honor Hispanic Heritage Month,[2] was traded to the New England Patriots for a fifth round draft choice in 2012 and sixth round draft choice in 2013. Even though he played in Super Bowl XLVI for the Patriots, Johnson contributed very little in 2011 for New England, finishing with only 15 receptions for 276 yards and one touchdown. Disappointed by his production and his apparent inability to grasp their offense, the Patriots released Johnson on June 7, 2012.

Johnson didn't stay unemployed for very long. His hometown team, the Miami Dolphins signed him to a contract on June 11, 2012, anxious to see if he could rekindle the magic he performed while playing for the Bengals. Johnson would never give the Dolphins a chance to find out. Soon after he signed with Miami, Johnson was arrested on a charge of

---

[1] Johnson caught four passes for 59 yards in the Bengals infamous 2005 wild card playoff loss to the Pittsburgh Steelers.

[2] He legally changed his last name from Johnson to Ochocinco on August 29, 2008. On July 23, 2012, he legally changed his last name back to Johnson.

domestic battery and was summarily released by the Dolphins on August 12, 2012. While he played one season for the Montreal Alouettes in the Canadian Football League in 2014, Johnson never again played a down in the NFL following his arrest.

Even for those who don't follow professional football, Chad Johnson is a well-known commodity. Some know of him because of his one-furlong foot race against a racehorse in 2007.[1] Others recall his fourth place finish on Dancing with the Stars in the spring of 2010 or his finding love reality television show, Ochocinco: The Ultimate Catch. Or maybe they saw him riding a bull named DeJa Blue for 1.5 seconds on the Professional Bull Riding circuit in 2011.

But if you were or are a fan of the Cincinnati Bengals, you know Johnson was more than just a football player turned national celebrity. He was one of the best, if not the best, wide receivers in team history. He remains the franchise leader in career receptions (751) receiving yards (10,783), receiving touchdowns (66) and 100-yard receiving games (31). His 396 points scored is the seventh highest by any Bengals player and the most by any wide receiver in team history. Johnson recorded seven seasons of 1,000 or more receiving yards, the most by any Bengal, including the two highest, 1,440 yards in 2007 and 1,432 yards in 2005, and four of the top five seasons in franchise history. His 260 receiving yards against the San Diego Chargers on November 12, 2006 is still the most by a Cincinnati receiver in a single game.

His dominance of the team's record book notwithstanding, Johnson's lasting impact on the city of Cincinnati and the Bengals goes beyond his career averages of 75.1 receptions, 1078.3 receiving yards and 6.6 touchdown catches per season. Before he arrived in 2001, the Bengals were scorned more than they were cheered, a franchise dying on the vine and whose fan base's apathy was at an all-time low. Five years into his tenure as a Bengal, Johnson almost single-handedly made the team relevant and cool again, turning a perennial NFL doormat into a contender for Super Bowl championships. Not only did Johnson accomplish this feat with his incredible receiving skills but he did it with his larger-than-life personality

---

[1] Johnson was given a 100-meter head start and he defeated the horse by 12 lengths.

as well. At its height, the Bengals were must-see television and Johnson was the toast of the town. It was a relationship between a player and a city best expressed back in 2005 by the radio executive Horton that encapsulates Johnson's career with the Bengals as well.

"Thank God we have him."[175]

CHAPTER FORTY–SIX

PAT McINALLY

Mr. Perfect

After he completed the standard 50-question exam all potential NFL draft choices take as part of every team's player evaluation process known as the Wonderlic test in 1975, Harvard University wide receiver Pat McInally believed all of the hype surrounding the test's reputation as being difficult was somewhat overstated.

"It really did seem like an easy test at the time," McInally said years later.[176] Considering he was a NCAA Post-Graduate Scholar while at Harvard, it's no surprise he didn't find the group intelligence test used to assess a player's aptitude for learning and problem solving very difficult. What did surprise all of the NFL scouts and executives who used the Wonderlic as part of their draft selection process was McInally's score—a perfect 50 out of 50, making him the first and only NFL draft prospect to earn a perfect score. The error free test surprised McInally as well, even with his unique preparation for the pre-draft exam.

"One of the reasons I did so well is because I didn't think it mattered," McInally recalled. "So I think I didn't feel any pressure at all. It was definitely a once in a lifetime thing. I could probably take it 100 times and never do it again."[177]

McInally's performance on the Wonderlic, while notable on its own, wasn't the only lasting impression he made in the NFL. In a 10-year career played entirely with the Cincinnati Bengals, McInally was at times a fearless wide receiver and consistently one of the leading punters of his time. Better yet for long-time Bengals fans, he arguably was, as local radio host Lance McAllister put it, the most interesting Bengal of all time.[178]

McInally was a football and basketball star in the early 1970s at Villa Park High School in California and attended Harvard only after his mom suggested he apply. Once accepted, he fully intended to concentrate on basketball but decided to play football as well "because I didn't know anyone and figured it would be a good way to meet people."[179] McInally's decision to include football as part of his athletic agenda while at Harvard proved more than beneficial for the Crimson and set the course for his future career as an NFL and an entrepreneur star.

A three year letterman from 1972-1974 at Harvard, McInally was a first team All-Ivy League split end and a Newspaper Enterprise Association (NEA) second team All-American in his junior year in 1973. That breakthrough season included a 13 reception game against Brown University, at the time, the school record for receptions in a game[1] and a school record 56 receptions for the year that also was the fourth most receptions in the NCAA in 1973.[2] His performance as a junior, however, was just a prelude to his award winning and honor laden senior season in 1974.

McInally helped lead the Crimson to an Ivy League title in 1974 with his team leading 46 receptions, the tenth most in the NCAA and a school record eight receiving touchdowns in a season[3] and three touchdown receptions in a game against Rutgers. He was named first team All-Ivy League for the second consecutive season and first team All-American by the U.S. Coaches, the U.S. Football Writers and the Walter Camp Foundation, selections that made McInally a Consensus All-American. He also received second team All-American honors from the NEA, the AP and the UPI and was recognized by the New England Football Writers as the

---

[1] The 13 receptions in a game currently ranks third in Harvard University history.

[2] McInally held the school record for receptions in a season at Harvard for 28 years despite only playing nine games in 1973. It still remains tied for fourth most in school history.

[3] His eight touchdown receptions in 1974 is currently tied for second most in Harvard school history.

Outstanding Senior Football Player in New England in 1974. He ended his career at Harvard as the school's leader in receptions (108), receiving yards (1,485) and touchdown receptions (15). Those impressive statistics eventually led to his induction into the Harvard Athletic Hall of Fame in 1997 and the College Football Hall of Fame in 2016.

McInally's accomplishments in his senior season garnered him invitations to several college all-star games, including the East-West Shrine Game, the Hula Bowl and the Senior Bowl. These post-season exhibition games provided the relatively unknown Harvard graduate with the opportunity to showcase his football skills in front of a large number of NFL coaches, scouts and executives. Apparently, McInally's play at Harvard combined with his work at the college all-star games impressed the Bengals enough to take him in the fifth round of the 1975 NFL Draft with the 120th overall selection. As to whether his pre-draft perfect Wonderlic score affected where he was chosen, McInally has a theory.

"I think they (NFL teams) think guys who are intelligent will challenge authority too much,"[180] McInally believes. Whether his mistake free pre-draft exam affected the decision makers in Cincinnati, McInally isn't so sure. "The Bengals kept it from me for years and years," McInally said. "They didn't want me to know."[181]

In a move befitting a Harvard graduate, McInally negotiated his rookie contract on his own, agreeing to a deal he later described as being less than lucrative. "The only thing I can say about the contract is that it was bigger than my Harvard scholarship," he later deadpanned.[182] With his contract signed and in place, all that was left for McInally to do before competing for a spot on the Bengals roster was to play in the 1975 College All-Star Football Classic in August in Chicago, Illinois. It was a trip to an essentially meaningless exhibition game that would severely alter his path to the NFL.

The College All-Star Football Classic, also known as the Chicago College All-Star Game, was an annual pre-season game dating back to 1934 that pitted the defending NFL champions against a team of college seniors from the previous year. Even though it interrupted the training camp for an NFL rookie who played in the game, the event carried enough prestige that if a player was invited to play on the college all-star squad, he went to Chicago and participated. Such was the case for McInally who joined such other NFL rookies as Russ Francis, Steve Bartkowski, and future Hall of Famer, Walter Payton to face the defending Super Bowl Champion Pittsburgh Steelers at Chicago's Soldier Field.

Early on, it looked like McInally was well on his way to becoming the game's Most Valuable Player. On the college all-star team's first drive, he caught a 28-yard touchdown pass from Bartkowski. Unfortunately, while being tackled in the end zone, McInally fractured his leg. The injury ended his training camp with the Bengals and caused him to miss the entire 1975 season. Despite the injury, McInally does not regret playing in the exhibition game, and in hindsight, believes it may have been a blessing in disguise.

"It probably worked out for the best," McInally recalls. "They (Bengals) had a lot of good receivers, but a couple of them moved on by the next year and I was able to make the club.[183] That gave me a year to acclimate myself to pro football and the Cincinnati area. I wasn't sure I wanted to be a professional football player. And with that kind of attitude, I probably wouldn't have been very successful."[184]

Fully recovered from his leg injury, McInally did indeed make the club in 1976, but in 14 games that season he failed to catch one pass. Instead, he earned a roster spot as a team's punter, beating out the incumbent Dave Green. He remained the team's punter for the next nine seasons after 1976, earning several honors and routinely finishing in the top 10 in the NFL in several punting categories.

That's not to say, however, that McInally abandoned his wide receiver roots. In a five-year stretch from 1977-1981, he caught 57 passes for 808 yards and five touchdowns. He acquired a reputation as one of the toughest wide receivers in the league during this time, a quality best exemplified by his performance against the Cleveland Browns in the final game of the season on December 21, 1980.

Early on in the inconsequential game for the Bengals but imperative for the Browns as they needed a victory to qualify for the playoffs, McInally went across the middle of the field to catch a pass from quarterback Jack Thompson. Before he could secure the pass, McInally was brutally clotheslined with a forearm to the chin by Browns safety, Thom Darden. The hit knocked him unconscious and motionless for over 15 minutes before being taken off the field. But he surprised everyone at Riverfront

Stadium that day when he returned to action, capping off his improbable comeback by catching a 59-yard game-tying touchdown pass in the fourth quarter.[1] It was one of six concussions he sustained while playing wide receiver, a signal to McInally that his days of catching passes in the NFL were over once the 1981 season ended.

Those multiple concussions, meanwhile, did not prevent McInally from performing his punting duties for the Bengals, nor did it stop him from becoming one of the top punters in the NFL. In a nine year period from 1977-1985, McInally finished the season in the top 10 in the NFL in yards per punt seven times, including leading the league in 1978 with a 43.1 average yard per punt[2] and in 1981 with a 45.4 average, a mark that is the fifth highest average yards per punt in a season in Bengals history. The 1981 season was highlighted by a single game performance of 55.67 yards per punt against the Buffalo Bills on September 27, the second highest single game performance in team history.

McInally continues to hold several other spots in the team record book for punting accomplishments in a season and in a game. His 91 punts in 1978 are third most in team history and his 3,919 punting yards that same year ranks fourth. In two separate games, at Green Bay on October 5, 1980 and against Cleveland on October 21, 1984, McInally punted five balls inside the 20-yard line, the second most in a game in club history.

McInally also continued his high level of punting from the regular season into the four playoff games he played in, including Super Bowl XVI, as well. In the Bengals post-season record book, he currently stands third in average yards per punt (40.58 yards), net yards per punt (37.0 yards) and punts inside the 20 (2) and fourth in total punts (12), punting yards (487 yards) and longest punt in a playoff game (60 yards, January 3, 1982 against Buffalo in the AFC divisional round).

Before he retired after the 1985 season, McInally was recognized

---

[1] Given today's NFL environment and their emphasis on player safety as it pertains to concussions and head injuries, it is safe to assume McInally never would have been given the opportunity to return against the Browns. In another sign of the changing times in the NFL, Darden was not ejected from the game and was fined only $1,000 for his vicious hit.

[2] McInally was also The Pro Football Historical Abstract's Adjusted Punting Yards leader in 1978 as well.

as one of the league's best punters by the national media. In 1977 and 1978, the UPI named him second team All-AFC punter and in 1981 was named first team All-AFC by the UPI and Pro Football Weekly, first team All-NFL by the AP, The Pro Football Writers and The Sporting News and second team All-NFL by The Newspapers Enterprise Association. He was also chosen to appear in his first and only Pro Bowl in 1981, making him the first Harvard graduate selected to the Pro Bowl and the only Harvard grad to play in both the Pro Bowl and the Super Bowl.

Once he left the NFL, McInally began pursuing a new career, this time as an entrepreneur. While visiting a toy store in 1986, he noticed there were no sports stars who had figurines or action figures like G.I. Joe. Along with a former college friend who was running the day-to-day operations of Kenner Toys (later known as Kenner Products), McInally created the Starting Lineup brand of sports action figures, the 4.5-inch replica of famous sports stars that became enormously popular with kids and memorabilia collectors alike. In the toy's infancy stages, McInally approached several of his former NFL teammates and opponents to approve using their likeness as one of the action figures. One such player was Hall of Fame quarterback, Terry Bradshaw, and at first, the Steelers great was more than just a bit apprehensive.

"Terry looks at me—he had a big cigar in his mouth—and says, 'Who cares about that little toy?'", remembers McInally when he talked to Bradshaw about becoming a member of the Starting Lineup product line. "Then he pulls out his cigar and says, 'Will they give me hair? If they give me hair, I want to be one.'"[185]

Years later, McInally was immortalized with his own Starting Lineup action figure and based upon his career numbers as a punter, it's also time to acknowledge him as one of the finest players in Cincinnati Bengals history. In addition to his contributions at wide receiver, McInally was a stabilizing force in the team's kicking game for 10 years. He is ranked second in team history in career punts with 700 and punting yards with 29,307. His 157 punts inside the 20-yard line is the third most in Bengals history while his 41.87 career average yards per punt and his 34.0 career net yards per punt is fifth and sixth best respectively all-time in club history.

In the end, Pat McInally enjoyed a unique and excellent career in his 10 years with Cincinnati. Was it perfect? No, but it didn't need to be to establish him as one of the best players in team history.

Besides, McInally had already achieved perfection before he caught one pass or punted one ball in a Bengals uniform.

CHAPTER FORTY-SEVEN

JOHN COPELAND

It's Harder than You Think

If *you want to know* how difficult the transition is from being a standout collegiate football player to becoming a competent and successful NFL player, just ask John Copeland. A featured member of the University of Alabama's 1992 National Championship team who was recognized as one of, if not, the best defensive lineman in all of college football, Copeland believed, as did most every professional football evaluator, that his NFL career would equal, or even surpass, his accomplishments as a member of the Crimson Tide. However, once he was drafted by the Cincinnati Bengals in 1993, reality soon set in.

"You go there and you think you are going to play 20 years and you soon realize it doesn't work like that," Copeland said about his NFL experience. "People just don't understand what the NFL is like. There is no bad player. Everybody is good. The competition is fierce. People don't realize the speed of the NFL games even compared to college."[186]

Thankfully for the Bengals, Copeland's observations about life in the NFL, comments echoed by many who played before and after him, didn't prevent him from making a significant contribution to the history of the franchise. Despite playing on only one Bengals team that finished a season with a record of .500 or better (1996), the native of Lanett, Alabama still made a noteworthy impact in his eight seasons as a defensive lineman in a Cincinnati uniform.

Copeland's road to the NFL began in Valley, Alabama at Valley High School where he was a star on the school's football team. In his senior season in 1988, Copeland recorded 99 solo tackles, 136 total tackles and five quarterback sacks, an effort that earned him first team All-State honors and a spot in the 1988 Alabama vs. Mississippi High School All-Star Game.

After graduating from Valley High School, Copeland spent two seasons honing his football skills at Hinds Community College in Raymond, Mississippi. He dominated the junior college football scene in 1989 and 1990, earning National Junior College Athletic Association All-American honors in 1990 and induction into the Hinds Community College Sports Hall of Fame in 2012.

More importantly, Copeland's stellar play at Hinds impressed a significant number of NCAA Division I head football coaches who were eager to sign him to a scholarship for the final two years of college eligibility. One of those coaches was the University of Alabama's Gene Stallings, who saw the junior college standout as one of the key building blocks in his effort to assemble one of the nation's best defenses and to restore the reputation of a once proud football program. Copeland apparently envisioned the same, joining the Crimson Tide for the 1991 season.

But before he could dominate Division 1 and SEC opponents as he had done at Hinds Community College, Copeland had to become acclimatized to his new home of Tuscaloosa, Alabama. It wasn't easy and he struggled to fit in. Luckily for Copeland, he met fellow teammate and defensive lineman, Eric Curry, and a bond was instantly forged.

"I didn't know anyone," Copeland recalls about his early days on the Alabama campus. "I was in Bryant Hall and Eric Curry came up to me and talked and we ate lunch. We became roommates and the rest is history. Together we pushed and motivated each other and the competition each day between us spurred us on."[187]

Copeland and Curry started together on the defensive line in 1991 but the early results were not encouraging for them or the team. After losing to the University of Florida in the second game of the season, 35-0, Copeland and the rest of the Crimson Tide knew things needed to change.

"That game made the 1992 national champions," Copeland remembers about the blowout loss to the Gators in 1991. "We got together afterward in a team meeting following that game and vowed to do everything in our power to win football games and we won a lot of football games."[188]

The team meeting obviously worked. Alabama won their remaining 10 games following the loss to Florida, and all of their 13 games the following season in 1992, culminated by a National Championship game victory over Miami (FL), 34-13 in the Sugar Bowl. Copeland played a considerable role in Alabama having the nation's number one ranked defense and in the school's ascendance to the national championship, finishing the 1992 season with 21.5 tackles for loss (third most in school history) and 10.5 quarterback sacks (tied for fifth in school history). It also earned him All-SEC defensive end honors and a first team All-American as well.

Once the 1992 season ended, Copeland and his teammate Curry capitalized on the team's national championship success and their own individual performances on the nation's number one defense to become one of the top selections in the 1993 NFL Draft. In fact, the debate around the Alabama campus prior to the draft was would be chosen first, Curry or Copeland. As it turned out, Copeland edged out his former roommate by one selection when he was chosen by the Cincinnati Bengals with the fifth overall pick while Curry was drafted by the Tampa Bay Buccaneers with the very next selection.[1]

Copeland wasted no time in making an impact on the Bengals defense, playing and starting at left defensive end in 14 of the team's 16 games. He finished the 1993 season with an impressive 43 solo tackles, 48 total tackles, three sacks and two forced fumbles. More importantly, Copeland remained a fixture in the Bengals starting lineup for the six of the next seven seasons,[2] leading all of Cincinnati's defensive linemen in passes defended three times (1995, 1996 and 1999), solo and total tackles

---

[1] Curry played seven seasons in the NFL with three different teams (Tampa Bay, Green Bay Packers and Jacksonville Jaguars), finishing his career with 95 tackles and 12.5 quarterback sacks.

[2] The lone season Copeland was not a regular starter on the Bengals defensive front was 1998 when he played in only five games without a single start.

twice (1995 and 1997) and sacks (1995), forced fumbles (1995), fumble recoveries (1997) and interceptions (1999) once.

Sadly, the Bengals themselves failed to match Copeland's performance in his eight years with the team from 1993-2000. Cincinnati was a dreadful 39-89 (.305) during Copeland's time with the franchise, finishing only one season with a record of .500 or better (1996, 8-8). Despite the dismal won-lost record, Copeland was part of several team defensive milestones, including team records for sacks in a game (8, October 16, 1994 at Pittsburgh) and fewest net yards rushing allowed in a game (11 yards, December 12, 1999 at Cleveland). Copeland starred in his own personal highlight reel when he returned a fumble 25 yards for the only touchdown in his NFL career in a 38-31 victory over the San Diego Chargers on November 2, 1997.

Even though he played during a dark period of the Bengals franchise, Copeland's play from 1993-2000 was one of the few bright spots. In his eight seasons in Cincinnati, Copeland started in 95.3% of the games he played (102 games started, 107 games played) and 79.7% of the games the Bengals played from 1993-2000 (102 games started, 128 games played). He ended his career averaging 33.75 solo tackles, 40.25 total tackles, three sacks, 2.12 passes defended and one forced fumble per season, in addition to his three career interceptions and three career fumble recoveries.

Not a bad resume for someone who as a rookie doubted he had a chance to make his mark in the NFL.

THE INITIAL CLASS OF THE CINCINNATI BENGALS HALL OF FAME

"Next year is our 50th year, which seems an appropriate time to put whatever we do together. I'm going to wait another year before I say much more."

Mike Brown, on the idea of recognizing and honoring great players of the team's past
July 26, 2016[189]

S*ince I began this project,* the Bengals and Mike Brown have become more receptive to publicly and formally recognizing the best players in team history by either establishing a Ring of Honor inside Paul Brown Stadium or a Cincinnati Bengals Hall of Fame somewhere near the facility. Whether it happens sooner rather than later, or specifically when the team commemorates its 50th season as a professional football franchise in 2017, remains to be seen. Regardless of when it occurs, it does appear it will eventually come to pass.

In the meantime, while the powers that be determine when the time is right to honor the players of their past, I have chosen, based upon the work I completed in writing this book, the first five Bengals who merit induction into the team's initial Hall of Fame class or Ring of Honor. They are ranked 1-5 in order of most deserving but in essence all five of my initial class of inductees undoubtedly have the credentials for inclusion. What is important here is not the ranking but instead the prestige that goes with being the inaugural members of the team's Hall of Fame or Ring of Honor.

1. **ANTHONY MUÑOZ.** In reality, there are no official rules for determining who qualifies for a team's Hall of Fame. The whole process differs from team to team and is, for all intents and purposes, a totally subjective exercise. If there were a set of criteria, however, there is no doubt one of them, if not the most important rule, would require a team to induct a player who already is a member of the sport's Hall of Fame. That's what makes the selection of Muñoz to the Bengals initial class a slam-dunk choice. It also doesn't hurt that many regard Muñoz as the greatest offensive lineman in NFL history.

2. **KEN ANDERSON.** Even though he played during a time when the reliance on the passing game in the NFL was far less prevalent than it is today, you can make the case that Anderson is not only the best quarterback in Bengals history but one of the top quarterbacks in league history. He remains over 30 years after his last game, the franchise leader in career total passing attempts, completions, passing yards and touchdown passes and was the league's Most Valuable Player when the Bengals made their first ever Super Bowl appearance. If that's not enough, consider the words of four-time Super Bowl champion and NFL Hall of Famer, Terry Bradshaw, a quarterback who knows greatness when he sees it. "He'll go down as one of the greatest quarterbacks who ever played," Bradshaw remarked about his division rival on a broadcast of one of Anderson's last games in the NFL. "One of the most accurate arms, [and] an uncanny mind to pick up blitzes."

3. **BOB JOHNSON.** Some might argue that the inclusion of Johnson, the Bengals first ever draft choice and the only player to have his number retired by the team, in the initial class is mostly ceremonial. While it's a factor that can't totally be dismissed, it

would unfairly dismiss the importance he played in the early years of a brand new professional football franchise. Anchoring the offensive line as the team's center in their first 10 seasons, Johnson played a large role in the Bengals' unprecedented early success that included two division titles and three post-season appearances in the team's first eight years of existence. Yes, Johnson's selection in the initial class is somewhat sentimental but it is more about the impact he had on the performance of the Bengals as they attempted to make their presence known first in the AFL and then the NFL. Without Johnson's play and his leadership, that road to NFL success would have been longer and tougher.

4. **CHAD JOHNSON.** There is no denying that the discussion of Johnson and his NFL career begins and ends with his personality and his antics on and off the field. It made Johnson, or Ochocinco if you prefer, relevant throughout the entire NFL. It should not, however, overshadow his production on the field in his 10 seasons in Cincinnati. Johnson is the team leader in career receptions, receiving yards, receiving touchdowns and 100-yard games and his 1,440 receiving yards in 2007 remains the most by a Bengal in a single season. Anyone who doesn't believe Johnson deserves inclusion in the team's inaugural Hall of Fame should heed the word of Johnson himself: "Child, please!"

5. **KEN RILEY.** The franchise leader in most games played, Riley's inclusion in the initial class of Bengals legends is more than just about his longevity and durability. Despite playing his last game in 1983, "The Rattler" remains the team leader in career interceptions, interception return yards and interception returns for touchdowns. His pairing with fellow cornerback, Lemar Parrish, made the Bengals defensive backfield one of the most formidable in the entire NFL in the early to mid-1970s. There are some NFL historians and long-time journalists who believe Riley deserves a place in the Pro Football Hall of Fame in Canton, Ohio. At the very least, he has earned a spot in the Bengals Hall of Fame in Cincinnati, Ohio.

So there is my list of candidates for the inaugural Cincinnati Bengals Ring of Honor or Hall of Fame. Now the challenge is two-fold. First, make your own list of who you believe deserves recognition as one of the best Bengals of all-time. Second, convince Mike Brown and the rest of the Bengals organization it's time to honor these players who performed at an elite level while wearing the Cincinnati uniform with a place for all current and future fans to visit and admire.

The team, its players and coaches, past and present, and most of all, the fans, deserve it.

CINCINNATI BENGALS 40TH ANNIVERSARY TEAM

Quarterback: Carson Palmer

Running Back: James Brooks

Fullback: Ickey Woods

Wide Receivers: Chad Johnson and T.J. Houshmandzadeh

Tight End: Dan Ross

Offensive Tackles: Anthony Muñoz and Willie Anderson

Offensive Guards: Max Montoya and Dave Lapham

Center: Rich Braham

Kicker: Shayne Graham

Defensive Ends: Justin Smith and Ross Browner

Defensive Tackles: Tim Krumrie and Mike Reid

Linebackers: Reggie Williams, Takeo Spikes and Brian Simmons

Cornerbacks: Ken Riley and Lemar Parrish

Safeties: David Fulcher and Solomon Wilcots

Punter: Lee Johnson

NFL TEAMS WITH HALL OF FAME

NEW ENGLAND PATRIOTS

PLAYERS	YEARS WITH TEAM
Mike Haynes	7
Steve Grogan	16
Andre Tippett	12
Bruce Armstrong	14
Stanley Morgan	13
Ben Coates	9
Jim Nance	7
Sam Cunningham	10
Jon Morris	11
Drew Bledsoe	9
Troy Brown	15
Tedy Bruschi	13
Ty Law	10
John Hannah	13
Nick Buoniconti	7
Gino Cappelletti	11
Bob Dee	8
Jim Lee Hunt	11
Steve Nelson	14

Babe Parilli	7
Houston Antwine	11
Willie McGinest	12
Kevin Faulk	13

TOTALS: 23 Players, 253 Years with Team, Average Year Per Player: 11.0

SEATTLE SEAHAWKS

PLAYER	YEARS WITH TEAM
Dave Brown	11
Kenny Easley	7
Walter Jones	13
Cortez Kennedy	11
Dave Krieg	12
Steve Largent	14
Curt Warner	7
Jim Zorn	9
Jacob Green	12

TOTALS: 9 Players, 96 Years with Team, Average Year Per Player: 10.7

ATLANTA FALCONS

PLAYER	YEARS WITH TEAM
Steve Bartkowski	11
Deion Sanders	5
William Andrews	6
Gerald Riggs	7
Jeff Van Note	18
Jessie Tuggle	14
Tommy Nobis	11
Mike Kenn	17
Claude Humphrey	11

TOTALS: 9 Players, 100 Years with Team, Average Year Per Player: 11.1

SAN DIEGO CHARGERS

PLAYER	YEARS WITH TEAM
Emil Karas	7
Frank Buncom	7
Bob Laraba	2
Jacque MacKinnon	9
Lance Alworth	9
Ron Mix	10
Paul Lowe	9
Keith Lincoln	8
Ernie Ladd	5
Walt Sweeney	11
John Hadl	11
Chuck Allen	9
Gary Garrison	11
Earl Faison	6
Dan Fouts	15
Charlie Joiner	11
Speedy Duncan	7
Russ Washington	15
Kellen Winslow	9
Rolf Bernischke	10
Gill Boyd	10
Gary Johnson	10
Doug Wilkerson	14
Wes Chandler	7
Stan Humphries	6
Louie Kelcher	9
Don Macek	14
Ed White	8
Fred Dean	7
Junior Seau	13
Darren Bennett	9

| Leslie O'Neal | 10 |
| LaDainian Tomlinson | 9 |

TOTALS: 33 Players, 307 Years with Team, Average Year Per Player: 9.3

INDIANAPOLIS COLTS

PLAYER	YEARS WITH TEAM
Bill Brooks	7
Chris Hinton	7
Jim Harbaugh	4
Marvin Harrison	13
Edgerrin James	7
Eric Dickerson	5
Marshall Faulk	5
Jeff Saturday	13

TOTALS: 8 Players, 61 Years with Team, Average Year Per Player: 7.6

NEW YORK JETS

PLAYER	YEARS WITH TEAM
Joe Namath	12
Curtis Martin	8
Joe Klecko	11
Larry Grantham	13
Freeman McNeil	12
Wesley Walker	13
Marty Lyons	11
Matt Snell	9
Don Maynard	13
Winston Hill	14
Gerry Philbin	9
Al Toon	8
Mark Gastineau	10

Wayne Chrebet   11

Emerson Boozer   10

TOTALS: 15 Players, 164 Years with Team, Average Year Per Player: 10.9

DENVER BRONCOS

PLAYER	YEARS WITH TEAM
Goose Gonsoulin	7
Rich Jackson	6
Floyd Little	9
Lionel Taylor	7
Charley Johnson	4
Paul Smith	11
Frank Tripucka	4
Billy Thompson	13
Craig Morton	6
Haven Moses	10
Jim Turner	9
Randy Gradishar	10
Tom Jackson	14
Louis Wright	12
John Elway	16
Karl Mecklenburg	13
Dennis Smith	14
Gary Zimmerman	5
Steve Atwater	10
Terrell Davis	7
Shannon Sharpe	12
Rod Smith	13
Tom Nalen	14
Gene Mingo	5
Rick Upchurch	9
Jason Elam	15

Simon Fletcher   11

John Lynch   4

TOTALS: 28 Players, 270 Years with Team, Average Year Per Player: 9.6

TAMPA BAY BUCCANEERS

PLAYER	YEARS WITH TEAM
Lee Roy Selmon	9
Jimmie Giles	9
Paul Gruber	12
Warren Sapp	9
Derrick Brooks	14
Mike Alstott	12
Doug Williams	5
John Lynch	11

TOTALS: 8 Players, 81 Years with Team, Average Year Per Year: 10.1

JACKSONVILLE JAGUARS

PLAYER	YEARS WITH TEAM
Tony Boselli	7
Fred Taylor	11
Mark Brunell	9

TOTALS: 3 Players, 27 Years with Team, Average Year Per Player: 9.0

CAROLINA PANTHERS

PLAYER	YEARS WITH TEAM
Sam Mills	3

NEW ORLEANS SAINTS

PLAYER	YEARS WITH TEAM
Archie Manning	11
Rickey Jackson	13
Willie Roaf	9
Morten Andersen	13

TOTALS: 4 Players, 46 Years with Team, Average Year Per Player: 11.5

MIAMI DOLPHINS

PLAYER	YEARS WITH TEAM
Larry Csonka	8
Bob Griese	14
Jim Langer	10
Paul Warfield	5
Nick Buoniconti	8
Larry Little	12
Dwight Stephenson	8
Bob Kuchenberg	15
Nat Moore	13
Dan Marino	17
Mark Clayton	10
Mark Duper	11
Dick Anderson	10
Richmond Webb	11
Bob Baumhower	10
Doug Betters	10
Jake Scott	6
Bill Stanfill	8
Jim Mandrich	8
Jason Taylor	13
Zach Thomas	12

John Offerdahl	8
Manny Fernandez	8

TOTALS: 22 Players, 235 Years with Team, Average Year Per Player: 10.2

TENNESSEE TITANS

PLAYER	YEARS WITH TEAM
Elvin Bethea	16
George Blanda	7
Earl Campbell	7
Ken Houston	6
Mike Munchak	12
Jim Norton	9
Bruce Matthews	19
Warren Moon	10
Eddie George	8
Steve McNair	11
Frank Wycheck	9

TOTALS: 11 Players, 114 Years with Team, Average Year Per Player: 10.4

BUFFALO BILLS

PLAYER	YEARS WITH TEAM
O.J. Simpson	9
Jack Kemp	8
Tom Sestak	7
Billy Shaw	9
Elbert Dubenion	9
Mike Stratton	11
Joe Ferguson	12
Joe DeLamielleure	8
Robert James	6
Bob Kalsu	1

George Saimes	7
Jim Kelly	11
Fred Smerlas	11
Kent Hull	11
Darryl Talley	12
Jim Richter	14
Thurman Thomas	12
Andre Reed	15
Steve Tasker	12
Bruce Smith	15
Booker Edgerson	8
Phil Hansen	11

TOTALS: 22 Players, 219 Years with Team, Average Year Per Player: 9.9

APPENDIX C

FOOTBALL OUTSIDERS DEFINITIONS[190]

DVOA—Defense adjusted Value Over Average

- Calculates team success based on down and distance of each play
- Determines how much more or less successful compared to league average
- Determines how much success offensive players achieved in each specific situation
  - o Compares to league average in each situation
  - o Adjusted for the strength of opponent
    - Getting to the end zone
      - Yards gained
      - First downs gained

Stops—The total number of plays which prevent a success by the offense

  - o Success
    - 45% of needed yards on first down
    - 60% of needed yards on second down
    - 100% of needed yards on third down

Defeats—The total number of plays which stop the offense from gaining first down yardage on third or fourth down, stop the offense behind the line of scrimmage or result in a fumble or interception.

Plays—The total number of defensive plays including tackles, pass deflections, interceptions, fumbles forced and fumble recoveries.

Stop Rate %--The percentage of total defensive plays resulting in a stop.

PRO FOOTBALL HISTORICAL ABSTRACT FORMULAS[191]

Adjusted Yards—Passing yards/2 + receiving yards/2 + rushing yards+ sack yards(-1) + interceptions (-35) + fumbles lost (-40) + punt return yards + kick return yards – (kick returns X 20) + (rushing touchdowns + kick return touchdowns + punt return touchdowns) X 10 + (passing touchdowns + receiving touchdowns) X 5

- o Average cost of an interception is 35 yards
- o Average cost of fumble lost is 40 yards
- o Quarterback and receiver should receive ½ credit for total yards on each pass play
- o Ignore first 20 yards of kickoff due to touchbacks

Adjusted Punting Yards—Gross punting yards + punts inside the 20 X 10 + touchbacks X -20 + blocked punts X -65 + punts X (-30)/ 2

Adjusted Kicking Yards—FG (field goals) missed 0-19 yards X -48 + FG missed 20-29 yards X -42 + FG missed 30-39 yards X -32 + FG missed 40-49 yards X -22 + FG missed 50 yards or more yards X -12 + FG made 0-19 yards X 2 + FG made 20-29 yards X 8 + FG made 30-39 yards X 18 + FG made 40-49 yards X 28 + FG made 50 yards or more X 38

Q Rating—Personal raw score/Highest position raw score X 10

Q3, Q6, Q9—3, 6, or 9 best Q scores combined

Q5, Q10, Q15—5, 10 or 15 best Q scores combined

Player Career Score—Q3+ (Q6X1.25) + (Q9X1.5)

Net Wins—Quarterback net wins in which were team's starting quarterback

Quarterback Career Score—Q5 + (Q10X1.25) + (Q15X1.5)

BIBLIOGRAPHY

Articles

Fabrikant, Geraldine, "Talking Money with Boomer Esiason, Quarterback Lets Advisor Call the Plays", *New York Times*, April 26, 1998

CBS News.com Staff, "Bengals Cut Johnson after Comments", *CBS Sportsline*, December 17, 1998

Daugherty, Paul, "Vengeance Is Mine Sayeth Bengals Overlord", *Cincinnati Enquirer*, December 8, 1998

Hobson, Geoff, "A Hall Hiss for the Rattler", bengals.com, February 10, 2015

Kirkendall, Josh, "Hall of Fame Weekend Reminds Us of Ken Riley's Snub", cincyjungle.com, August 3, 2013

Dehner Jr., Paul, "Ken Riley Inducted into HCBU Hall of Fame This Weekend", cincinnati.com, February 27, 2015

Crippen, Ken, "Where Are They Now: Ken Riley", NFPost.com, December 19, 2013

Freedman, Samuel G., "Omission of Bengals Riley from Hall of Fame Is A Striking Oversight", *New York Times*, August 3, 2013

Nix, J.W., "Crazy Canton Cuts: Lemar Parrish", bleacherreport.com, April 9, 2009

Kirkendall, Josh, "Best Bengals Draft Pick #2: Lemar Parrish", cincyjungle.com, April 27, 2011

Ward, Robert, "Reggie Jackson in No Man's Land", *Sport*, June 1977

Jacob, Bonnie, "A Real High", *Cincinnati Magazine*, August 1976

"Viking Offensive Coach Myers Dead at 53", *Lubbock Avalanche-Journal*, February 24, 1999

Bruton, Mike, "For Returning Cunningham, A Coach's Death Tempers Joy He Came to Receive an Award. But He Mourned a Man Who Had Made His Sport Fun Again", philly.com, February 24, 1999

"A Local Law Firm Founded by Former NFL Players—Cameron, Davis, Gonzalez and Marroney", www.prlog.com, June 14, 2010

Andreu, Robbie and Dooley, Pat, "No. 43: Glenn Cameron", *Gainesville Sun*, July 22, 2006

University of North Dakota Athletics Media Relations, "UND's Jim LeClair, Terry Abram Named to Inaugural Class of South St. Paul High School Athletic Hall of Fame", www.undsports.com, September 7, 2007

Associated Press, "Wilkinson Apologizes to Cincinnati For 'Racist' Comment", espn.go.com, December 14, 2005

Daugherty, Paul, "Ex-Bengal Reggie Williams Fighting to Save His Leg", *USA Today*, August 26, 2013

Ballard, Sarah, "He Knows Where of He Speaks", Sports Illustrated, December 21, 1987

United Press International, "Bengals Linebacker Reggie Williams Wins City Council Election", www.upi.com, November 8, 1989

Dehner, Paul Jr., "Mike Brown: 'Lack of Honoring Former Players' Probably My Fault'", www.cincinnati.com, July 28, 2015

Gola, Hank, "32 Years Ago in Cincinnati, Hell Froze Over with a Super Bowl Trip on the Line", *New York Daily News*, January 4, 2014

Dehner, Paul, Jr. "Scribe Session Series: Joe Walter." *The Cincinnati Enquirer*, July 10, 2014. www.cincinnati.com.

Rolling, Chris. "Former Guard Bobbie Williams Signs with the Baltimore Ravens." *Bleacher Report*, June 11, 2012. www.bleacherreport.com.

Bass, Mike. "Magical '88 Season Lingers, But Only In Bengals Memory." *The Chicago Tribune*, October 24, 1993.

Hardin, Marc. "Five Questions: Bruce Kozerski." *The Cincinnati Enquirer*, December 7, 2011.

Baker, Chris. "Bengals Learn Montoya's House in Cincinnati Is Not His Home." *The Los Angeles Times*, July 25, 1990.

Vrentas, Jenny. "Super Bowl Injuries: What It's Like to Get Hurt in the Game of Your Life." *Sports Illustrated*, January 12, 2016. www.si.com.

Bannon, Terry. "These Deals Didn't Work." *The Chicago Tribune*, August 25, 2004.

"Ex-Grid Star Mayes All-American Person." *The Toledo Blade*, January 11, 1990.

Hobson, Geoff, "Voices of '05: Willie Banking on Defense", bengals.com, January 9, 2016

University of Texas 2015 Football Media Guide, "Football History: University of Texas", www.TexasSports.com, May 27, 2015

Pro Football Hall of Fame, "1976 NFL Expansion Draft", www.profootballhof.com, January 1, 2005

Kirkendall, Josh, "Best Bengals Draft Picks #8: Eddie Edwards", www.cincyjungle.com, April 20, 2011

University of Miami Sports Hall of Fame, "Eddie Edwards: Inducted 1989", www.umsportshalloffame.com

Hobson, Geoff, "Sack Master Edwards Weighs In", www.bengals.com, September 21, 2009

Fragale, Michael, "West Virginia University: Sports Hall of Fame", www.wvusports.com, 2007

Kirkendall, Josh, "The Impact Rich Braham Had for the Cincinnati Bengals", www.cincyjungle.com, May 17, 2013

Iowa State University, "Bruce Reimers: Hall of Fame Class of 2009", www.cyclones.com, April 28, 2009

Hobson, Geoff, "Ex-Bengal Vern Holland Dies", *Cincinnati Enquirer*, April 22, 1998

Donaldson, Kelly, "Wilson Has Close Ties to Today's Big Game", gainesvilletimes.com, February 5, 2006

Associated Press, "Former Hawk Happy Being Parent, Coach", *Seattle Times*, September 26, 1990

Winters, Kelly, "Muñoz, Anthony, 1958-, Former Professional Football Player, Contemporary Hispanic Biography", encyclopedia.com, 2003

Greenberg, Jay, "The King of the Block", *Sports Illustrated*, September 10, 1990

University of Notre Dame, "Ross Browner Bio: Notre Dame Football", www.und.com/sports, 2000

Chival, Craig, "Browner Made Impact Immediate and Often", www.und.com, November 3, 1999

Monaco, Mike, "Waking the Echoes: Ross Browner", *The Observer*, October 30, 2014

Ruman, Steve, "Warren's Ross Browner Made A Big Splash on the Gridiron", Vindy.com, September 13, 2013

Kirkendall, Josh, "Cris Collinsworth Always Remembers Super Bowl Losses", cincyjungle.com, January 31, 2015

Underwood, John, "Catch a Catching Star", *Sports Illustrated*, December 14, 1981

Murphy, Austin, "Dude With a 'Tude", *Sports Illustrated*, August 26, 1991

Robbins, Danny, "Pickens Didn't Exactly Volunteer to Go Both Ways", *Los Angeles Times*, December 29, 1989

Hobson, Geoff, "Pickens Rips Coslet, Then Recants", *Cincinnati Enquirer*, December 30, 1999

Nadeau, Rene, "Where Are They Now? Former Tulane and NFL Tight End Rodney Holman", www.sportsnola.com, May 2, 2013

"McGee Chooses Michigan", *Angus-Press*, January 27, 1989

Greene, Van, "Former Bengals Tight End Tony McGee Found Post-NFL Success with Logistics", *Sports Illustrated*, May 24, 2015

Campbell, David, "Reggie Kelly's Value Went Beyond Numbers for Bengals", *Bleacher Report*, August 4, 2009

Florio, Mike, "Reggie Kelly Has Great Advice for Today's Players", *Pro Football Talk*, May 27, 2013

Hobson, Geoff, "Prepared", bengals.com, May 14, 2010

Rowe, Don, "Dreams, Hard Work Helped Kelly Reach NFL", *The Dispatch*, April 3, 2012

Kane, Dave, "Central Illinois Famous Bob Trumpy, Football Star, Broadcaster", *State Journal Register*, February 22, 2014

"Isaac Takes Glory from Trumpy", *Piqua Daily Call*, October 18, 1974

"Bengals Reverse Way Past Miami to Stay In Picture", *Albuquerque Journal*, November 21, 1977

"Trumpy Sizes up Career", *Los Angeles Times*, December 6, 1987

Kay, Joe, "T.J. More Than Chad's Sidekick on Bengals", *Associated Press*, November 30, 2005

O'Neil, Danny, "Seahawks New Wide Receiver T.J. Houshmandzadeh is Out for Recognition", *The Seattle Times*, April 19, 2009

Corbett, Jim, "C.J. and T.J.—The Bengals Odd Couple—One's Flash, the Other's Polish", *USA Today*, November 1, 2006

"Bears' Isaac Curtis Declared Ineligible", *Ellensburg Daily Record*, June 3, 1971

Hamilton, Tom, "Who Was the Best Back? Orange County's Veteran Prep Coaches Offer Some Suggestions", *The Los Angeles Times*, October 9, 1985

Hobson, Geoff, "Bengals like Ike to Make Draft Call", bengals.com, April 23, 2012

Eskenazi, Gerald, "Bengals Curtis: More Than A Just Sprinter", *New York Times*, January 21, 1982

Hobson, Geoff, "Difference Maker", bengals.com, June 30, 2009

"All-District Football Team", *Elyria Chronicle Telegram*, December 1, 1981

Maxsie, Joe, "Eight Greats to Be Inducted Next Week," *Cleveland Plain-Dealer*, September 3, 2008

Hobson, Geoff, "Still Tough to Take", bengals.com, February 7, 2014

"Tim McGee Returns to Hometown of Cleveland as a Cincinnati Star", *United Press International*, November 29, 1989

Corbett, Jim, "Bengals Johnson Talks the Talk and Walks the Walk", *USA Today*, October 19, 2005

Hobson, Geoff, "Best of the Best?" bengals.com, April 5, 2016

Crowe, Jerry, "McInally's Life off the Field Has Eclipsed Playing Career", *The Los Angeles Times*, April 24, 2011

Merron, Jeff, "Taking Your Wonderlics, ESPN.com, 2007

Starr, Cindy, "It's A Kick for McInally to Break into the Lineup", *Kentucky Post*, May 22, 1997

Klepal, Dan, "The Deadline Deals That Built a Stadium: Seven Years in the Making, Paul Brown Stadium Almost Didn't Happen", *Cincinnati Enquirer*, August 13, 2000

Albergotti, Reed and McWhirter, Cameron, "A Stadium's Costly Legacy Throws Taxpayers for a Loss", *Wall Street Journal*, July 12, 2011

McClellan, Bob, "McInally Continues to Perfect the Wonderlic", rivals.com, June 15, 2006

McCurdie, Jim, "Life is More Than Just Football for McInally", *Los Angeles Times*, October 30, 1985

Zimanek, Brad, "Copeland Thrilled to Be Around Football, Tuscaloosa", *Montgomery Adviser*, August 19, 2015

Skinner, Richard, "Mike Brown Moves Step Closer to Honoring Bengals Past", local12.com, July 26, 2016

Books

Brennan, Jack, Combs, P.J. and Moore, Inky, *The Cincinnati Bengals 2016 Media Guide*, Cincinnati Bengals, Inc., Cincinnati, Ohio, 2016

Lahman, Sean, *The Pro Football Historical Abstract"*, Lyons Press, Guilford, Connecticut, 2008

Boyles, Bob and Guido, Paul, *The USA Today College Football Encyclopedia 2010-2011*, Skyhorse Publishing, New York, New York, 2010

University of Maryland, *2015 Maryland Football Record Book*, College Park, Maryland, 2015

Carr, Don, *2015 Lincoln University Football Media Guide*, Jefferson City, Missouri, 2015

Auburn Athletics Communications, *Auburn Football 2015 Media Almanac*, AuburnTigers.com, Auburn, Alabama, 2015

Baylor University Department of Athletics, *2015 Baylor Football Media Almanac*, AMA Nystrom, Waco, Texas, 2015

University of Tennessee and UTSports.com, *The 2015 Tennessee Football Media Guide*, CCM Photo Books, Tampa, Florida, 2015

Powell, Ryan, *North Dakota 2015 Football Media Guide*, UND Media Relations Department, Grand Forks, North Dakota, 2015

Best, Kevin and Hundley, Bobby, *2015 North Carolina Football Media Guide*, North Carolina Athletic Communications Office, Chapel Hill, North Carolina, 2015

Ghorbi, Camron and Symonds, Tom, *2015 University of Miami Football Media Guide*, University of Miami Communications, Coral Gables, Florida, 2015

2015 Iowa State University Football Media Guide, Ames, Iowa, 2015

Office of Athletic Media Relations, *2015 Tennessee State University Football Media Guide*, TSU Xerox Service, Nashville, Tennessee, 2015

2015 Georgia Football Media Guide, UGA Sports Communications Office, Athens, Georgia, 2015

2015 USC Football Media Guide, USC Sports Information Office, Los Angeles, California, 2015

Apple, Dan, *2015 Florida Gators Football Media Guide*, UAA Communications Office, Gainesville, Florida, 2015

Carlson, Norm, *University of Florida Football Vault: The History of the Florida Gators*, Whitman Publishing, Atlanta, Georgia, 2007

Akey, Curtis, Dunaway, Roger and Weaver, Richie, *2015 Tulane Football Media Guide*, Tulane Athletics Communications Office, New Orleans, Louisiana, 2015

Ablaaf, David, Shepard, Chad, Johns, Joey and Eisendrath, Zach, *University of Michigan 2015 Football Media Guide*, University of Michigan, Ann Arbor, Michigan, 2015

Martin, Bill, *2015 Mississippi State University Football Media Guide*, Mississippi State University, Starkville, Mississippi, 2015

Abel, Liz, *2016 Utah Football Media Guide*, University of Utah, Salt Lake City, Utah, 2016

Cerritos College Falcons 2015 Football Media Guide, Norwalk, California, 2015

2016 Oregon State Football Media Guide, Oregon State University, Corvallis, Oregon

California Golden Bears 2016 Football Information Guide, Berkeley, California, 2016

May, Mike, *San Diego State 2015 Football Media Guide*, San Diego State University Athletic Media Relations Office, San Diego, California, 2015

Carter, Lemar and Stepp, Jordan, *Cal 2016 Track and Field Record Book*, Berkeley, California, 2016

Robinson, Ryan, Burns, M.J., Lee, Stephen K., Hiser, Kellen and Yellin, Jason, *Tennessee Football Media Guide 2016*, CCM Photo Books, Knoxville, Tennessee, 2016

Harvard 2016 Football Media Guide, Harvard University, Cambridge, Massachusetts, 2016

University of Alabama 2016 Football Media Guide, Alabama Athletics Communications Office, Tuscaloosa, Alabama, 2016

Schatz, Aaron, *Football Outsiders Almanac 2016: The Essential Guide to the 2016 NFL and College Football Seasons*, Create Space Independent Publishing Platform, Colorado Springs, Colorado, 2016

Websites

The Official Home of the BYU Cougars, www.byucougars.com

"About Augustana College", www.augustana.edu

"Tribe Vikings Hall of Fame", The Official Site of Augustana College Athletics, www.athletics.augustana.edu

"Lemar Parrish Player Page", www.databasefootball.com

"Hall of Fame—Phil Myers", The Official Athletic Site of the Northwestern Oklahoma State University Rangers, www.riderangersride.com

History Record Book, North Carolina Central University Athletics, www.nccueaglepride.com

"Gator Greats", www.gatorfclub.org

Cameron, Gonzalez and Marroney, PLLC, West Palm Beach Trial Lawyers, www.attorneysofwestpalmbeach.com

"Hall of Fame, Jim LeClair", www.goldeneaglessports.com

Official Website of Dartmouth College Varsity Athletics, www.dartmouthsports.com

Pro Football-Reference, www.pro-football-reference.com

SR/College Football, www.sports-reference.com/cfb

Football Outsiders, www.footballoutsiders.com

Podcasts

Dehner Jr., Paul, "Enquirer Podcast Series: Inside the 2005 Bengals", cincinnati.com-bengals-football/id39749633? mf=8, June 23, 2015

McAllister, Lance, "Willie Anderson, Former Bengals OL", www.700wlw.com, October 22, 2015

Goodpaster, Mike, "Bruce Reimers Former Cincinnati Bengals Offensive Lineman!" *Grueling Truth Radio Network*, February 24, 2016

Dehner Jr, Paul, "Scribe Session: Tony McGee", *Cincinnati Enquirer*, June 19, 2014

ENDNOTES

1   Klepal, Dan. "The Deadline Deals That Built a Stadium: Seven Years in the Making, Paul Brown Stadium Almost Didn't Happen." *The Cincinnati Enquirer*, August 13, 2000.

2   Ibid.

3   Albergotti, Reed, and Cameron McWhirter. "A Stadium's Costly Legacy Throws Taxpayers for a Loss." *The Wall Street Journal* (New York, New York), July 12, 2011.

4   Ibid.

5   Roling, Chris. "Bengals 2014 Salary Cap: Breaking Down Overall, Position-Specific Cap Space." *Bleacher Report*, January 15, 2014. www.bleacherreport.com.

6   Dehner, Paul, Jr. "Mike Brown: Lack of Honoring Former Players' Probably My Fault." *Cincinnati. com*, July 28, 2015. www.cincinnati.com.

7   Hanzus, Dan. "NFL Study Finds 6.86-Year Average Career for Players." *National Football League*, September 15, 2011. www.nfl.com.

8   "Bengals Cut Johnson after Comments." *CBS Sportsline*, December 7, 1998. www.cbsnews.com.

9   Daugherty, Paul. "Vengeance Is Mine Sayeth Bengals Overlord." *The Cincinnati Enquirer*, December 8, 1998.

10   Kirkendall, Josh. "Hall of Fame Weekend Reminds Us of Ken Riley's Snub." *Cincy Jungle*, August 3, 2013. www.cincyjungle.com.

11   Freedman, Samuel G. "Omission of Bengals Riley from Hall of Fame Is A Striking Oversight." *The New York Times*, August 3, 2013.

12   Hobson, Geoff. "A Hall Hiss for The Rattler." *Cincinnati Bengals*, February 10, 2015. www.bengals.com.

13   Ibid.

14   Gola, Hank. "32 Years Ago in Cincinnati, Hell Froze Over with a Super Bowl Trip on the Line." *New York Daily News*, January 4, 2014.

15   Ibid.

16   Ward, Robert. "Reggie Jackson in No Man's Land." *Sport*, June 1977.

17   Jacob, Bonnie. "A Real High." *Cincinnati Magazine*, August 1976.

18 Bruton, Mike. "For Returning Cunningham, A Coach's Death Tempers Joy He Came to Receive an Award." *The Inquirer*, February 24, 1999. www.philly.com.

19 "Viking Offensive Coach Myers Dead at Age 53." *Lubbock Avalanche-Journal*, February 24, 1999.

20 Ibid.

21 Bruton, Mike. "For Returning Cunningham, A Coach's Death Tempers Joy He Came to Receive an Award." *The Inquirer*, February 24, 1999. www.philly.com.

22 Jacob, Bonnie. "A Real High." *Cincinnati Magazine*, August 1976.

23

24 "A Local Law Firm Founded by Former NFL Players—Cameron, Davis, Gonzalez and Marroney." News release, June 14, 2010. Press Distribution Log. www.prlog.com.

25 Cameron, Gonzalez and Marroney, PLLC, West Palm Beach Trial Lawyers. www.attorneysofwestpalmbeach.com.

26 Powell, Ryan. *North Dakota 2015 Football Media Guide*. Grand Forks, ND: UND Media Relations Department, 2015.

27 "Wilkinson Apologizes to Cincinnati for "Racist" Comment." *ESPN*, December 14, 2005. www.espn.go.com.

28 Ballard, Sarah. "He Knows Whereof He Speaks." *Sports Illustrated*, December 21, 1987.

29 "Bengals Linebacker Reggie Williams Wins City Council Election." November 8, 1989. www.upi.com.

30 Ballard, Sarah. "He Knows Whereof He Speaks." *Sports Illustrated*, December 21, 1987.

31 Gola, Hank. "32 Years Ago in Cincinnati, Hell Froze Over with a Super Bowl Trip on the Line." *New York Daily News*, January 4, 2014.

32 Ibid.

33 Ibid.

34 Dehner, Paul, Jr. "Scribe Session Series: Joe Walter." *The Cincinnati Enquirer*, July 10, 2014. www.cincinnati.com.

35 Ibid.

36 Ibid.

37 Ibid.

38 Rolling, Chris. "Former Guard Bobbie Williams Signs with the Baltimore Ravens." *Bleacher Report*, June 11, 2012. www.bleacherreport.com.

39 Bass, Mike. "Magical '88 Season Lingers, But Only In Bengals Memory." *The Chicago Tribune*, October 24, 1993.

40 Hardin, Marc. "Five Questions: Bruce Kozerski." *The Cincinnati Enquirer*, December 7, 2011.

41 Baker, Chris. "Bengals Learn Montoya's House in Cincinnati Is Not His Home." *The Los Angeles Times*, July 25, 1990.

42 Vrentas, Jenny. "Super Bowl Injuries: What It's Like to Get Hurt in the Game of Your Life." *Sports Illustrated*, January 12, 2016. www.si.com.

43 Ibid.

44 Ibid.

45 Bannon, Terry. "These Deals Didn't Work." *The Chicago Tribune*, August 25, 2004.

46 "Ex-Grid Star Mayes All-American Person." *The Toledo Blade*, January 11, 1990.

47 Ibid.

48 Ibid.

49 Ibid.

50 "Willie Anderson, Former Bengals OL." Interview. *700 WLW* (audio blog), October 22, 2015. www.700wlw.com.

51 Hobson, Geoff. "Voices of '05: Willie Banking on Defense." Cincinnati Bengals. January 9, 2016. www.bengals.com.

52 Ibid.

53 "Eddie Edwards: Inducted 1989." University of Miami Sports Hall of Fame. www.umsportshalloffame.com.

54 Kirkendall, Josh. "Best Bengals Draft Picks #8: Eddie Edwards." SB Nation. April 20, 2011. www.cincyjungle.com.

55 Ibid.

56 Hobson, Geoff. "Sack Master Edwards Weighs In." Cincinnati Bengals. September 21, 2009. www.bengals.com.

57 "Bruce Reimers Former Cincinnati Bengals Lineman." Interview. *The Grueling Truth Radio Network* (audio blog), February 26, 2016. www.thegruelingtruth.net.

58 Ibid.

59 Ibid.

60 Ibid.

61 Ibid.

62 Hobson, Geoff. "Ex-Bengal Vern Holland Dies." *The Cincinnati Enquirer*, April 22, 1998.

63 Ibid.

64 "Former Hawk Happy Being Parent, Coach." *The Seattle Times*, September 26, 1990.

65 Donaldson, Kelly. "Wilson Has Close Ties to Today's Big Game." The Times. February 5, 2006. www.gainesvilletimes.com.

66 Ibid.

67 Ibid.

68 Ibid.

69 Ibid.

70 Ibid.

71   Lahman, Sean. *The Pro Football Historical Abstract*. Guilford, CT: Lyons Press, 2008.

72   Winters, Kelly. "Muñoz, Anthony: 1958--: Former Professional Football Player." *Contemporary Hispanic Biography*. 2003. www.encyclopedia.com.

73   Lahman, Sean. *The Pro Football Historical Abstract*. Guilford, CT: Lyons Press, 2008.

74   Winters, Kelly. "Muñoz, Anthony: 1958--: Former Professional Football Player." *Contemporary Hispanic Biography*. 2003. www.encyclopedia.com.

75   Lahman, Sean. *The Pro Football Historical Abstract*. Guilford, CT: Lyons Press, 2008.

76   Greenberg, Jay. "The King of the Block." *Sports Illustrated*, September 10, 1990.

77   Ibid.

78   Ibid.

79   Ibid.

80   "Anthony Muñoz Charges into Pro Football Hall of Fame." www.thegoal.com.

81   Ruman, Steve. "Warren's Ross Browner Made a Big Splash on the Gridiron." The Vindicator. September 13, 2013. www.vindy.com.

82   Ibid.

83   Monaco, Mike. "Waking the Echoes: Ross Browner." The Observer. October 30, 2014. www.ndsmcobserver.com.

84   Chival, Craig. "Browner Made Impact Immediate and Often." University of Notre Dame. November 3, 1999. www.und.com.

85   Ibid.

86   Ruman, Steve. "Warren's Ross Browner Made a Big Splash on the Gridiron." The Vindicator. September 13, 2013. www.vindy.com.

87   Monaco, Mike. "Waking the Echoes: Ross Browner." The Observer. October 30, 2014. www.ndsmcobserver.com.

88   Ibid.

89   Underwood, John. "Catch a Catching Star." *Sports Illustrated*, December 14, 1981.

90   Ibid.

91   Ibid.

92   Ibid.

93   Ibid.

94   Ibid.

95   Kirkendall, Josh. "Cris Collinsworth Always Remembers Super Bowl Losses." SB Nation. January 31, 2015. www.cincyjungle.com.

96   Underwood, John. "Catch a Catching Star." *Sports Illustrated*, December 14, 1981.

97   Robbins, Danny. "Pickens Didn't Exactly Volunteer to Go Both Ways." *The Los Angeles Times*, December 29, 1989. www.articles.latimes.com.

98   Ibid.

99   Murphy, Austin. "Dude with a 'Tude." *Sports Illustrated*, August 26, 1991. www. si.com.

100   Robbins, Danny. "Pickens Didn't Exactly Volunteer to Go Both Ways." *The Los Angeles Times*, December 29, 1989. www.articles.latimes.com.

101   "Jeff Blake Interview on Deep Bombs to Carl Pickens, Tasting Turf at Riverfront Stadium and Deer Antler Spray." Interview. *Sports Douchebags* (web log), March 27, 2015. www.sportsdouchebags.com.

102   "Pickens Rips Coslet, Recants." CBS News. December 29, 1999. www. cbsnews.com.

103   Hobson, Geoff. "Pickens Rips Coslet, Then Recants." *The Cincinnati Enquirer*, December 30, 1999. www.bengals.enquirer.com.

104   Nadeau, Rene. "Where Are They Now? Former Tulane and NFL Tight End Rodney Holman." SportsNOLA. May 2, 2013. www.sportsnola.com.

105   Ibid.

106   Ibid.

107   Ibid.

108   Ibid.

109   Ibid.

110   Ibid.

111   Ibid.

112   Ibid.

113   Ibid.

114   Ibid.

115   Greene, Van. "Former Bengals Tight End Tony McGee Finds Post-NFL Success with Logistics." *Sports Illustrated*, May 24, 2015. www.si.com.

116   Ibid.

117   Lahman, Sean. *The Pro Football Historical Abstract*. Guilford, CT: Lyons Press, 2008.

118   "Scribe Session: Tony McGee." Interview. *The Cincinnati Enquirer* (audio blog), June 19, 2014. www.enquirer.com.

119   Ibid.

120   Hobson, Geoff. "Prepared." Cincinnati Bengals. May 14, 2010. www. bengals.com.

121   Ibid.

122   Rowe, Don. "Dreams, Hard Work Helped Kelly Reach NFL." The Dispatch. April 3, 2012. www.cdispatch.com.

123   Hobson, Geoff. "Prepared." Cincinnati Bengals. May 14, 2010. www. bengals.com.

124   Campbell, David. "Reggie Kelly's Value Went Beyond Numbers for Bengals." Bleacher Report. August 4, 2009. www.bleacherreport.com.

125 Ibid.
126 Florio, Mike. "Reggie Kelly Has Great Advice for Today's Players." Pro Football Talk. May 27, 2013. www.profootballtalk.nbcsports.com.
127 Lahman, Sean. *The Pro Football Historical Abstract*. Guilford, CT: Lyons Press, 2008.
128 "Isaac Takes Glory from Trumpy." *Piqua Daily Call*, October 18, 1974.
129 "Bengals Reverse Way Past Miami to Stay in Picture." *Albuquerque Journal*, November 21, 1977.
130 Ludwig, Chick. *Legends: Cincinnati Bengals: The Men, The Deeds, The Consequences*. Wilmington, OH: Orange Frazier Press, 2004.
131 Lahman, Sean. *The Pro Football Historical Abstract*. Guilford, CT: Lyons Press, 2008.
132 Corbett, Jim. "C.J. and T.J.--The Bengals Odd Couple--One's Flash, the Other's Polish." *USA Today*, November 1, 2006. www.usatoday30.usatoday.com.
133 O'Neil, Danny. "Seahawks New Wide Receiver T.J. Houshmandzadeh is Out for Recognition." *The Seattle Times*, April 19, 2009. www.old.seattletimes.com.
134 Ibid.
135 Ibid.
136 Ibid.
137 Corbett, Jim. "C.J. and T.J.--The Bengals Odd Couple--One's Flash, the Other's Polish." *USA Today*, November 1, 2006. www.usatoday30.usatoday.com.
138 O'Neil, Danny. "Seahawks New Wide Receiver T.J. Houshmandzadeh is Out for Recognition." *The Seattle Times*, April 19, 2009. www.old.seattletimes.com.
139 Corbett, Jim. "C.J. and T.J.--The Bengals Odd Couple--One's Flash, the Other's Polish." *USA Today*, November 1, 2006. www.usatoday30.usatoday.com.
140 Ibid.
141 Ibid.
142 O'Neil, Danny. "Seahawks New Wide Receiver T.J. Houshmandzadeh is Out for Recognition." *The Seattle Times*, April 19, 2009. www.old.seattletimes.com.
143 Ibid.
144 Hobson, Geoff. "Bengals like Ike to Make Draft Call." Cincinnati Bengals. April 23, 2012. www.bengals.com.
145 Hamilton, Tom. "Who Was the Best Back? Orange County's Veteran Prep Coaches Offer Some Suggestions." *The Los Angeles Times*, October 9, 1985.
146 Hobson, Geoff. "Bengals like Ike to Make Draft Call." Cincinnati Bengals. April 23, 2012. www.bengals.com.
147 Inman, Cam. "For Don Coryell, to Air was Devine." *The Mercury News* (San Jose, California), July 4, 2010. www.mercurynews.com.
148 Eskenazi, Gerald. "Bengals Curtis: More than Just a Sprinter." *The New York Times*, January 21, 1982. www.nytimes.com.
149 Ibid.

150 Hobson, Geoff. "Difference Maker." Cincinnati Bengals. June 30, 2009. www. bengals.com.

151 Hobson, Geoff. "Bengals like Ike to Make Draft Call." Cincinnati Bengals. April 23, 2012. www.bengals.com.

152 Hobson, Geoff. "Difference Maker." Cincinnati Bengals. June 30, 2009. www. bengals.com.

153 Ibid.

154 Ibid.

155 Ibid.

156 Hobson, Geoff. "Still Tough to Take." Cincinnati Bengals. February 7, 2014. www.bengals.com.

157 "Tim McGee Returns to Hometown of Cleveland as a Cincinnati Star." *United Press International*, November 29, 1989. www.upi.com.

158 Ibid.

159 Hobson, Geoff. "Still Tough to Take." Cincinnati Bengals. February 7, 2014. www.bengals.com.

160 Lahman, Sean. *The Pro Football Historical Abstract.* Guilford, CT: Lyons Press, 2008.

161 Corbett, Jim. "Bengals Johnson Talks the Talk and Walks the Walk." *USA Today*, October 19, 2005. www.usatoday.com.

162 Ibid.

163 Ibid.

164 Kiper, Mel. "Some Players' Stock on the Rise." ESPN. January 23, 2001. www. espn.com.

165 Ibid.

166 Kiper, Mel. "1st Round Projection." ESPN. March 30, 2001. www.espn.com.

167 Hobson, Geoff. "Best of the Best?" Cincinnati Bengals. April 5, 2016. www. bengals.com.

168 Corbett, Jim. "Bengals Johnson Talks the Talk and Walks the Walk." *USA Today*, October 19, 2005. www.usatoday.com.

169 Ibid.

170 Ibid.

171 ESPN Radio. *Mike and Mike in the Morning.* January 13, 2008.

172 Corbett, Jim. "Bengals Johnson Talks the Talk and Walks the Walk." *USA Today*, October 19, 2005. www.usatoday.com.

173 Ibid.

174 Ibid.

175 Ibid.

176 McClellan, Bob. "McInally Continues to Perfect the Wonderlic." Rivals.com. June 15, 2006. www.rivals.com.

177 Ibid.

178 "Pat McInally, Former Bengals Punter/Wide Receiver." Interview. *ESPN 1530* (audio blog). Accessed January 18, 2016. www.espn1530.iheart.com.

179 Crowe, Jerry. "McInally's Life Off the Field Has Eclipsed Playing Career." *The Los Angeles Times*, April 24, 2011. www.articles.latimes.com.

180 McClellan, Bob. "McInally Continues to Perfect the Wonderlic." Rivals.com. June 15, 2006. www.rivals.com.

181 Crowe, Jerry. "McInally's Life Off the Field Has Eclipsed Playing Career." *The Los Angeles Times*, April 24, 2011. www.articles.latimes.com.

182 Messerschmidt, Michael. "Pat McInally Signs Pact with AFC's Cincinnati Bengals." *The Harvard Crimson*, March 11, 1975.

183 McClellan, Bob. "McInally Continues to Perfect the Wonderlic." Rivals.com. June 15, 2006. www.rivals.com.

184 McCurdie, Jim. "Life is More Than Just Football for McInally." *The Los Angeles Times*, October 30, 1985. www.articles.latimes.com.

185 Starr, Cindy. "It's a Kick for McInally to Break Into the Lineup." *The Kentucky Post*, May 22, 1997.

186 Zimanek, Brad. "Copeland Thrilled to Be Around Football, Tuscaloosa." *The Montgomery Advertiser*, August 19, 2015. www.montgomeryadvertiser.com.

187 Ibid.

188 Ibid.

189 Skinner, Richard. "Mike Brown Moves Step Closer to Honoring Bengals Past." WKRC Cincinnati. July 26, 2016. www.local12.com.

190 Schatz, Aaron. *Football Outsiders Almanac 2016: The Essential Guide to the 2016 NFL and College Football Seasons*. Colorado Springs, CO: Create Space Independent Publishing Platform, 2016.

191 Lahman, Sean. *The Pro Football Historical Abstract*. Guilford, CT: Lyons Press, 2008.

Printed in the United States
By Bookmasters